FOR BOTH CROSS AND FLAG

IN THE SERIES *Urban Life, Landscape, and Policy,*
EDITED BY ZANE MILLER, DAVID STRADLING, AND LARRY BENNETT

For Both Cross and Flag

Catholic Action, Anti-Catholicism, and National Security Politics in World War II San Francisco

William Issel

TEMPLE UNIVERSITY PRESS
Philadelphia

TEMPLE UNIVERSITY PRESS
1601 North Broad Street
Philadelphia PA 19122
www.temple.edu/tempress

Published 2010
Printed in the United States of America

This book is an expansion of the article by William Issel, "'Still Potentially Dangerous in Some Quarters': Sylvester Andriano, Catholic Action, and Un-American Activities in California," *Pacific Historical Review* 75, no. 2 (May 2006), 231–270.

♾ The paper used in this publication meets the requirements of the American National Standard for Information Sciences—Permanence of Paper for Printed Library Materials, ANSI Z39.48-1992

Library of Congress Cataloging-in-Publication Data

Issel, William.
For both cross and flag : Catholic Action, anti-Catholicism, and national security politics in World War II San Francisco / William Issel.
p. cm.
Includes bibliographical references and index.
ISBN 978-1-4399-0028-4 (cloth : alk. paper)
1. Andriano, Sylvester, 1889–1963. 2. Italian Americans—California—San Francisco—History—20th century. 3. Catholic Action—California—San Francisco—History—20th century. 4. Catholic Church—California—San Francisco—History—20th century. 5. Anti-Catholicism—California—San Francisco—History—20th century. 6. Religion and politics—California—San Francisco—History—20th century. 7. World War, 1939–1945—Italian Americans. 8. Italian Americans—Civil rights. 9. San Francisco (Calif.)—Ethnic relations. 10. San Francisco (Calif.)—Politics and government—20th century. I. Title.

F869.S39I85 2009
305.6'827946108951—dc22 2009021168

2 4 6 8 9 7 5 3 1

Contents

A photo gallery begins on page 7

Acknowledgments

This book could not have been written without the assistance of Jeffrey M. Burns, the director of the Chancery Archives of the Archdiocese of San Francisco; Susan Goldstein, Pat Akre, Christina Moretta, Tami J. Suzuki, and their colleagues at the San Francisco History Center of the San Francisco Public Library; Susan Sherwood and Catherine Powell of the Northern California Labor Archives and Research Center of San Francisco State University; and Linda Wobbe, the archivist of the College of St. Mary's of California. Thanks are also due to the librarians and staff of the Bancroft Library at the University of California, Berkeley; the Anne Rand Research Library of the International Longshoremen's and Warehousemen's Union; the Southern California Library for Social Studies and Research; the California State Archives, for supplying a copy of the Tenney Committee hearings shortly after they were made available for research; and librarians and archivists at the National Archives and the Library of Congress.

I thank Robert W. Cherny, Jeffrey M. Burns, Constance Holmes, Mary Claire Heffron, and Marjorie Lasky for reading and commenting on all or parts of the manuscript, and Kathleen Maggiora Rogers of the Associazione Piemontesi nel Mondo of Northern California for her interest in and support of my research about the Piemontesi. Thanks are also due to Kenneth Burt for sending me copies of several useful documents that he discovered in his own research on Catholics and California politics. Further, I thank Andrew Canepa, Peter D'Agostino, John P. Diggins, Stefano Luconi, Matteo Pretelli, and Stephen Schwartz, who generously replied to my e-mail research queries; David Cicoletti, who supplied information about the Andriano family; Rose Marie Cleese, who provided information about the close friendship between her grandfather, mayor Angelo Rossi, and Sylvester Andriano; and my research assistants, George Malachowski, Giovanna Palombo, and John Rosen.

A brief account of the subject of this book appeared in print as "'Still Potentially Dangerous in Some Quarters': Sylvester Andriano, Catholic Action, and Un-American Activities in California," *Pacific Historical Review* 75, no. 2 (May 2006), 231–270. I thank the University of California Press for permission to reprint some of the text of that article, the editors of the journal and their readers for comments on the manuscript for the article, and the readers who commented on the book manuscript for Temple University Press. Responsibility for any errors or omissions that may have escaped my attention is mine alone.

I also thank Zane Miller for suggesting that I consider publishing my book in his Temple University Press series, and I acknowledge the friendly and professional assistance of the Temple team: Mick Gusinde-Duffy, Lynne Frost, Gary Kramer, Emily Taber, Kimberley C. Vivier, and David M. Wilson.

Introduction

Massachusetts Congressman Thomas P. O'Neill once famously remarked that in the United States, "all politics are local." O'Neill made a good point, but it was only half true, because local politics in the United States, especially during wartime, have also been shaped by the political and religious loyalties that immigrants bring with them. Government officials who fail to take account of such loyalties and rivalries may find themselves duped into becoming partisans on one or another side of local political battles when they make decisions about who is and who is not a security risk during wartime. Their commendable zeal to protect the nation from harm can lead them to violate the constitutional rights of citizens while doing nothing to protect domestic security. That is exactly what happened in the case of Sylvester Andriano, an Italian-born San Francisco attorney and local government official who was forcibly removed from the West Coast in 1942 on the basis of politically inspired false charges that he was a Fascist agent. The Andriano case provides a cautionary tale about the sometimes deleterious impact on our national life of religious and ideological zealotry in our communities, no-holds-barred political competition in our big cities, and fallible power-seeking public officials in our national security agencies during wartime.

This book is about the ordeal of Sylvester Andriano, but it is first and foremost a book that means to restore our appreciation of the impact of European political and religious rivalries in the political cultures of American cities in the first half of the twentieth century. The setting is San Francisco, California, the second-largest city west of the Mississippi River at the time. During the World War II years most of the city's residents were Irish, German, or Italian immigrants, their children, and their grandchildren. These men, women, and children made up nearly two-thirds of the city's population at a time when 94 percent of San Franciscans were persons of European descent. The devout Catholics among them asserted their faith-based convictions in public debates about a range of issues, as did a variety of zealous anti-Catholic residents, including Communist Party members. And San Franciscans kept informed about and were deeply concerned with, disturbed by, and divided over the political crises that roiled European affairs, from Mussolini's March on Rome in October 1922 to Hitler's Blitzkrieg against Poland in September 1939. When the United States entered World War II, anti-Catholic activists seized on the fact that Italy was now allied with Germany and Japan against America to convince domestic security officials that Sylvester Andriano was a Fascist agent.

Anti-Catholic zealots targeted Andriano because he served as president of the Catholic Men of San Francisco, a Catholic Action program established by Archbishop John J. Mitty in 1938. After Mussolini and Hitler signed their Pact of Steel agreement on May 22, 1939, and especially after Italy declared war against the United States on December 10, 1941, Andriano's anti-Catholic Masonic, Socialist, and Communist enemies seized the opportunity to remove the Catholic attorney from political influence by accusing him of being a Fascist agent. Federal and state loyalty investigating committees, the FBI, and the U.S. Army accepted the truth of the bogus charges and issued Andriano an "individual exclusion order," forcing him to be relocated away from coastal states on the grounds that he was a security risk.

In order to better understand the story of Andriano's ordeal, I begin by detailing the transnational political rivalries that divided many American cities between the First and Second World Wars: rivalries between devout Catholics and committed anti-Catholics in Italian communities and between Catholic anti-Communists and their Communist Party competitors. Then I zero in on the operations of the California and federal legislative loyalty investigating committees in 1941 and 1942 and on the consequences of J. Edgar Hoover's expansion of the FBI's domestic security responsibilities at the beginning of the war.

During the 1930s Sylvester Andriano emerged as the leading figure in a faith-based cultural and political reform movement known as Catholic Action. Along with other militant lay men and women, Andriano joined his local archbishop in using church resources to battle communists, socialists, freethinkers, and anarchists, as well as reformers who advocated birth control, divorce, eugenics, and the undoing of traditional gender role definitions. He also participated in the cultural and business outreach programs of the Fascist government of Italy. To Andriano, this seemed legitimate; after all, Italy and the United States maintained friendly relations, and ethnic pride could arguably coexist with loyalty to America. Once war broke out, however, Italian American Catholics such as Andriano, who regarded themselves as nonpolitical, became vulnerable to charges that their attempts to foster ethnic pride in their Italian heritage constituted collaboration with the enemy.

On August 19, 1940, six days after the Luftwaffe unleashed its deadliest attack in the Battle of Britain, a witness testified before the House Un-American Activities Committee (HUAC) that Andriano was "indubitably the fountain head of all Fascist activities on the Pacific coast." In May 1942 the California legislature's Joint Fact-Finding Committee on Un-American Activities (known as the Tenney Committee for its chair, Jack Tenney) announced that Andriano and two other San Franciscans, journalist Ettore Patrizi and attorney Renzo Turco, were the ringleaders of California Fascism. Andriano denied all the charges under oath in 1942, but the Tenney Committee nonetheless declared him a security risk, and in September the U.S. Army served him with an order that excluded him from the Western Defense Region.

Andriano's public career included both city politics and Catholic Church activities, and by the early 1920s he counted himself among the *prominenti,* the North Beach Italian American district's leading business and professional figures. In the late 1920s Andriano and his friend and law client Angelo Rossi had both gained citywide influence by serving on the San Francisco Board of Supervisors. Rossi became mayor in 1931, sent Andriano to Europe as the city's delegate to an international conference, and appointed him to the police commission. Andriano also served on a local draft board. A close associate of Archbishop Edward J. Hanna in the latter's efforts to promote greater religious activity among San Francisco Italian Catholics during the 1920s, Andriano developed even stronger ties with Hanna's successor, coadjutor Archbishop John J. Mitty, who officially replaced Hanna in 1935. Mitty delegated Andriano to organize a new Catholic Action program called the Catholic Men of San Francisco. With the mayor's support and assistance, Andriano and Archbishop Mitty commenced a citywide campaign to shape municipal reform and labor relations according to a program based on Catholic moral principles.

Andriano's assumption of leadership in San Francisco Catholic Action triggered a campaign *against* Catholic activism from three different local sources linked to transnational political competition. One assault came from the leaders of the city's Italian Masonic organization, who regarded Andriano as an embodiment of the monstrous political offspring produced by the Vatican's illicit embrace of Fascist evil. A second set of attacks came from the anticlerical critics of Pope Pius XI among the anti-Fascist political exiles from Italy (*fuorusciti*), who regarded devout local Catholics as morally equivalent to the bureaucrats running Benito Mussolini's allegedly criminal regime. A third offensive against Andriano, Rossi, and Catholic Action derived from the local Communist Party (CP). Local party leaders followed up their success in shaping the strategy and tactics of the 1934 waterfront and general strikes with a vigorous program of labor organizing and electoral politics. Like its counterparts in leading cities in the United States and Europe, the San Francisco CP followed the program of the Communist Third International organization (Comintern) and denounced Catholic cultural authority and political influence in its San Francisco publications and public meetings.

On December 7, 1941, Japan attacked Pearl Harbor, and three days later Italy declared war on the United States. Self-appointed superpatriots and public officials joined forces in the weeks to come and set out to identify dangerous and disloyal Italian-born residents. Andriano's and Rossi's various critics seized the opportunity provided by the national emergency to discredit the leadership of Catholic Action and weaken Catholic political power in the city. International Longshoremen and Warehousemen's Union (ILWU) president Harry Bridges (a secret member of the Communist Party who went by the name "Rossi" in clandestine communications with the Comintern) and several other critics of Catholic activism volunteered to testify before state and federal un-American investigating committees that the mayor and his former police commissioner were Fascist agents "potentially dangerous" to the United States.

Previous historians, beginning with John P. Diggins in 1972, have illuminated the complex divisions within California's Italian American communities during the period. They have established that the investigation and exclusion of Andriano, Patrizi, and Turco were the products of accusations by anti-Catholic critics within the Italian American community who harbored political grievances, as well as of post–Pearl Harbor security considerations and anti-Italian ethnic prejudice on the part of public opinion shapers and government officials outside the community.

This book demonstrates that Andriano's exclusion also derived from his militant Catholic activism and the reaction it engendered both inside and outside the Italian American community. Local Bay Area political and religious rivalries between Catholics and anti-Catholics in the Italian American community and between Catholic anti-Communists and their Communist Party adversaries played a major role in Andriano's designation as an "un-American" citizen who was "potentially dangerous" to the security of the nation.

Andriano's ordeal was also the product of a separate set of dynamics related to J. Edgar Hoover's expansion of the FBI's counterintelligence responsibilities from 1936 through the years of World War II and beyond. Hoover's zeal in seeking to increase his bureau's power and public prominence by expanding its role in counterintelligence has been documented by several historians, but the Andriano case and its demonstration of the influence of anti-Catholicism and local politics on national security investigations have been lost to history.

I became interested in Sylvester Andriano while engaged in a project documenting the competition between the Communist Party and the Catholic Church in San Francisco during the 1930s and 1940s. As I read through one after another collection of archival records, including correspondence between Andriano and a Catholic Action colleague, Communist Party records, the National Archives, Andriano's FBI file, army and navy documents, and letters and reports in the Chancery Archives of the Catholic Archdiocese of San Francisco, I learned about Andriano's ordeal and discovered that he was innocent of the charges and had suffered a terrible injustice at the hands of government authorities. But I did not write this book merely to correct the record and defend Sylvester Andriano's good name.

My major purpose is to demonstrate how international and national events impinged on the political culture of a major American city from World War I to World War II, eventually influencing domestic security politics after Pearl Harbor. Throughout the book I draw extensively on the historical record to present the actual voices of the participants in the events. I begin with a brief account of Andriano's background and career and then provide a detailed narrative of his role in Catholic Action and San Francisco politics, including local consequences of the victory of Fascism in Italy, the Lateran Accords between the Italian state and the Vatican, the labor conflicts of the Great Depression, the Communist Party's role in local politics, and the outbreak of World War II in Europe and the Pacific. The final chapters describe the security investigations of Andriano and discuss the implications of his case for our understanding of the impact of loyalty investigations on civil liberties in time of war.

Figure 1 "This Is the May Day Celebration We Want." The Catholic Church's Catholic Action perspective was pronounced explicitly when the archdiocesan newspaper ran this cartoon in the *Monitor* on May 4, 1935. The Communist Party's class-conflict perspective is replaced with one in which the employer and the worker, who is depicted as a larger and more imposing figure, cooperate in the community interest. *(The Monitor, May 4, 1935.)*

Figure 2 The Catholics of San Francisco's "Little Italy" turned out for a procession outside Saints Peter and Paul Church on November 3, 1935, marking the church's Golden Jubilee. Archbishop John J. Mitty celebrated a High Mass. *(Photo permission of San Francisco History Center, San Francisco Public Library.)*

Figure 3 Sylvester Andriano did not sympathize with or serve as an agent of the Italian Fascist government, but large numbers of Italian Americans expressed public support for Mussolini. Here, on May 6, 1936, residents of San Francisco's North Beach district, some apparently giving the Fascist salute, wave Italian and U.S. flags while viewing photographs illustrating the Fascist conquest of Ethiopia. *(Photo permission of the San Francisco History Center, San Francisco Public Library.)*

Figure 4 The success of the Catholic Action program was dramatized when Mayor Angelo Rossi administered the oath of office to Sylvester Andriano (*right*) and J. Ward Mailliard Jr. (*left*) as members of the San Francisco Police Commission, July 20, 1937. *(Photo permission of the San Francisco History Center, San Francisco Public Library.)*

Figure 5 Catholic Action influence in San Francisco increased after the 1934 waterfront and general strike, as evidenced in the annual Labor Day Mass at St. Mary's Cathedral, this one in 1938. Archbishop Mitty is in the front row, with Mayor Angelo Rossi standing at his left. John F. Shelley is the tall man behind and to the mayor's left in the second row. *(Photo permission of the Chancery Archives of the Archdiocese of San Francisco.)*

Figure 6 The officers of the Young Ladies Institute (YLI) of the San Francisco Archdiocese at their annual Communion Mass in 1939. The YLI worked throughout the archdiocese to implement the Catholic Action moral apostolate program. *(Photo permission of the Chancery Archives of the Archdiocese of San Francisco.)*

Figure 7 The Communist Party attempted to increase its political influence by electing its members to political office, as illustrated by this Communist Party campaign flyer from the 1939 San Francisco election. The party ran Oleta O'Connor Yates for city assessor and Elaine Black and Archie Brown for seats on the Board of Supervisors. The coupon at the bottom requested name and address information and included a line where voters could check "Tell me more about Communist Party." *(From the author's collection.)*

Figure 8 Sylvester Andriano's political enemies testified that he was a Fascist agent in hearings called by the California legislature's anti-subversive committee. Here Andriano responds to questions from Richard Combs, attorney for the Tenney Committee, at the San Francisco hearings, May 25, 1942. *(Photo permission of the San Francisco History Center, San Francisco Public Library.)*

Figure 9 Carmelo Zito, who was highly critical of both Sylvester Andriano and Mayor Angelo Rossi testified against them at the Tenney Committee hearings. Here he is shown at his desk in the office of *Il Corriere del Popolo.* This photo appeared in a laudatory article in the Communist Party newspaper *People's World* on May 26, 1942, the day after Zito testified against Sylvester Andriano. *(Photo permission of the Northern California Labor Archives and Research Center.)*

Figure 10 Harry Bridges testifies at the Tenney Committee hearings, May 27, 1942. Like Zito, Bridges claimed that Mayor Angelo Rossi was a Fascist and that his Catholic Action–inspired labor relations policies had aided and abetted the Axis powers. *(Photo permission of the San Francisco History Center, San Francisco Public Library.)*

I

Sylvester Andriano, a Catholic Attorney in San Francisco

The comforts offered by American free-life appeal to them and almost before they know it, they have learned to love America. When this stage is reached none are more eager than Italians to become full-fledged American citizens.

—Sylvester Andriano, "Italian Immigrants in America," 1909

'Little Italy' is no longer so little, for the Italians, 60,000 strong, are San Francisco's largest and most powerful national minority.

—*San Francisco: A Guide to the Bay and Its Cities,* 1940

Sylvester Andriano began his lifelong practice of combining the promotion of Catholicism with the preservation of Italian culture during his student days at St. Mary's College of California. Then located in Oakland, across the bay from San Francisco, the men's college attracted the aspiring sons of Catholic families to study under a faculty drawn from the Christian Brothers religious order. Andriano graduated from St. Mary's in 1911, ten years after he arrived in San Francisco from his birthplace in Castelnuovo d'Asti, ten miles southwest of Turin in the Piedmont region of Italy.[1]

Sylvester's older brothers Giuseppe and James were the first to leave the family orchards in Castelnuovo d'Asti for opportunities in San Francisco, arriving in 1895 and 1898, respectively. Giuseppe bought a restaurant and married a fellow immigrant named Eugenia, who, assisted by a servant, ran a household that included several lodgers and members of the extended family. Sylvester lived with Giuseppe, Eugenia, and their daughter Edna, working in the restaurant after school, until he graduated from St. Mary's. Another older brother, Angelo, a Roman Catholic priest ordained in Turin, arrived in 1905 and became the pastor of a series of Bay Area churches. Angelo was one of two siblings who became priests, but the other, Pasquale, died shortly after being ordained into the Salesian religious order and never came to the United States.[2]

Five years after Sylvester arrived in the city, the great San Francisco earthquake and fire destroyed two-thirds of the city, but he and his family survived the catastrophe unhurt and undeterred in their goal of establishing an Andriano family branch in California. Like other up-and-coming Piedmontese immigrants to San Francisco, Giuseppe moved out of the North Beach Italian colony, bought a large new residence on Polk Street, and filled it with his family members and seven lodgers. Their sister Serafina joined them in 1908 and lived in Giuseppe and Eugenia's household until she married a waiter in the restaurant and moved a few blocks away to start her own family. James married and bought a house in the city's Eureka Valley district (today's Castro neighborhood), working as a gardener in Golden Gate Park. Their brother Angelo returned to Italy in 1929, with the expectation (false, as it turned out) that the Lateran Accords between the Vatican and the Fascist regime would restore the Catholic Church's power and prestige in Italy. None of the other siblings returned to Italy except on visits, and all became naturalized citizens even while marrying fellow Italians or California-born children of Italians. During the Prohibition years, Giuseppe and Eugenia, now parents of three children, traded the restaurant business and city life for a fruit orchard and the rural Valley of Heart's Delight—today's Silicon Valley in Santa Clara County. Country life also appealed to Sylvester, who once he had established himself in San Francisco purchased a ranch in nearby Los Altos, to which he retired on weekends and vacations as a respite from his professional responsibilities in the city.[3]

While all the Andriano siblings made a successful transition from Italy to America, Sylvester stood out as the scholar, becoming the only college graduate in the family and later an influential lay activist in Catholic Church affairs, both Italian and citywide. He excelled in his studies at St. Mary's (and played varsity basketball), won the Cottle Medal for Oratory in his junior year, and graduated maxima cum laude, having won medals for excellence in both modern languages and Christian doctrine. Andriano also served three years on the editorial board of the *Collegian,* a monthly literary review, and his articles exuded love for his native country and earnest Catholic piety in equal measure.[4]

In "An Italian Hill Town" the nineteen-year-old imagined himself back in his birthplace.

> After a two blocks' walk we reach the Via Maestra (Main Street) with its large and well kept plaza. In the middle is the monument of Don Bosco, the founder of the Salesian order, and a native of this town. At the end of this street there is a beautiful avenue lined with horse-chestnuts, where the people come to promenade of evenings. We proceed up Main Street until we reach the church. It is old and magnificent and surpasses in grandeur and dignity any church in the United States. It has a very high campanile with four huge bells which can be heard for several miles around. It is now six o'clock. The Angelus is ringing. Far over the distant hills the sun has disappeared from view, but its refulgent rays still linger. But even they finally disappear and leave the azure sky tinted with a beautiful crimson hue, and "the splendor falls on castle walls / and snowy summits old in story."[5]

The three places that received special attention in the article were all religious sites: the monument to Don Bosco, another native of the town and founder of the Salesian (Society of St. Francis de Sales) order of Catholic priests; the church; and the Salesian College. (Today Don Bosco is a Catholic saint and the town is named Castelnuovo Don Bosco.)

Andriano's subsequent contributions to the *Collegian* continued to highlight Catholic piety and Italian culture, including an article on the life of Saint (then Venerable) Giovanni (Don) Bosco. In "The Apostle of the Little Ones" Andriano explained how Don Bosco chose his life's work after seeing "how many ragged and uncared-for boys roamed languidly" through the streets of the city of Turin.

> It was here that he recognized his life work; he felt as if a voice from heaven had called unto him, "You are a shepherd; these are your flocks. Feed my lambs." The good work of Don Bosco soon spread all over the city and boys flocked to him. He built technical schools and workshops and aided his boys in choosing suitable professions. Other priests, realizing the great spiritual benefit to be derived from such work, soon joined him, and little by little the order spread, first into other Italian cities, and then into the whole world.[6]

Andriano's Catholic piety and his faith in the power of prayer were evident in his 1911 autobiographical essay about the seemingly miraculous powers of "That Old Statue"—a statue of the Madonna and Child ("La Madonna") on the road between Castelnuovo and nearby Valmartina. In his article Andriano recounted how "that same statue or she whom the statue represented—which I leave to you to decide—actually saved my life and that of three other little children" when they were walking home from school after a torrential rainstorm.

> Presently we noticed that the creek which ran parallel to the road was constantly swelling and that at some places it even threatened to overflow. Suddenly we were startled by a rumbling noise from behind. We looked back, and as we did so, one of my companions shrieked: "The flood, the flood!" I gasped in a subdued voice, "La Madonna!" re-echoed my companions simultaneously; and we started to run toward it. We felt that once at the feet of Mary we should be safe. Higher and higher the waters rose, first to our knees then to our waists; once or twice we were all but overpowered and almost despaired, but that same secret force kept us standing. With arms outstretched we made one ultimate, desperate effort which brought us to the pedestal. Saved! After muttering a few "Ave Marias," the most fervent that I have ever uttered, we turned to contemplate the awful sight about us. For one endless hour the flood continued its

> work of devastation, after which the waters having abated, we said one last "Ave Maria" to our kind protectress, and went home, none the worse for wear, but with a wonderful experience to narrate.[7]

In "The Italian Dialects," written in his junior year, the young student of languages—who became proficient in English, Italian, Spanish, and French—argued that the dialects were "very rough and crude" except for Tuscan: "The national language of Italy is nothing but the Tuscan dialect."

> A great many Americans are at a loss to account for the saying that the Italian language is so sweet and musical when to them the speech of Italians sounds anything but sweet and musical. This is because they seldom hear the real Italian spoken. On the other hand, their ears are quite familiar with the harsh monotone of the language of the bootblack, the street laborer and the garbage man. But the truth is that none of these speaks the real Italian, but some dialect of which does indeed sound very outlandish.[8]

Andriano pointed out that "the Italian which is ridiculed or tried to be imitated on the American stage is that of the Neapolitans and southern Italy," which he considered "abominable and sounds very repulsive."

In an article titled "Italian Immigrants in America" Andriano deplored critics who regarded Italians as "inferior to the rest of European immigrants," and took issue with those who claimed that Italians lacked "the Americanizing spirit." In reality "the comforts offered by American free-life appeal to them and almost before they know it, they have learned to love America. When this stage is reached none are more eager than Italians to become full-fledged American citizens." At the same time, he continued (in a passage that foreshadowed his later work to promote Italian cultural preservation among San Francisco Italian Americans), "it is true that they always retain the highest respect for their fatherland, but nobody can call that a bad trait; on the contrary, it would be a sign of weakness if they didn't. It is not an unusual thing to enter an Italian cottage and see hanging, side by side over the fire-place, the portraits of King Victor and President Lincoln." In reply to critics who argued that Italians lacked an essential cultural quality necessary for loyalty to the United States, Andriano pointed to the response of Italian residents to the 1906 conflagration in San Francisco.

> If they do not Americanize, why did they not after the fire leave San Francisco to its fate and go somewhere else? But they didn't. On the contrary, they stuck to her as steadfastly and even more so than any other class of people. With her they fell; with her they rose again. And who among you who has witnessed the phenomenal and phoenix-like rise of our beloved metropolis will deny that the Italians were among the very first to recuperate from the disaster? The smoke of the conflagration had scarcely cleared away, when a new and jubilant "Little Italy" was already flourishing under the shadows of Rincon and historical Telegraph Hill,—I dare say, far ahead of any other section in the burnt district. Extend that brotherly hand which is so characteristic of Americans, and you will find before you know it that you shall have acquired a worthy and grateful compatriot as fully American as the most patriotic of our great republic.[9]

In his junior year at St. Mary's the twenty-year-old Andriano became a member of the Salesian Council of the Catholic Young Men's Institute, the first of numerous local Catholic Italian American organizations he joined during a professional career that spanned nearly five decades. The council admitted only native Italians or Italian Americans, and it operated in connection with Saints Peter and Paul Church, one of the three parish churches delegated by the San Francisco Archdiocese to the Salesian priests for the pastoral care of the Italian community. Andriano returned to Italy after graduation and then traveled in Europe while improving his French and Spanish language skills, and when he returned he enrolled in the University of California's Hastings College of the Law in San Francisco. He became a naturalized citizen while a student at Hastings and graduated with his law degree in 1915, the same year he served as president of the Salesian Council. By the time Andriano passed the bar exam, he was already well known in citywide Catholic circles, and the official archdiocesan newspaper, the *Monitor,* predicted "a very successful career" for the "brilliant young graduate" of St. Mary's, a "gifted young man of exceptionally fine character and ability."[10]

In the autumn of 1915 Andriano opened a law practice with another Hastings graduate, James A. Bacigalupi. Bacigalupi graduated from the Jesuit Santa Clara College in 1901 before attending Hastings and was the American-born son of Italian immigrants who had arrived in California in the 1870s. Two years later twenty-seven-year-old Sylvester Andriano and twenty-four-year-old Leonora Cicoletti, the daughter of an Italian-born San Jose businessman and a California-born Italian American, drove to the coastal town of Half Moon Bay thirty miles south of San Francisco, where they were married in Our Lady of the Pillar Church by Sylvester's brother Angelo, the pastor. They moved into a new house in the western part of the Marina district, a recently developed neighborhood two miles from Little Italy, where they had a view across the Golden Gate to the Marin headlands. For families like the Andrianos, a move to the Marina or the adjacent Pacific Heights district represented a deliberate step toward the American mainstream. The Marina district was popular among well-to-do Italian American business and professional families, but they were now surrounded not by the sights and sounds of the old country but by 1920s American consumer culture; Italian Americans were only some 2–5 percent of the district's population, which was primarily U.S.-born and non-Italian.[11]

Andriano joined the law practice of James A. Bacigalupi at an auspicious moment. Their offices occupied the floor above the new headquarters of Amadeo P. Giannini's Bank of Italy, and their practice included Giannini's bank as well as the Italian consulate. Two years after Andriano joined him, Giannini offered Bacigalupi a position in the bank, where he served as president from 1924 to 1931. Andriano and attorney Michael Cimbalo then took over

Bacigalupi's clients, including the Italian consulate. They represented the consulate in a variety of cases, such as those involving industrial accidents or nonresident heirs to estates left by deceased Italian San Francisco residents. When Cimbalo moved to New York City, Andriano kept the consulate account, but he was not—as the California state antisubversive Tenney Committee would later claim—"the attorney of the local Italian Consulate."[12]

Andriano then joined forces with William R. Lowery, a fellow graduate of the St. Mary's College class of 1911. By this time, the city's Italian-born residents and their American-born offspring numbered some 46,000, which made them nearly 9 percent of the city's total population of 506,676. The decade of the 1920s witnessed the high point in the demographic expansion of the city's Italian American population. After 1930, when the population reached 58,000 (just over 9 percent of the total), the numbers began a gradual decline all the way down to 29,000 (4 percent) in 1970. Catholic Italians belonged to a vast archdiocese that contained 171 parishes, some six hundred priests, and over four hundred thousand Catholics living in thirteen Bay Area counties from Santa Clara in the south to Mendocino in the north.[13]

During the first half of the 1920s, as he expanded his law practice, Sylvester Andriano also became a leading builder of Catholic cultural infrastructure in San Francisco's Little Italy. The groups he organized or cofounded included the Dante Council of the Knights of Columbus, the Salesian Boys' Club, and a chapter of the Boy Scouts of America. He also served as president and board member of several other institutions: the Italian School, which offered afterschool Italian-language classes; the Italian Sports Club; the Italian Chamber of Commerce; the Bank of Italy; and a community center called the Fugazi Building. The boys' club operated in quarters provided by Saints Peter and Paul Church, which would soon be the focus of anti-Catholic hostility.

2

Anti-Catholicism in Little Italy

We are now in the heart of the business section of the Latin Quarter, and as we pass through the crowds we catch phrases of French, Portuguese, Spanish, and the various musical dialects of Italy. Many quaint shops are to be found here, their windows displaying an infinite variety of foreign goods. Little marble figures such as Italians like, Mexican glass and pottery, and French embroideries. Hardly an American name or sign is in evidence.

—Elizabeth Gray Potter, *The San Francisco Skyline,* 1939

This is one of the largest concentrations of Italian-Americans in the United States. Their influence in San Francisco has been tremendous. Italian life in San Francisco is hearty, colorful and uninhibited. The Latin Flavor of the city; its tradition of European Sunday, the habitual wine-bibbing, its sensitivity to the picturesque is due largely to the Italian population and they have contributed greatly to the city's folklore and night life.

—Leonard Austin, *Around the World in San Francisco,* 1959

Sylvester Andriano, firmly committed to Catholicism, Americanization, and the maintenance of his Italian cultural heritage, built his law practice in the growing community of Little Italy. But most of the city's Italian community demonstrated little interest in citizenship or Americanization. As the decade of the twenties began, 80 percent of the city's Italian immigrants maintained their Italian citizenship, and ten years later only 44 percent of the men and 31 percent of the women were United States citizens. And as the number of Italian residents in San Francisco grew from the beginning of the century to the 1920s, so did Little Italy's contingent of anti-Catholic anarchists, socialists, and masons.

The new Sts. Peter and Paul Church quickly attracted anti-Catholic hostility. Between 1922 and 1924 Andriano raised over one hundred thousand dollars toward the construction of this church, which stood on Filbert Street, facing Washington Square. The largest of three Catholic churches established to serve the growing Italian American community between 1897 and 1914, this new (second) Sts. Peter and Paul Church was in the heart of Little Italy and quickly acquired the status of a cultural landmark for the city as well as the neighborhood. Its massive Carrara marble altar and similar embellishments earned the edifice the title of "the Italian Cathedral of the West."[1] Built in the Romanesque Revival style, the church, its twin spires towering 191 feet above the neighborhood, announced that Italian Catholics intended to practice their faith in a dignified and impressive structure second to none. In 1923, while it was still under construction, Cecil B. DeMille used the church for scenes in his spectacular movie *The Ten Commandments*. San Francisco Catholics celebrated when craftsmen completed the work three years later and the parish dedicated the new altar. But others scoffed at the celebration and regarded the new church as a symbol of ancient superstition and popular ignorance, its priests and their lay confidants as recipients of undeserved wealth and power, and after the new Sts. Peter and Paul was dedicated, dynamiters attacked it. Between January 1926 and January 1927, four separate church bombings shook the neighborhood, causing substantial but not extensive damage. Anti-Catholic resentments smoldered beneath the sounds of the Italian Colony's "musical dialects" and behind its facade of "quaint shops" and "colorful and uninhibited" folk culture.[2]

After the fourth bombing, city police announced to the press that they could no longer afford to protect the church, but secretly, Detective Sgt. Thomas DeMatei organized a squad that kept watch on the church twenty-four hours a day. The detective's cousin was a Salesian priest, and it was the Italian Salesian religious order that staffed the church. In the early morning hours of March 6, 1927, two men approached the church; one stood guard and the other struck a match to light the fuse of a bundle of dynamite. DeMatei and his men shot them, killing one and wounding the other.

City police were familiar with Celsten Eklund, the wounded man, who died in custody several months later. He was a well-known figure in the community of single men who lived in boardinghouses and residential hotels in the South of Market Street neighborhood, the area Jack London made famous as a hotbed of radicalism in his 1909 short story "South of the Slot." Eklund's talents as a soapbox orator extended well beyond San Francisco, and Seattle police had arrested him during a demonstration by backers of the Industrial Workers of the World (IWW). The IWW's militant and uncompromising anticapitalist rhetoric and its call for "One Big Union" that would unite workers regardless of nationality, race, or skills attracted anarchists as well as respectable skilled craftsmen, and the organization enjoyed considerable support in San Francisco. There is no evidence that Eklund carried an IWW membership card, however, and while the organization called for the destruction of capitalism and for sabotage, neither its program nor its leaders advocated the use of dynamite against public officials, government buildings, corporate property, or churches.[3]

Eklund and his fellow dynamiter's penchant for explosives put them closer to the operations of the Galleanisti groups than to the program of the IWW. These groups operated independently across the nation in the first three decades of the twentieth century, but they were all inspired by the writings of Luigi Galleani, who lived in the United States from 1901 until he was deported in 1917. Galleani, who published the newspaper *Cronaca Sovversiva* (Subversive Chronicle) and wrote do-it-yourself manuals for making bombs, criticized those anarchists who preached an end to capitalism but refused to destroy the people and places associated with capitalist power. Spontaneous violence, he argued, would prepare the way for the crumbling of the old order. His heroes included Gaetano Bresci, who assassinated King Umberto I of Italy in August 1900, and Leon Czolgosz, who shot President William McKinley in August 1901. Nicola Sacco and Bartolomeo Vanzetti, anarchists executed by the state of Massachusetts in April 1927 for robbery and murder after a sensational trial that made them martyrs for the cause of worker justice, contributed articles to Galleani's newspaper.[4]

The Galleanisti were responsible for a series of bombings from 1914 to 1920, including a bomb in Milwaukee that killed ten police officers and detectives at a police station as they attempted to defuse it; one that exploded prematurely in front of the house of United States Attorney General A. Mitchell Palmer, killing the deliverer, Carlo Valdinoci; and one that went off on Wall Street at one minute past noon on September 16, 1920, killing thirty-eight and injuring four hundred. The Galleanisti targeted Catholic churches as well as court buildings and Wall Street temples of commerce. Their most prestigious religious target, St. Patrick's Cathedral in New York City, narrowly escaped damage: an informant tipped off authorities beforehand, and the bombers aborted their plans. In 1916 Nestor Dondoglio (aka Jean Crones), a Galleanisti chef, tried to eliminate the civic elite of Chicago by poisoning the soup at a three-hundred-person banquet welcoming the newly appointed leader of the city's Catholics, Archbishop George William Mundelein. The archbishop never touched his soup, and the other guests escaped harm because a sous-chef had disliked the aroma and diluted the soup.[5]

Were Eklund and his partner active Galleanisti, and did their attack on Sts. Peter and Paul represent a gesture of defiance against a hated symbol of complicity with an allegedly brutal capitalist order? Were they outraged like others across the nation in 1924, when they heard the news that Judge Webster Thayer in Boston had denied four motions for a new trial of Sacco and Vanzetti? Had Eklund read or heard about Felix Frankfurter's article in the latest *Atlantic Monthly* which raised questions about the impartiality of the prosecutors and the judge and cast doubt on the guilty verdict in the Sacco and Vanzetti trial?[6]

Eklund died without disclosing the answers to such questions, and he refused to provide any details about the identity of his dead accomplice beyond his Italian last name, Ricca. The man killed by police as he tried to light the dynamite on Filbert Street that early morning may have met Celsten Eklund while passing the time in the dining room of a South of Market boardinghouse. Or the two may have met while working in orchards up and down the Pacific states, living in rooming houses and hotels in Seattle, Portland, San Francisco, Los Angeles, and San Diego when the work dried up.[7] Whatever brought them together, Ricca and Eklund ended their lives determined to accomplish a destructive act of anti-Catholic terrorism.

The bombings signaled to San Franciscans that anarchist anti-Catholicism was still a force to be reckoned with, despite the well-publicized police raid in 1919 that resulted in the closing of the most visible organized presence of anarchism in the city, the IWW Latin Branch. In contrast to socialism, which attracted a wide spectrum of city residents, relatively few of whom were Italian American, San Francisco anarchism was for the most part an Italian concoction, with a bit of Spanish and French flavoring. City *anarchica* heaped scorn on the Italian Catholics, especially the Salesian priests. Anarchists plastered their anticlerical broadsheet *L'Asino* (The Donkey) on the doors of Sts. Peter and Paul, they organized *feste anarchiche* in competition with Catholic festivals, and they published the anarchist monthly newspaper *La Protesta Umana*. San Francisco activists also contributed to the anarchist publications *Cronaca Sovversiva* and *La Questione Sociale,* providing material on local developments for a larger national readership. In November 1906 a San Francisco correspondent decried Catholic Italian religious devotion in the city, which was especially manifest in the months after the great earthquake and fire.

> Religious fervor is at its apex. The Italian element—without distinction between southern and northern—gives us an unsettling spectacle, which is both servile and idiotic. . . . The moment they have a baby [they] hurry to call the priestly enemy to have the child baptized. The strongest propagandist would give everything up when faced with these people. It is therefore useless to speak to them about the slavery and misery in which one lives. Each one accepts resigned the fate that god has decreed. If I confront them with the causes of their misery when they complain, they just abandon me and flee. I can only hope for an awakening of these masses.[8]

Four years later, Italian socialists organized the Latin Branch of the IWW, which welcomed anarchists and syndicalists as well as socialists. In the pages of its newspapers *Il Proletario* and *Il Lavoratore Industriale* the Latin Branch targeted the city police department, American Federation of Labor (AFL) unions, Italian business owners and professionals (*prominenti*), and the Catholic population and church leadership. What the Latin Branch lacked in numbers, with never more than several hundred members, it made up for in rhetorical flourish and revolutionary noise. Every week, soapbox orations at outdoor meetings competed with Catholic homilies at Sts. Peter and Paul Church, only a few blocks away. The church building was renamed "quell sacro pastribolo delle coscienze" (that sacred gallows of conscience), and the pastor earned the sobriquet "infame l'uomo nero, la bestia, malefica, il prete" (infamous black man, the evil beast, the priest).[9]

Latin Branch anarchists made the front page after a speech on Sunday, August 13, 1911, by Filippo Perrone, a peripatetic Italian anarchist who had recently arrived in San Francisco from Baja California, where he had been organizing anarchist communes with the Mexican revolutionary Ricardo Flores Magón. San Francisco police normally operated according to a "live and let live" policy toward street speakers, but Perrone seems to have particularly annoyed the detectives on duty, who arrested him after he shouted "disparagingly about the American flag, condemning law and order, and denouncing all form of government, and ending with a tirade against the Pope." *Cronaca Sovversiva* lost no time condemning "un vergognoso sopruso dei polizziotti di San Francisco" (a shameful abuse by San Francisco police). *L'Italia,* a politically conservative North Beach newspaper, also objected to the arrest, arguing that the police had violated both Italian dignity and American free-speech rights. But Father Rafaelle Piperni, the pastor of Sts. Peter and Paul, disagreed, criticizing Perrone for his incendiary irreligious discourse and *L'Italia* for its mistaken belief that the official guardians of civic law and order should tolerate public advocacy of an erroneous philosophy.[10]

Father Piperni, who served as pastor of Sts. Peter and Paul from 1897 to 1929, battled Italian members of the Masonic Order as well as socialists and anarchists. The pope condemned freemasonry in 1738, and Catholics lost their good standing in the church if they joined a Masonic lodge. Freemasonry came to Little Italy in 1872 (twenty-five years before the first Salesian priests arrived), when Andrea Sbarboro and his colleagues founded a lodge by the name of Speranza Italiana. The city's Italian masons declared their anti-Catholicism by setting up business on the second anniversary of Victor Emmanuel II's defeat of the soldiers of Pope Pius IX and the end of the Papal States, associating "the hope of Italy" in the lodge's name with the secular monarchy instead of the Catholic papacy. Tensions between Masonic anti-Catholics and Catholic anti-Masons came to the boiling point when Ernesto Nathan, the mayor of Rome, came to San Francisco to represent Italy at the Panama Pacific International Exposition, the 1915 world's fair. Mayor Nathan's Jewish family background and his membership in the Masonic Order provoked consternation among the city's Catholics, especially Italian Catholics. They could recall Nathan's speech at the opening of the 1911 Rome Exhibition, a speech made on the anniversary, once again, of the 1870 victory of Italian government troops over the army of the Papal States. For Nathan, Italy aspired to be "the champion of liberty of thought," except that the Catholic Church blocked the way: the Vatican represented "the fortress of dogma where the last despairing effort is being made to keep up the reign of ignorance." Archbishop Hanna, who had lobbied unsuccessfully to have Nathan replaced by a Catholic, lamented, "It makes one burn with shame to think of the Italy so glorious, so Catholic is represented here by a free-mason, a socialist, a Jew."[11]

Archbishop Hanna moderated his anti-Semitism in the years to come, but he gave no quarter to anarchism, socialism, or masonry, Italian or otherwise. His predecessor, Archbishop Patrick W. Riordan, tried to distract Italian residents from anti-Catholic ideologies by inviting Italian priests such as Angelo Andriano and Rafaelle Piperni to San Francisco. Hanna followed suit, recruiting zealous priests to expand services to Italian Catholics and encouraging Italian laymen such as Sylvester Andriano to build new social infrastructure to foster Catholic cultural power. The most eminent of the newcomers was Father Albert Bandini, a native of Florence trained in classical studies and the law. Hanna had served with the Florentine on the faculty of St. Andrew's College, a seminary in Rochester, New York, before moving to San Francisco in 1912. In 1915, when newly installed as archbishop of San Francisco, Hanna invited his former colleague to the city. Bandini arrived eight months after Nathan's controversial visit.[12]

By 1919 Father Bandini had become both a U.S. citizen and a member of the California Bar Association, and he ministered to the growing number of Italians in the San Francisco archdiocese. That same year, Sylvester Andriano and James Bacigalupi, although no longer law partners, collaborated in mounting the city's first Columbus Day celebration. They also organized the Italian Catholic Union (ICU), which promoted Columbus Day and provided the funds to publish a Catholic weekly to reach the Italian-speaking residents of Little Italy and the growing number of Italian Americans living well beyond North Beach. By the end of 1923 the four-year-old paper, *L'Unione,* with Archbishop Hanna serving as its honorary president, boasted accurately that it had "the Largest Circulation of any Italian-American Weekly published in San Francisco." Italian priests served as the paper's first two editors, Bandini succeeding Father Oscar Balducci.[13]

The business staff included Luigi Providenza, the twenty-six-year-old former chairman of the Genoa branch of the Popular Party. The Popular Party (Partito Popolare Italiano, or PPI) was founded in 1919 by the former head of Italian Catholic Action, a Sicilian priest named Don Luigi Sturzo. PPI activists like Providenza were targeted by the hardliners who organized the Communist Party of Italy in January 1921, and he left Italy after surviving three assassination attempts. The new pope, Pius XI, preferred a Vatican-controlled Catholic Action program to a Catholic Action–oriented political party. By the end of 1922, with Mussolini the prime minister of Italy and the Fascists in power, the PPI's days were numbered.[14] Providenza left Italy and became one of the Catholic *fuorusciti* who would continue their anti-Fascist work outside their native country.

Resettled in San Francisco, his PPI days behind him, Providenza turned his attention toward the apathetic non-churchgoing Italian population in the city. Anti-Catholic political doctrines offered a serious challenge to the faith, but so did the waterfront and Barbary Coast saloons, dance halls, and bordellos adjacent to Little Italy. As Providenza went door-to-door to sell subscriptions to *L'Unione* to Catholic families in North Beach, he was "appalled to find that most of them had lost their Faith." So in 1924 he joined forces with Father Bandini to create the Italian Catholic Federation (ICF), a parish-based, Bay Area–wide "lay apostolate" dedicated to the revitalization of religious observance, mutual benefits for members and families, and charity work. With backing from devout *prominenti* like Sylvester Andriano, the ICF sent missionary priests into Italian neighborhoods, sponsored retreats, and organized parades, processions, and public prayer devotions called novenas. Founded to promote Catholic practice, the ICF also boosted ethnic pride, and its by-laws included a "PATRIOTIC" clause: to "keep alive the respect and love of its members for their original Fatherland, encouraging and promoting at the same time some methods of enlightened Americanization among them."[15]

Promoting Americanization while maintaining love and respect for the fatherland was not as simple a proposition as the ICF made it appear. German Americans had found it necessary to distinguish between affection for the homeland and support for the kaiser and his regime during World War I, and Italian Americans in the mid-1920s found themselves disagreeing over the legitimacy of Mussolini's Fascist regime. Most Americans, San Franciscans included, regarded Mussolini positively until the late 1930s. But that was not the case for Italian secular liberals, socialists, and communists, especially those political exiles (*fuorusciti*) who were anti-Catholic. They condemned *Time* for putting Il Duce on its cover and cringed at such popular culture tributes as Cole Porter's "You're the tops, you're Mussolini." Most Italian American Catholics focused on "the reassuring and conservative aspects of his regime: the re-establishment of law and order, the repression of communism, the abolition of the right to strike, the agricultural projects for draining and reclaiming wastelands, the Crucifix again placed in the public schools, the trains which ran on time." But critics of the Italian American Catholic accommodation seethed. The biographer of Gaetano Salvemini, a historian member of the anti-Fascist exile community, recalled that "it was hardly possible to pronounce the words 'on time' in Salvemini's presence, without his rising to his feet in a rage."[16]

Writing from his San Francisco office, Father Bandini critiqued even the rather mild dissent against Fascist theory published by Father John A. Ryan, a professor at the Catholic University of America. Ryan criticized "the political doctrine of Fascism" when he reviewed the English translation of a speech of that title by Alfredo Rocco, the Fascist minister of justice, in two issues of the weekly Catholic magazine *Commonweal* in November 1926. Ryan's argument that Fascism demonstrated principles and practices offensive to Catholics roused the ire of Father Bandini. In a letter to the magazine, Bandini accused Ryan of "overstating his objections to Fascism" and insisted that "any form of civil society, if safeguarding the authority of the Church and allowing the spiritual development of man, does not contradict Catholic doctrine. . . . [Ryan] probably does not mean to say that a good Fascist cannot be a good Catholic." Ryan replied that Fascism includes "the monstrous propositions that the state is an end in itself, that it is justified in using any means to attain its objects, and that it is the source of all individual rights—in other words, that the human person has no natural rights." Bandini had the last word in a second letter to *Commonweal,* defending "the many Catholics, high and low, churchmen and laymen, who support Fascism in Italy."[17]

3

Catholic Action, from Rome to San Francisco

The action of Catholics, of whatever description it may be, will work with greater effect if all of the various associations, while preserving their individual rights, move together under one primary and directive force.

—Pope Leo XIII, "Graves de Communi Re," 1901

The field of Catholic Action is extremely vast. In itself it does not exclude anything, in any manner, direct or indirect, which pertains to the divine mission of the Church.

—Pope Pius X, "Il Fermo Proposito," 1905

It is not possible for a Catholic to accept the claim that the Church and the Pope must limit themselves to the external practices of religion (such as Mass and the Sacraments).

—Pope Pius XI, "Non Abbiamo Bisogno," 1931

We have a duty to make a contribution of Christian ideals and principles to the nation.

—Coadjutor Archbishop John J. Mitty, "Sermon on Catholic Action," 1932

When Father Albert Bandini insisted that one could support Fascist Italy and still be a good Catholic, he was expressing the mainstream view among the nation's Catholics during the 1920s. They could justify their position by citing the practice of the Vatican itself, which criticized certain practices of the regime but did not declare the Fascist state incompatible in principle with Catholic natural law theology. Italian Fascism became even more acceptable to American Catholics after the Pope agreed to the Lateran Accords of February 11, 1929. Through this treaty the Vatican acquired sovereignty over its Roman properties, diplomatic relations opened with Italy, Catholicism became the official state religion, Catholic marriages and Catholic school diplomas acquired legal standing, elementary and secondary school students studied religion with books and teachers approved by the church, and Catholic lay organizations, specifically the Vatican's Catholic Action lay organizations, received state sanction.[1]

Catholics in the United States, Italian and otherwise, expected the Lateran Accords to open a new era of Catholic influence in Italy. Certainly, this was the view of Father Angelo Andriano, who gave up his parish church and his chaplaincy in the Italian Catholic Federation and returned to Italy four months after Vatican secretary of state Cardinal Pietro Gasparri signed the treaty. Angelo's brother Sylvester understood the reasons for the decision, but he confided to Archbishop Edward A. Hanna his belief that Angelo was taking "a most ill-advised step."[2]

> Providence may have decreed that he, with his twenty odd years' diversified experience in the Catholic life of this country, should play a part in the reflowering of religion in Italy, following the settlement of the Roman question, for the honor of God and his Church? Of course, when I think of the tremendous work that remains to be done among our Italian people here and how well he was doing his share of that work and how few there are to do it, I find it hard to believe that he has not made a mistake.

By the mid-1920s Sylvester Andriano was a member of the archbishop's inner circle of laymen, relied on for his knowledge of and influence in the Italian community. At the same time, the attorney was venturing beyond his work with Catholic and Italian causes into the larger arena of San Francisco municipal politics and public office. In 1925 he joined the executive committee of a local Association Against the Prohibition Amendment, bringing a specifically Catholic social policy viewpoint to the debate when he lectured audiences that such legislation belonged to the sphere of local, not national, control.[3] Three years later he joined attorneys Maurice Harrison and Chauncey Tramutolo in a "young men's Smith club" in support of the nomination of New York governor Alfred E. Smith as the Democratic Party's candidate in the presidential election of 1928. And in the same year, San Francisco mayor James Rolph Jr. appointed Andriano to a three-year, nine-month term on the city Board of Supervisors, replacing a member who had died in office. Then, in 1931, Andriano's friend and client Angelo Rossi became the city's first Italian American mayor, and that summer Rossi sent Andriano to Paris as the city's representative in a delegation of U.S. mayors to the Paris International Exposition.[4]

During his trip abroad Andriano visited his brother Angelo. Angelo was now resettled in Turin but was reconsidering his decision to return to Italy, given the Fascist regime's attack on several of the church's Catholic Action programs there. These programs, religious educational and recreational organizations run by lay men and women, were designed to revitalize Italian culture and politics along the lines of Catholic teaching. Mussolini had never intended the Lateran Treaty agreements with the church to open the door to Catholic competition with his regime's program of Fascist political socialization, and he quickly made it clear (as did his local Fascist party "enforcers") that less Catholic Action was more than enough.[5]

The term Catholic Action came into general usage after 1901, when Pope Leo XIII (1878–1903) urged lay Catholics to mobilize, under the guidance of their bishops, on behalf of Christian Democracy and against Social Democracy, which he equated with "bad philosophical and ethical teaching," criticizing "the error which was lurking in the utterances of socialism." Pius X (1903–1914) extended the concept two years later in his "Il Fermo Proposito" (On Catholic Action in Italy), which urged lay men and women, under the direction of their priests and bishops, to organize

> bands of Catholics who aim to unite all their forces in combating anti-Christian civilization by every just and lawful

> means. They use every means in repairing the serious disorders caused by it. They seek to restore Jesus Christ to the family, the school and society by re-establishing the principle that human authority represents the authority of God. They take to heart the interests of the people, especially those of the working and agricultural classes, not only by inculcating in the hearts of everybody a true religious spirit (the only true fount of consolation among the troubles of this life) but also by endeavoring to dry their tears, to alleviate their sufferings, and to improve their economic condition by wise measures. All these works, sustained and promoted chiefly by lay Catholics and whose form varies according to the needs of each country, constitute what is generally known by a distinctive and surely a very noble name: "Catholic Action," or the "Action of Catholics."[6]

Catholic Action work became a central element of the program outlined by Pope Pius XI (1922–1939) in his first encyclical, "Ubi Arcano Dei Consilio" (On the Peace of Christ in the Kingdom of Christ), issued in December 1922, ten months after he took office. Reflecting on the cultural impact of the Great War, the pope expressed concern that "public life is so enveloped, even at the present hour, by the dense fog of mutual hatreds and grievances that it is almost impossible for the common people so much as freely to breathe therein. If the defeated nations continue to suffer most terribly, no less serious are the evils which afflict their conquerors." In addition to the tensions among countries dissatisfied with the provisions of the peace treaties signed at Versailles, Pius XI was particularly distressed by "the war between the classes, a chronic and mortal disease of present-day society, which like a cancer is eating away the vital forces of the social fabric, labor, industry, the arts, commerce, agriculture—everything in fact which contributes to public and private welfare and to national prosperity." Despite "our much praised progress, we behold with sorrow society lapsing back slowly but surely into a state of barbarism." Catholics, including "that whole group of movements, organizations, and works so dear to Our fatherly heart which passes under the name of 'Catholic Action,'" could lead the way in restoring "the fundamental principles of Christianity" to a central place in world affairs "both in public and private life." In his enumeration of the activities particularly crucial for lay activism, the pope emphasized "the *holy battle* waged on so many fronts to vindicate for the family and the Church the natural and divinely given rights which they possess over education and the school."[7]

San Francisco's Archbishop Edward Hanna involved himself personally in Catholic Action work by expanding the church's outreach activities to poor immigrants and migrants, fostering Catholic activism in local trade unions, and serving as an arbitrator in the city's labor disputes. Perhaps the most dramatic public demonstration of the archbishop's commitment to Catholic Action came on October 5, 1924, the anniversary of the founding of the Holy Name Society, when 80,000 Catholics displayed their solidarity by marching the length of Market Street, San Francisco's major downtown thoroughfare, in a demonstration against the Ku Klux Klan. Sylvester Andriano supported a variety of Catholic Action youth programs during the 1920s. Whether it was because he was responding directly to Pius XI's call for waging a "*holy battle*" on the educational front, or was influenced by the model of Don Bosco's work with boys, or was compensating for the fact that he and his wife were childless, or perhaps for all these reasons (the record is silent), Andriano became especially active in North Beach Catholic youth programs and served as the chairman of the statewide Knights of Columbus Catholic education committee. St. Mary's College depended on him as a guest instructor in their "transition course" for members of the graduating class, where he suggested Catholic alternatives to "the curse of individualism," and in 1929 the Italian government awarded Andriano the honorific title of "Insignia of the Cross of Italian Knighthood" in recognition of his educational work among Italian youth.[8]

Five months before Andriano received his knighthood award, Benito Mussolini addressed the Italian Chamber of Deputies and clarified the provisions of the 1929 Lateran Accords. The accords did not establish a "free and sovereign church, free and sovereign state."

Instead, "in the state the church is not sovereign and not even free. . . . The Fascist state categorically reaffirms its ethical character. It is Catholic, but it is Fascist—indeed, it is exclusively, essentially Fascist." "In this we are intractable! Education must belong to us."[9]

The pope replied the next day with "a stinging indictment of Mussolini's contention that children belonged to the state" and, two weeks later, with a line-by-line reply to Il Duce's argument in the Vatican newspaper. There the controversy stood until April and May 1931, when members of the Gruppo Universitari Fascisti (GUF), angered by Catholic youth groups in northern Italy, took to the streets. Seeing their Catholic Action rivals as a "Catholic cyst within the Italian body politic," they ransacked the offices of Catholic Action groups, burned Catholic books, mocked Catholic worship with blasphemous parodies, and shouted "Death to Catholic Action" and "Down with the pope."[10]

The Fascist attacks on Catholic Action leaders forced Igino Righetti, president of the leading Catholic university organization, to seek refuge in the Vatican during the last week of May. Sylvester Andriano was in France that week and may have seen the headlines announcing Mussolini's May 29 decision to make all non-Fascist youth groups illegal, to padlock their offices, and to confiscate their records. Priests and bishops all over Italy launched protest demonstrations. In Turin, where Andriano reunited with his brother Father Angelo several weeks later, Mussolini's order—according to the Fascist party local prefect—"exasperated the clergy mightily and they have thrown themselves into the work of sabotage." The pope issued his own protest on July 5, when he published the encyclical "Non Abbiamo Bisogno" (Concerning Catholic Action in Italy) in the Vatican newspaper. Written in vigorous Italian rather than in academic Latin, smuggled out of Italy to avoid confiscation by government censors, and published by Monsignor Francis Spellman of New York, the letter denounced the regime's attack on Catholic Action as a thinly veiled excuse to justify what the London *Tablet* characterized as attacks by "Fascismo's bullies" designed to "secure all Italy and all Italians for the totalitarian and omnivorous State."[11] The pope declared that it was the Catholic Church, not the Fascist state, that had a "universal and divine mandate to educate children," and he condemned Mussolini's premise that children should be educated

> for the sole and exclusive benefit of a party and of a regime based on an ideology that clearly resolves itself into a veritable pagan worship of the state. A conception of the State which makes the rising generations belong to it entirely, without any exception, from the tenderest years up to adult life, cannot be reconciled by a Catholic either with Catholic doctrine or with the natural rights of the family. It is not possible for a Catholic to accept the claim that the Church and the Pope must limit themselves to the external practices of religion (such as Mass and the Sacraments), and that all the rest of education belongs to the State.[12]

The pope's uncompromising language in "Non Abbiamo Bisogno" did not translate into papal intransigence regarding Catholic Action. Instead, the pontiff approved a series of eleven cooling-off meetings between Vatican and Fascist representatives to resolve the differences between the state and the church without further violence. In September the Vatican announced a compromise designed to satisfy both sides: Catholic Action would be restructured as a strictly local endeavor operating within diocesan limits under the watchful eyes of bishops; and the most militant anti–Catholic Action university leaders, Carlo Scorza and Giovanni Giurati, would be removed from their positions in the GUF. Scorza, who had directed the Fascist Youth organization (Gioventù Fascista), was also removed from that post and expelled from the Fascist Party Directorate. The compromise punished the most militant of the anti-Catholic leaders, but it hurt Catholic Action organizations more because they were reduced to the status of "religious discussion groups," bereft of political and policy influence. Don Luigi Sturzo, the exiled former head of the now defunct Catholic political party, characterized the September compromise as "the complete triumph of the Fascist state over the church."[13] The crisis ended, and relations between the church and the regime entered what historian Richard A. Webster has described as "idyllic years."[14]

Twelve years later Andriano recalled the significance of his 1931 visit to Italy: the pope was "stoutly defending Catholic Action against the unwarranted attacks of the Fascists and denouncing some of the teachings and practices of Fascism including the Fascist oath. I became really interested in Catholic Action and upon my return to San Francisco undertook the study of it in earnest."[15] Andriano's decision to make Catholic Action a preoccupation came at an auspicious moment with both an international and a local dimension. If the pope's decision to downsize Catholic Action into a diocesan endeavor applied to the United States as well as Italy, American lay persons could make it a high-priority local option, provided their bishop approved. And a strong proponent of the papal initiative, Bishop John J. Mitty, arrived six months later to become San Francisco's coadjutor archbishop. As coadjutor, Mitty worked in concert with Archbishop Hanna for three years and then succeeded him as archbishop when Hanna retired in March 1935.

When he arrived in San Francisco, Mitty was a forty-eight-year-old former bishop of Salt Lake City, Utah. A battlefield chaplain during World War I, he participated in the Meuse-Argonne offensive in France. His leadership style combined efficient administration of archdiocesan business affairs with zealous evangelism in connection with the message of the papal encyclicals. He chose as the official motto of his episcopal office the phrase "Mihi Vivere Christus Est" (To me, to live is Christ).[16]

Mitty's arrival in San Francisco coincided with a nationwide discussion among Catholic clergy and laity about how best to implement the teachings contained in two papal encyclicals issued by Pius XI in 1931. The discussion concerned both "Non Abbiamo Bisogno" (On Catholic Action in Italy) and "Quadragesimo Anno" (On Reconstruction of the Social Order). The latter reasserted the principles of Pope Leo XIII's 1891 encyclical on labor and capital, which had urged Catholics worldwide to insist on a moral economy. Pius XI reiterated the condemnation of what he considered utopian left-wing ideologies and social movements as well as materialist business practices backed by laissez-faire governments that ignored the general good of the community. He urged Catholics to take the lead in organizing new community institutions designed to foster cooperation among workers, business owners, and government officials, and he excoriated the notions that class conflict was natural, that irreconcilable differences separated working people and the business class, and that an overthrow of all existing things would accomplish paradise on earth for the workers of the world.[17] Scarcely a year after the Vatican promulgated the two 1931 encyclicals, Archbishop Mitty launched a Catholic Action campaign in San Francisco that would continue through the 1930s and into the World War II years and beyond.

The occasion was a sermon at a reception for the Archdiocesan Council of the National Council of Catholic Women (NCCW) on May 7, 1932. Mitty told his audience that he wanted "greater effort and activity on your part" on behalf of Catholic Action, which "has been preached to us in season and out of season, especially by our present Holy Father, Pope Pius XI. By Catholic Action we mean the intelligent cooperation of the laity in all Catholic interests and activities under the direction of the Hierarchy."

> The purpose and object of our organization is not political. Neither as a Church nor an organization are we interested in any political aim or any political party. Our aim and purpose is to bring the ideals and principles of Christ into every phase of human life, into our own individual life, into family, social, economic, professional, political and national life. We are striving to advance the interests of Christ, to bring the spirit of Christ into our homes, our reception halls, our workshops, our offices, our legislative assemblies. We cannot separate human activity into separate compartments; we cannot accept the ideals of Christ in our personal lives and ignore them in business, social and political relations. We have a duty to make our contribution of Christian ideals and principles to the nation.

He continued, "We cannot live as if we were not part of the country. We are Americans with the obligation to serve the best interests of the nation. And we do that best of all when the spirit of Christ animates and vivifies all our activities and our relations and when we band ourselves together to bring the spirit of Christ into every phase of human life and activity." We must "work unceasingly for both Church and country, for both Cross and Flag."[18]

Mitty could not know, as he spoke in May 1932, that two years later a series of events would occur in San Francisco that would challenge the church and its lay activists to define more carefully the boundaries between the political and the nonpolitical in Catholic Action work. These events, a local expression of the national contest between labor and management in the context of New Deal labor relations reforms, were the tumultuous waterfront strike of May–July 1934 and the four-day general strike of July 16–19, 1934. Because Andriano was closely connected with the archbishop and the Chancery Office, and because he served on Mayor Rossi's citizens' advisory committee during the strike, he would thereafter be associated with the positions they took during those emotional and sometimes violent weeks.

4

Catholic Action Theory and Practice in San Francisco

Enroll in this great movement . . . there is no more important outlet for Catholic Action in these distressing times.

—Academy of San Francisco Organizing Committee, April 18, 1933

The members of the Academy . . . stood up like men. They have assumed real leadership in the fight for the application of the ideals of Christian justice, probably to a greater extent and to greater advantage than any similar group of Catholic gentlemen in America.

—*Leader,* July 21, 1934

The Pacific Coast maritime strike from May through July 1934 challenged church leaders and lay men and women to confront an ambiguity created by the pope's September 1931 agreement with the Fascist government of Italy. Pius XI had agreed to shrink Catholic Action by removing it from electoral politics and restricting its remaining activities to diocesan boundaries. But the pope issued no corresponding reduction in the theory of Catholic Action; its scope and limits had in fact expanded with the Vatican's encyclical of May 15, 1931, "Quadragesimo Anno," which called for "reconstruction" of the social order. What did this ambiguity portend for Catholics in the United States? Did American bishops, priests, and lay men and women reduce Catholic Action interest group efforts in the fields of education, labor and capital, anti-Communism, and other issue areas, such as birth control and public morals?

U.S. bishops responded not by reducing their efforts but by intensifying them, working to create more effective diocesan Catholic Action work nationwide along the lines of the encyclicals of

Pius XI. The coordinating agency for this work was the National Catholic Welfare Conference, an interest group that represented American bishops. Although it was based in Washington, D.C., its chairman during this period was Archbishop Edward Hanna of San Francisco. It was in this context that Coadjutor Archbishop Mitty called for a revitalization of Christian practice by means of a robust new Catholic Action initiative. Mitty's call demonstrated that he and Archbishop Hanna intended to increase, not reduce, faith-based public activism in the city. This decision set the stage for an aggressive assertion of Catholic principles two years later when San Franciscans confronted the tumultuous events of May–July 1934. But even beforehand, Catholic Action work moved steadily forward.[1]

In September 1932, four months after Mitty issued his call for a Catholic Action initiative to the women of the local branch of the NCCW, New York City laymen organized the Catholic League for Social Justice and sent out calls to their counterparts in cities across the nation to follow suit. Six months later Catholics in fifty-four dioceses in the United States, including New York City, had established branches. Sylvester Andriano and his law partner William R. Lowery took up the call and organized a San Francisco branch called the Academy of San Francisco, which operated out of their office at 550 Montgomery Street in the heart of the city's financial district. By April 1933 Archbishops Hanna and Mitty had approved the academy's work and it had enrolled three dozen members, including several judges, numerous attorneys and physicians, and Gordon O'Neill, the editor of the archdiocesan newspaper the *Monitor.* Each member pledged "to inform myself on Catholic doctrine on Social Justice, to conform my life to its requirements, and to do everything in my power, in my home and religious life, in my social and business contacts, to promote its principles." They explained that their object was "to mobilize the combined strength of all these existing [San Francisco Catholic devotional and social] societies to enable their members to answer the call of our Holy Father." Members established committees devoted to specific aspects of public policy, and Andriano agreed to chair the Committee on Catholic Education in California.[2]

The San Francisco response to the call for intensified Catholic Action work attracted the attention of the pope's representative in the United States, Apostolic Delegate Archbishop Amleto Giovanni Cicognani, who praised Archbishop Hanna's efforts "to prepare laymen for Catholic Action." "It is becoming urgently necessary," Cicognani wrote, "to prepare laymen who under the guidance of the Bishops and priests will speak for the Church. Students of our Universities and Colleges should give special attention to the Social Question so that they may assume a lay leadership which is truly Catholic and which will resourcefully make popular Catholic principles. This is but complying with the wish of the Holy Father. It will make practical His Holiness' plan of Catholic Action."[3]

Attorney Roy A. Bronson advertised the work of the academy in a letter sent to the pastors of every Catholic church in the San Francisco area, urging them to provide "the Catholic laity with a program of Catholic action and an opportunity to exercise their full moral and civic duty in the reconstruction of our social and economic order in the Christian spirit of justice, charity, moderation and fortitude." In August the academy announced its first project, a year-long program of biweekly lectures devoted to "finding out the facts in connection with Education in our country and to test the value of these facts in the light of Catholic principles." When members assembled at the Hotel Cecil that fall and winter, they heard a variety of presentations analyzing education from the perspective of Catholic Action; for example, Sylvester Andriano praised "the Catholic educational program" in California, and Judge Robert McWilliams critiqued secular attempts "to nationalize the system of education in this country."[4]

Two weeks after McWilliams's lecture, the *Monitor* published a lengthy attack on the school reform work of Columbia University professor John Dewey, a leading critic of Catholic natural law philosophy who had repelled Catholic intellectuals by rejecting the concept of an absolute deity while cynically acknowledging the utility of religion in society. Dewey was only the tip of the iceberg, according to the editorial "A Revolution by Professors," which warned against an insidious process under way throughout the nation: "teachers in the American public schools are invited and urged to become agents of a revolution; which has as its objective the American brand of communism." Echoing Pope Leo XIII's condemnation of social democracy in 1901, the editorial warned against "a monopolistic State, governed by materialist university men."

> The appalling phenomenon is that the encroachment of the State as directed by the professors occasions little articulate alarm on the part of Catholics. We seem to rest content that President Roosevelt will permit nothing to be done to offend Catholics. The charm, the good will, the high degree of courage of the President are worthy of unreserved praise. But, must we suffer all of the brain trustees and other wonder boys in the government to manoeuvre toward the totalitarian state without challenge? The kindest service to Mr. Roosevelt is criticism and vigilance over the public servants upon whom he depends. A century ago, even to-day under less charming and less tolerant a ruler, Catholics would have spoken against the absorption of life by civil government.
>
> We are in danger, as a people, of slow spiritual death because the services of the Church, in which services we should participate, are appropriated by the State that is directed by professors, who intend to make certain that the Church shall remain irrelevant. Our only hope is to make the Church felt in practical political and communal life.[5]

On March 3, just over a month after the *Monitor* urged its readers to make their presence felt, the union representing dockworkers on the Pacific Coast set in motion a series of events that provided Catholic Action activists an opportunity to demonstrate that they were a force to be reckoned with in public life. Emboldened by the Roosevelt administration's support for union organizing and collective bargaining, the longshoremen's associations demanded worker-controlled unions, union-controlled hiring halls, higher wages and a bonus for overtime work, and a thirty-hour week. Two months later their demands were still unmet, and after voting to strike, some ten thousand dockworkers left their jobs in port cities up and down the coast. The following day, May 10, thousands of San Francisco strikers demonstrated their strength when they marched in a picket line along the waterfront.[6]

By the end of the first month of the strike, despite personal mediation attempts by Mayor Rossi and Assistant Secretary of Labor Edward J. McGrady, the conflict had intensified. Seamen and other maritime workers joined the strike, and sympathetic teamsters refused to move "scab" (non-union) cargoes. The Waterfront Employers Association flatly refused to consider the key demand of a union-controlled hiring hall and enlisted the support of the city's Chamber of Commerce and its union-busting Industrial Association. The employer organizations condemned the strike as a Communist-inspired revolt, not a genuine labor dispute, and they urged the mayor to crush it with military force. Archbishops Hanna and Mitty acknowledged the role of Communists but insisted that the strikers had legitimate grievances that should be addressed by the employers. Sylvester Andriano, serving on Mayor Rossi's informal citizens' committee, urged the mayor not to use force against the strikers, and Andriano's San Francisco Academy endorsed the demand for a union hiring hall. The academy joined the two archbishops in criticizing the employers for their refusal to consider moderating their position on the strike demands.

Communist activists did play a role in setting the strategy and tactics of the strike. The Communist Party district organization decided to build up its membership in San Francisco at a meeting in spring 1932, and several experienced agents, including Sam Darcy and Harrison George, moved to the city to recruit new members, especially waterfront and maritime workers, into the Communist movement. To attract the attention of radical and potentially radical maritime workers, party agents decided to publish a mimeographed newspaper, the *Waterfront Worker* (coincidentally, this was one week after Archbishop Mitty called for the Catholic Action program). For two years, the Communist Party built up the circulation of the newspaper and recruited new members. Several of the *Waterfront*

Worker inner circle became members of the executive committee of the dockworkers' union, Local 38-79 of the International Longshoremen's Association, and one of those men, Harry Bridges, was elected chairman of the strike committee in March 1934.[7]

Bridges came under attack both because of his alleged Communist affiliations and because the Australian-born longshoreman had lived in San Francisco for over a decade but had never become a U.S. citizen. Bridges was a secret member of the Communist Party who went by the name "Rossi" in clandestine communications with the Communist Third International organization (Comintern), but he never admitted to being a member of the party, never explained why he chose the name "Rossi," and never slavishly followed "the party line." The independent Catholic newspaper the *Leader,* continuing the policy of its founder, Father Peter Yorke, of supporting the rights of labor as vigorously as it did full and complete Irish independence from England, condemned the charges of Communist influence as "vicious misrepresentation" by "callous capitalists and the servile press and radio stations." The *Monitor,* while critical of "materialists on both sides," especially castigated the "rugged individualists among the shipping executives who hate resistance to their lust for power and for profits." The official archdiocesan newspaper warned that settlement of the strike would come only when business agreed to "break away from the code of hate and contempt that has characterized too many American captains of industry and finance."[8]

On June 9, at the end of the first month of the strike, the archdiocesan newspaper presented the Catholic Church's point of view in a front-page editorial titled "The Maritime Strikes." "The rights of the ship-owners over their ships do not give them the right to impoverish the whole community; nor do the rights of the striking workers include the right to pursue their aims regardless of the consequences to the third party in the dispute, namely the people who are not directly involved, but whom [*sic*] depend upon cargoes for their livelihoods and sustenance." Sounding a theme that would prove continuous through the 1934 events, the *Monitor* urged "all Catholics, who are employers, or who are in any way directly connected [with management] to read and know the contents of the encyclicals . . . that treat of the problems of capital and labor . . . and to acquaint their associates and acquaintances with the contents of these encyclicals and to give them copies of them." Should Catholic San Franciscans fail in this duty, according to the editorialist, "then those Catholics will be held to answer."[9]

In addition to prescribing the moral responsibility of all San Franciscans to involve themselves personally in helping to settle labor conflicts according to Catholic principles, the editorial alerted Catholics to the particular danger posed by extremism. "Shipowners have a perfect right to refuse to deliver the management of their business to a soviet. Longshoremen have a perfect right to organize in a union and to bargain collectively for wages and hours that will enable them to support their families in frugal comfort, to educate their children, and to lay something by for sickness and old age. But these rights are obscured because of the laissez faire extremists on the one hand and the communist fanatics on the other. The public has had enough of both." It continued, "We regret that hate motivates both of these groups. The Communists hate injustice more than they love justice. The ruthless 'individualists' among employers do not consider justice at all, but hate all who check their lust for power and money."[10]

San Franciscans needed to organize a Catholic counterforce:

> If Christian workers would stem the tide of Communism, they must bring to the workers' cause as devoted an energy and as strict a discipline as members of the Communist Party manifest. Communism is a religion—a materialistic religion [and] appeals to many workers because the apostles of Communism work with a zeal worthy of a better cause. They can be challenged and checked only by men, who for the love of God study the Catholic teaching as thoroughly as Communists study the Communist theory; who devote as much energy to the propagation of the principles contained in the encyclicals on labor as the Communists do in spreading the doctrine of Marx; who labor as industriously to apply Catholic principles as the Communists work to apply the principles of Lenin.[11]

Given the influence of Catholic social teaching on labor activism in the city, San Francisco Catholics had long regarded principled anti-Communism and militant trade unionism as fitting together as comfortably as the two halves of a walnut. Mayor Rossi, determined to discredit Communism, also took steps to educate the public on the differences between legitimate union activity compatible with Catholic teaching and illegal radical violence. Presiding over a meeting at city hall, in the midst of the business paralysis induced by the strike, the mayor proclaimed the week of June 21–28 "American Legion Week." Flying squadrons of "three minute men" would take their patriotic message, with musical accompaniment, into all the downtown and neighborhood theaters. This effort "to stamp Communism out of American life . . . represents crystallized efforts of civic, religious, labor and group leaders . . . brought to active educational functioning through the exigencies of the situation, locally and nationally." At the end of the week's events a committee representing the waterfront employers met with the mayor and his advisory committee and demanded that the city break the strike by forcibly opening the port. Sylvester Andriano disagreed and argued, against the objections of the majority of the group, not to approve such a plan or be a party to it.[12]

Andriano was the mayor's friend as well as his personal attorney, but he also commanded a degree of influence because of his previous service on the city Board of Supervisors and his extensive nongovernmental civic activities. He was singled out as a model of impartial judgment on May 27, when the board unanimously supported a resolution by Supervisor Andrew Gallagher that Rossi appoint a commission to investigate the role of the police during the strike to that point. The commission should include "one or two public spirited citizens whose sense of social justice and of fair play has appealed to me as much, for example, as that of my two former and undefeated colleagues on this board, Supervisors Andriano and Harrelson." Rossi never appointed such a commission, but now he decided to follow Andriano's advice and announced that the city's fight was against Communists, not labor unions, and that it would not put its authority at the disposal of the Chamber of Commerce and the Industrial Association.[13]

Archbishop Hanna, appointed by President Roosevelt the chairman of the National Longshoreman's Board, with authority to oversee a settlement of the strike, joined the mayor in asking the Industrial Association to postpone its attempts to force open the port. When time ran out on the postponement, on July 3, the Industrial Association began moving freight from the docks to warehouses, and that action precipitated battles all that day and on July 5 (all parties observed the July 4 holiday). Strikers tried to stop the trucks by intimidating the non-union drivers, threatening to turn over their vehicles, and by raining bricks and cobblestones on them. When the city police used tear gas and clubs to discourage such behavior, the predictable result was outrage that the police had violated the mayor's promise to maintain neutrality. And when police resorted to shotguns, riot guns, and pistol fire, killing two men who were bystanders at an intersection filled with unruly demonstrators, Mayor Rossi was blamed along with his police department. California's governor ordered the National Guard to occupy the waterfront and warehouse districts, and the employers reopened the port with non-union workers.

The killings on July 5 ("Bloody Thursday") generated a huge wave of sympathy for the strikers, who held a dramatic funeral procession on July 9 (by agreement with a chastened police department), marching solemnly up the entire length of Market Street to the accompaniment of Beethoven's funeral march. Then, on July 13, Archbishop Hanna addressed San Franciscans in a speech broadcast over radio stations KGO, KPO, and KFRC. Hanna approached the issues of the strike by reemphasizing the principles of Pope Pius XI's encyclical of 1931, "Reconstruction of the Social Order." "A bargain cannot be just unless the human character of the worker is fully recognized"; and "rights must be religiously respected wherever they are found and it is the duty of the public authority to protect each one in the possession of his own rights." Returning to the themes enunciated in the *Monitor*'s June 9 editorial, the archbishop explicitly endorsed both labor unions and collective bargaining, and he condemned employer exploitation that ignored "the human character of the worker." Then, in a blunt rejection of the Communist Party slogan "class against class," Hanna criticized unionists who premised their activities on the necessity of "conflict between class and class." Both sides in the waterfront strike, Hanna insisted, should move quickly to accept the results of arbitration, keeping in mind the "underlying principles which have ever been the teaching of Christianity during 2000 years."[14] The teamsters, then one after another of San Francisco's unions, put themselves on the side of the striking longshoremen and maritime workers by carrying out a general strike that lasted from July 16 to July 19. For seventy-seven hours, the city experienced what the Joint Maritime Strike Committee, in a statement of July 20, described as a "mass strike of organized labor and the united sympathy of the public at large."[15]

Two business groups, an Ad Hoc Citizen's Committee headquartered at the Palace Hotel and the Junior Chamber of Commerce requested a declaration of martial law during the general strike. National Guard troops were already posted on the waterfront, but putting the entire city on a wartime basis would have satisfied those employers described by the president of the Waterfront Employers Association as having "urged war from the beginning."[16] Roger D. Lapham, president of the American Hawaii Steamship Company, expressed the point of view of this faction in a July 18 telephone conversation with Secretary of Labor Frances Perkins: "We can cure this thing best by bloodshed. We have got to have bloodshed to stop it. It is the best thing to do." The governor, however, refused to declare martial law unless Mayor Rossi made the request. Rossi consulted his Citizens Committee of 25, and according to Andriano, who attended the meeting, "I was the only member of that committee on the side of labor and vigorously opposed the almost unanimous attempt of the committee to terrorize and brow-beat Mayor Rossi into petitioning the Governor to call in the militia."[17]

On July 20, John Francis Neylan, a Catholic attorney close to Archbishop Hanna who represented the Hearst interests on the

West Coast, hosted a meeting of the employers at his Woodside home and reminded them of the future damage to the city's business reputation should they continue their uncompromising stance. The San Francisco Academy reiterated its argument that "Rerum Novarum" and "Quadragesimo Anno" mandated approval of the strike committee's major outstanding demand: a union hiring hall controlled by the International Longshoremen's Association. Archbishop Hanna's arbitration board continued its deliberations as the teamsters returned to their jobs on July 21, and nine days later Hanna announced an end to the strike after negotiating a jointly operated hiring hall.[18]

Mayor Rossi's refusal to give in to the pressure to declare martial law earned praise from the labor press and the Catholic papers. The *Leader* described Rossi as "the mayor of all the people of San Francisco," not "an ineffectual tool of vested wealth and a foe to honest labor." The *Monitor* argued that San Francisco businessmen needed a new departure: "just businessmen . . . must present some other group of principles than those upon which the two brutalizing programs of laissez-faire and Communism are to be founded." The time had come for "the parting of the ways," and the choice was clear: "Society must be reconstructed on the lines set out in the Communist program and initiated in Russia, or on definitely Christian principles."[19]

Mayor Rossi received praise from the church leadership and from Catholic Action activists, but he received more criticism than credit from the quarters of conservative business and radical labor. Chamber of Commerce president J. W. Mailliard Jr., by agreeing to arbitration, demonstrated a pragmatic accommodation to the upwelling of sympathy for the strikers that followed the killings of Bloody Thursday. But Mailliard continued to describe the general strike as "treason" and demanded that in the future "constituted authority be upheld and that the rights of every man and woman in San Francisco from this day on shall be protected." He also minimized the responsibility of business for the conditions that led to the strike demands, admitting only that "it is our duty to see that those isolated instances in which labor has been exploited shall be corrected." The Communist Party, whose national leadership secretly visited the city during the strike, regarded San Francisco as "the party's greatest organizing success in 1934," but the party's ability to build on that success was jeopardized by Mayor Rossi and the clerical and lay Catholic activists on whose support he depended. And the hostility of the radical left toward Rossi and Catholic activists would only grow as Archbishop Mitty and Sylvester Andriano expanded the Catholic Action program in the months after the settlement of the strike.[20]

5

Sylvester Andriano and Catholic Action in San Francisco

How fitting it would be for San Francisco to take the lead in fostering Catholic Action among American cities . . . it is necessary,—I was about to say, it is imperative, that Catholic Action be established along parish and diocesan lines.

—Sylvester Andriano to Archbishop John J. Mitty, March 2, 1936

What is wrong with the world today, which has divorced Christ from so many phases of human life? The supernatural is being excluded. We cannot exclude the supernatural from our lives and from the world without ourselves and the world drifting back to a pagan conception of human life.

—Archbishop John J. Mitty, May 29, 1937

In the months following the waterfront and general strikes of 1934, Sylvester Andriano and Archbishop John J. Mitty intensified their relationship and collaborated in expanding the Catholic Action presence in San Francisco beyond the academy that Andriano and William Lowery had organized in 1933. On May 12, 1935, the archbishop and the attorney participated in the graduation exercises at St. Mary's College in Moraga. Mitty awarded the diplomas to the eighty-six graduates, and Andriano gave the commencement address, praising the accomplishments of the class of 1935 but bemoaning "the lapse of Catholic Action" in the curriculum of Catholic schools and colleges. He suggested the importance of not only learning the theory of Catholic Action but also "developing workers in the ranks," and urged his audience to make Catholic Action an integral part of their private and public lives.[1]

Andriano's and Mitty's collaboration represented an expression of their mutual interest in Catholic Action, dating back to 1931 and

1932, respectively. But it also had a foundation in their experience in bringing Catholic values to bear on the settlement of the 1934 waterfront and general strikes and their desire to implement the Vatican's plan for the program as detailed in the 1935 *Manual of Catholic Action* by Monsignor Luigi Civardi. Written and published in Italian in 1933, Civardi's work appeared in English translation two years later; the translator, Jesuit priest C. C. Martindale, suggested that the term "lay apostolate" served as the best translation of the Italian *Azione Cattolica.* The official archdiocesan newspaper published an extensive summary of Civardi's description of the theory and practice of this lay apostolate work in a series of articles from February through April 1935, concluding with a discussion of education—"the Scholastic Field"—which stressed that "the school is among the most efficacious instruments of ideal propaganda and education. This is so well understood by the enemies of Christ, that they have at all times and everywhere attempted to mould the school system to their false educational standards."[2]

After the St. Mary's commencement, Archbishop Mitty turned to Andriano again, this time for advice about "the condition of the Italians in California with regard to religion," and the attorney responded with a detailed analysis. Then, after a ten-page discussion of the Italian question, Andriano addressed himself to a new topic: "the one point of Catholic doctrine in which the Italians in this country, in common with many of their American brethren, have strayed farthest from the faith and succumbed to the evil influence of liberalism and laicism, is in the matter of discipline, obedience and respect for authority, without which there can be no unity."

> Catholic Action, the essence of which is participation and cooperation with and subordination to the bishops and pastors, seems admirably fitted to counteract this un-Catholic tendency on the part of so many of the laity. You will pardon me if I seem to digress from my subject to speak of Catholic Action but . . . if it be desired to develop a lay apostolate worthy of the name, resort must be had to Catholic Action properly so called.

> The study of the encyclicals on the teachings of the Church on various questions is both useful and necessary but it is not an end in itself and unless it culminates in action it is of no very great avail. I doubt if in the day of reckoning we will be given very much credit for our knowledge of the encyclicals if we have never converted that knowledge into action. Too many of us are growing old doing little else but studying. What the world needs today are men of faith, of action and of courage.[3]

Andriano confided that "at one time I was hopeful that the San Francisco Academy would undertake the work, but upon reconsidering the matter, I think it would be preferable to form an entirely new group of men." They would be "prepared to do whatever the Archbishop wishes them to do" in order to accomplish Pius XI's vision of "a single, compact and disciplined army" of Christian activists to work toward Catholic faith-based goals.

> Can any one doubt that a true Catholic Action organization would greatly help the Catholic press, the retreat movement, the increase of vocations, the Catholic schools and, perhaps, eventually make possible a victory at the polls on the question of exempting them from taxation? The League of Decency would not only become more effective in its campaign against indecent movies, but might extend its sphere of activity to indecent books, newspapers, magazines, dress and speech and might give rise to a league for temperance (not total abstinence) which is just as needful today as the others. The ineffectual campaign which is being waged against divorce, the declining birth rate and sterilization could by means of Catholic Action really be made effective.
>
> While activities in the social and economic fields are not strictly speaking part of Catholic Action because their ends are different, such activities are no more alien to it than they are to the Church itself for the reason that social and

> economic questions are fundamentally moral and religious questions and Catholic Action can also play its legitimate part in those fields, especially by forming the public conscience in conformity with Christian principles and by sending forth from among its ranks competent leaders who apply themselves to the solution of those questions.[4]

Andriano worried that the archbishop might consider his unsolicited advice an expression of "ill-regulated zeal," and if so, he asked the archbishop to "forgive me for it." But rather than criticize the layman for his enthusiasm, Mitty asked him to participate in an even more important occasion. After indicating that the Catholic school board members unanimously recommended Andriano, the archbishop asked him to present the commencement address for the 1936 graduation ceremony of all seven San Francisco Catholic high schools and academies, some seven hundred fifty graduates, at the city's Dreamland Auditorium. "I feel it is a splendid opportunity for a Catholic layman to present the Catholic viewpoint on education . . . I would esteem it a great favor if you would be kind enough to accept this invitation and to help us in our efforts to impress upon our own people, as well as the non-Catholics, the work that we are trying to do in the field of Catholic education."[5]

Mitty's satisfaction with Andriano's speech before an audience of nearly ten thousand in the Dreamland Auditorium moved the attorney to draft a "Plan for Catholic Action," which he shared with the archbishop in September. Perhaps in an ironic reference to his own commencement addresses, Andriano began with a criticism of "flowery statements" and then proceeded to a downbeat list of problems: "Catholicity is not making much progress. Perhaps barely holding it's [*sic*] own. Perhaps really losing. Not only in numbers but also in fervor and fidelity." "Birth control, practical cessation of immigration, the American materialistic environment, atheistic anticlericalism. The old self-sacrificing, self-denying Catholicity would seem to be rapidly dying out. A fervent few . . . an overwhelming majority of normal Catholics. Communistic propaganda may have made far more inroads than it appears."[6]

Andriano's remedy was couched in terms that might have come from his days playing varsity basketball for St. Mary's College: "The best defense is an attack." The San Francisco project would be part of a "systematic, coordinated, directed, expository, Nation-wide evangelization [underscoring in original]. Under direction and control of the Apostolic Delegate and Bishops. Centralized in Washington. Perhaps N.C.W.C. [National Catholic Welfare Council]." Andriano cited as authority the popes who had spoken out on Catholic Action and Archbishop Celso Benigno Luigi Costantini, an Italian priest who had been a chaplain in the Italian army during World War I and then spent thirteen years as the apostolic delegate to China. Costantini had recently been appointed secretary of the Vatican's Society for the Propagation of the Faith, and he described Catholic Action tactics in unmistakably militaristic fashion. "Good preaching, efforts to spread Catholic truth, development of the native clergy and right social action are the four weapons that can defeat 'the missionaries of Satan.'"[7]

Andriano suggested a fifteen-point "plan of action" premised on a willingness to launch "a constant, patient, consistent Crusade [underscoring in original]." Leadership would come from "two men at least" willing to agree to "a three month intensive concentrated training," after which they would begin "arousing the zeal of pastors for this work by propaganda, assistance, suggestions, and contact." The lay activists would assist "Bishops in their particular problems in particular places. Communism, Mormonism, Adventists, Country Districts and High School Students." Appealing to Mitty's experience during his six-year service as bishop of Salt Lake City before he came to San Francisco, Andriano suggested that the San Francisco program include an "adaptation of Mormon, and various other missionary methods for laymen and laywomen." He also suggested that the archdiocese establish "diocesan mission bands" made up of devout "young, zealous, enthusiastic Americans" who were "interested in non-Catholic mission work" in order "to thoroughly work through [the] diocese, especially the country districts and smaller communities." To combat "indifferentism," activists would write and distribute pamphlets, produce radio programs, increase the numbers of Catholic books in public libraries, and convince the editors of "secular newspapers and magazines" to carry more articles about Catholic topics.[8]

In early October the archbishop confided to Father Thomas N. O'Kane, a professor at St. Joseph's College, the preparatory seminary of the archdiocese, that he was impressed with Andriano's proposal of having a very limited group of laymen make a study of real Catholic Action. "Mr. Andriano has probably read everything that has been published on the subject and has the Catholic ideal of it, and he wants to get a dozen or more laymen imbued with the same principles, so that we can get real Catholic Action instead of some of the fool things that parade under the name." Mitty asked O'Kane to be his personal representative and to work with Andriano as he developed his plans further, "so that the group would keep within the reservation."[9]

Andriano met with Father O'Kane in October and then began buttonholing fellow members of the San Francisco Academy and other Catholic Action enthusiasts who were likely to share his ambitious vision to build a more extensive "real Catholic Action" program. One of the first men he approached was a St. Mary's College philosophy professor, James L. Hagerty. Hagerty had graduated from St. Mary's College in 1919 and began teaching at his alma mater immediately afterward. He earned a master's degree in 1921 and commenced a career as a philosophy professor at St. Mary's, and in 1930 he began publishing a Catholic literary review, the *Moraga Quarterly*. Hagerty was a lifelong bachelor who sported a Clark Gable mustache, and students flocked to his popular classes. He mentored a number of students who would later become leading figures in Bay Area Catholic circles, and in November one of his protégés, a senior from Little Italy named Joseph L. Alioto, who would later become mayor of San Francisco, addressed the Young Men's Institute on Catholic Action.[10]

Alioto's speech, "The Catholic Internationale," marked the degree to which the papal program of Catholic Action had already made an imprint on the public discourse of Catholic San Francisco. Alioto began with a rhetorical evocation of Communism; since the

Russian Revolution, "like an enormous, hideous octopus it has reached out over the world with its black tentacles to engulf other lands within the darkness of its soulless philosophy."

> Germany and Italy were able to stave off the threat only by running to another extreme, which in many of its manifestations is just as despicable. Today France stands on the brink of havoc, and in Spain the very foundations of order are swept away. With a satanic ruthlessness that could not have been exceeded by Vandals, Turks, or Moors the Communist passions of absolutism and hate are destroying Christianity, civilization, and all the sweet fruits which art and culture have bequeathed. Communism has attained the position of a universal power [and] stands today as a cancer in the world's social organism.[11]

Alioto argued that given Communism's international scope and its appeal as a "counterfeit religion," only a true religion "that is likewise international" would be able "to cut away this cancerous growth." "There is only one power in the world which answers that description: the Roman Catholic Church. The battle lines . . . are clearly marked: It is to be the Catholic Internationale arrayed against the Communist Internationale; Rome against Moscow; Christ against Anti-Christ." He ended his speech with an explicit endorsement of the Catholic Action strategy, noting that the "Catholic Church in its scheme of organization into parishes and diocese affords the effective means whereby we may infiltrate the social organism. From the individual the Catholic Internationale must build itself upward to the family, to the parish, to the diocese, until it permeates the whole world with its rich and happy philosophy. Then shall the emptiness and the stupidity of Communism be exposed."[12]

Alioto's speech focused on Communism, but its larger message about the importance of Catholic Action brought him to the attention of Archbishop Mitty, who called on him for service in a variety of diocesan activities in the years to come. The speech appeared in the winter issue of the *Moraga Quarterly,* which was fast becoming a vehicle for spreading the Catholic Action message under the editorial guidance of Professor Hagerty.

Hagerty soon became Andriano's partner in the Catholic Action program, and scarcely a month after Alioto's speech at the Young Men's Institute, Andriano reported to the archbishop that several others had joined the planning process. They included his law partner William Lowery; Harold McKinnon, from the law firm Bronson, Bronson, and McKinnon; Jack Casey, San Francisco city engineer; physician Dr. Milton Lennon; public schoolteacher Peter Conmy; and Santa Clara College professor Umberto Olivieri. From Little Italy came Armand Demartini, brother of one of the priests at Sts. Peter and Paul Church. Andriano also consulted with aging Catholic teamster union officials Michael Casey and John P. McLaughlin "with a view of selecting two young, active, Catholic-minded labor leaders to join the group." In January, after the holiday season, Andriano distributed copies of Civardi's *Manual of Catholic Action* to his associates, and they met for the first time on February 12, 1937.[13]

Most of the men who attended this first meeting continued to gather every other week during that year for focused discussions on how to move from the theory of Catholic Action to the practice. By the autumn of 1937 Andriano and Hagerty had met with the pastors of each of the sixty parishes in San Francisco to solicit support for the new citywide Catholic Action lay organization, and on December 22 Archbishop Mitty invited several dozen men from throughout the city to meet to discuss "uniting the parishes of San Francisco in a definite program of Catholic Action." In addition to representatives from the largest parishes, the invitees included Police Chief William J. Quinn, high-ranking officers from important municipal government departments, and executives from the city's largest and most prestigious business firms. On the Feast of the Epiphany, January 6, 1938, some two hundred men gathered in the cathedral's basement and formally inaugurated the Catholic Men of San Francisco. Hagerty announced that "Confirmation is the Sacrament of Catholic Action, making men soldiers," and suggested that the assembled volunteers regard themselves as part of the "priesthood of the layman."[14]

Mitty appointed Andriano and Hagerty to the positions of president and executive secretary of the new organization, and in March, Andriano traveled to Rome to secure official Vatican approval of San Francisco's Catholic Action initiative. Pope Pius XI gave the group his blessing, and Giuseppe Cardinal Pizzardo, the chief assistant for Catholic Action in Italy, and Monsignor Luigi Civardi, author of the *Manual of Catholic Action,* assured the San Franciscan that his plan was a sound one. After his return from Rome, Andriano and Mrs. John Murray of the Archdiocesan Council of Catholic Women laid the plans for a massive outdoor rally on behalf of Catholic Action. And on Sunday afternoon, October 29, fifty thousand Bay Area Catholics filled Kezar Stadium in the city's Golden Gate Park to celebrate the Feast of Christ the King. Archbishop Mitty led a procession carrying the Blessed Sacrament and then gave a benediction from an ornate, oversized altar on the fifty-yard line. The archbishop began his "Address on Catholic Action" by announcing, "We must first of all get a grasp upon what the Holy Father wants in Catholic Action. What is it all about? I like to sum it up in one phrase: That what the Holy Father wants you to do is to vitalize your religion, make it something really vital in your lives." Mitty criticized the notion that

> religion is not supposed to come out of that [certain limited] compartment and overflow into our being. We have a feeling of inferiority about religion, due to an historic situation where we were out-numbered. But there is no necessity for it today. Human life has been practically denuded of Christian principles. What the pope wants is to vitalize them. That is the meaning of Catholic Action—no more, no less. . . . In doing that we not only make a contribution to the progress of the Church, but we are making a substantial contribution to the welfare of our own land, a contribution to America

> which it badly needs; we are making a contribution to human civilization, until we bring about a right balance between material and spiritual things, which are going topsy-turvy.[15]

From 1938 until the winter of 1941–1942, when their work was derailed first by the demands of the wartime emergency and then by the Tenney Committee's accusations that Andriano was a Fascist agent, Andriano and Hagerty built up Catholic Action's numbers and expanded the organization at the city and parish level. Andriano, Lowery, and McKinnon established a lawyers' guild called the St. Thomas More Society, and McKinnon served as the first president. Parish councils, charged with organizing Catholic Action Circles in each of the city's sixty parishes, pursued a three-part agenda of devotional revitalization involving individual sanctification, sanctification of the home, and sanctification of society. The program included participation in parish holy-hour devotions; regular celebration of annual feast days; blessing of homes, grace before meals, family communion, and renewal of marriage vows daily; parish Sunday mass crusades aimed at increasing regular attendance and punctuality; and the use of the missal and active participation in rosaries, benedictions, and Stations of the Cross.[16]

Catholic Action schools for parish priests and parochial schoolteachers began operations in San Francisco, Alameda, San Mateo, and Santa Clara counties. And in 1939 the Catholic Men published *Catholic Action: The Church in Action; Official Handbook of the Catholic Men of the Archdiocese of San Francisco,* with forewords by Archbishop Mitty and Cardinal Pizzardo, as well as *Catholic Action and the Priest,* a booklet by Father John J. Hunt, the group's chaplain. The archdiocesan council published a monthly newsletter and operated a speaker's bureau that dispatched lecturers to meetings and radio programs in all the Bay Area counties. St. Patrick's Seminary in Menlo Park added a required Catholic Action course to its curriculum. Even Catholic high schools in the Bay Area joined the campaign by establishing student Catholic Action Circles.[17]

By mid-1941, according to an official report, 160 of the 174 parishes in the archdiocese had established Catholic Action Circles, involving fifteen hundred men and three hundred women. For Sylvester Andriano and Archbishop Mitty, the establishment and growth of the Catholic Men of San Francisco represented the culmination of a decade-long effort to put Pope Pius XI's call for a lay apostolate into practice. Andriano's and Mitty's work in these campaigns extended beyond the founding of the organization. It involved both domestic and international issues, and it forthrightly announced that Catholic faith-based principles deserved a leading place in the making of public policy.[18]

6

The Catholic Action Social Apostolate

Catholic Action does not concern itself only with the support and defense of the Catholic faith. It concerns itself with all divine and human interests in this world: with morality, economics, social movements, legislation. The great problems with which every nation is wrestling—economics, social justice, international peace, human rights—are fundamentally moral.

—Stanislaus Riley, "Place of the Laity in Catholic Action," March 22, 1935

From the turbulent days of the general strike in July 1934 to Pearl Harbor, Sylvester Andriano, Archbishop Mitty, and their Catholic Action colleagues publicized and expanded what Andriano called "this new crusade" in a multifaceted campaign to establish "real Catholic Action" in northern California. Given the prominence of labor relations issues in San Francisco during the first decade of his service in the city, it is not surprising that Archbishop Mitty placed a high priority on the social apostolate aspect of Catholic Action, defined by Vatican spokesman Cardinal Pizzardo as "concerned with the spread of Catholic social teaching and the realization of Catholic principles in social institutions."[1] And Mitty used his office as a "bully pulpit" in public events and expressed himself in a forthright manner in private communications. Early in his administration the new archbishop lectured one of the city's business leaders, shipping executive Hugh Gallagher, saying that he should pay more attention to the principles laid out in Pope Leo XIII's labor encyclical. Mitty expressed his concern about the future, reminding Gallagher that "there is, then, grave danger of a duplication of the events of the summer of 1934—a general strike, violence, bloodshed and loss of life."[2] "To avert this calamity," he continued, "both groups should be willing to submit disputed points to an impartial board of arbitration. When conciliation and mediation have failed, this appears to be the only rational method of settling an industrial dispute on the basis of justice and equity, rather than on the basis of the economic power of the employers or the numerical strength and organization of the employees. San Francisco wants not a temporary truce but a permanent peace."

Throughout the first decade of his tenure Mitty rarely missed an opportunity to publicize the importance of conducting labor relations according to the principles expressed in the labor encyclicals. Mitty made sure that the *Monitor,* the official weekly newspaper of the archdiocese, provided its readers with front-page coverage of local and national news of the labor movement. News of events that included speeches on labor issues by church leaders often ran as the lead story, and the text of the sermon or speech was reprinted in full on the editorial page. The *Monitor* added its voice to the public discussion of a proposal by the Chamber of Commerce to formulate a cooperative, institutionalized working relationship with citywide central bodies of the American Federation of Labor (AFL) and Congress of Industrial Organizations (CIO). The paper promoted the need for such cooperation as a precondition for the future economic prosperity of the Bay Area. This issue and many others involving labor and capital were rivaled only by those of Communism and World War II for frequency of coverage in the *Monitor*'s editorial columns. These editorials consistently invoked the labor encyclicals, alternately emphasizing the rights of workers, the need for labor and capital to cooperate, and the responsibilities of the state.[3]

The archbishop also took advantage of a variety of public events to promote the labor encyclicals. Many of these events were directly related to either the city's workers in general or organized labor in particular. The celebration of Labor Day provided one such opportunity. Designated in 1910 by Archbishop Riordan an occasion for special ceremonies dedicated to the working man, the Labor Day Mass had become a city tradition by 1935. Archbishop Mitty used the Mass both as a forum in which to preach at length on labor issues and as an opportunity for the church hierarchy to appear in public with labor leaders in a dramatic gesture of support for unions. And in May 1937, when Archbishop Mitty presided over the funeral services for the long-time president of the San Francisco Teamsters' Union Michael J. Casey, he used the occasion to once again spread the Catholic Action social apostolate message. He praised Casey for his solidarity with members of his union who had voted their support for the general strike, even though Casey had opposed it. Casey had "put into practice the teachings of both Leo XIII and Pius XI," had been "fair and just in the demands that he made upon industry and he was likewise insistent that labor give its full meed of justice to industry." A staunch opponent of Communism, Casey and his conservative, Catholic unionism provided a model for the future, according to Mitty: "Here we have a fair solution of the problems that confront our city and country today."[4]

Archbishop Mitty personally spread the Catholic Action message, but he also delegated social apostolate work to both lay persons and clergy, and he chose young Father Hugh A. Donohoe to be the unofficial and informal coordinator of this aspect of Catholic Action work. Donohoe began his work immediately after being ordained in June 1930; when the school year started that fall, the twenty-five-year-old priest began teaching at the archdiocesan preparatory seminary, St. Joseph's College. Two years later he began doctoral studies at the Catholic University, where he received his Ph.D. in 1935, writing a dissertation under the direction of the nationally eminent scholar of Catholic social justice theory Monsignor John A. Ryan (1869–1945). Donohoe then began a seven-year tenure as a professor of social ethics at St. Patrick's, the archdiocesan seminary in Menlo Park, some thirty miles south of San Francisco. During that time he helped organized the local branch of the Association of Catholic Trade Unionists, and he served as its chaplain from its founding in 1938 through the 1940s. Mitty appointed Donohoe to serve as rector of St. Mary's Cathedral, and in 1942 Mitty appointed him editor of the official weekly newspaper, the *Monitor.* From 1935, when he returned from Washington, D.C., to 1962, when he left to become bishop of Stockton, Donohoe served as the archbishop's chief spokesman on Catholic Action in general and on issues of labor relations, social justice, and political socialization in particular.[5]

Like several other Catholic Action activists involved in social apostolate work, Donohoe was a product of San Francisco's predominantly Irish Catholic Mission District. He was born in 1905, the third child of Patrick and Frances Brogan Donohoe. Patrick hailed from Longford, Ireland, and Frances was a California daughter of Irish immigrants. As co-owner of Donohoe and Carroll Monuments in Colma, a small town just outside the city and the home of Holy Cross Cemetery, Patrick provided headstones and mausoleums for Catholic burials. Patrick died in 1923, when Hugh was eighteen.[6]

Hugh Donohoe's sister Patrice recalled that "there was lots of joy in our family but that didn't last after my father died." What did last was the Catholic religiosity and devotion to the church that Patrick had fostered. "We said the Rosary together every solitary night. My father had great devotion and I attribute our vocations to that." Two of Hugh's four brothers became priests in the Jesuit order, and three of his five sisters became Catholic nuns. A lifelong member of the Sisters of Notre Dame de Namur, Patrice recalled Hugh as "devoted to the Pope and his teachings" and "always positive" rather than negative when it came to spreading the Catholic Action message.[7]

From the time he assumed his duties as a professor at St. Patrick's, Donohoe prepared outlines for the archbishop's labor-related sermons, wrote drafts for the archbishop's correspondence on social ethics matters, organized conferences on social policy matters, and founded, managed, and taught in a diocesan labor school. The archbishop also called on him to serve as a mediator in a case of labor-management conflict in Notre Dame Hospital, an archdiocesan institution.[8]

One of Donohoe's first duties was the organization of a San Francisco Bay Area Social Action School for Priests (SASP). After the national meeting of U.S. bishops in November 1936, a call went out for setting up summer schools of social action for the clergy, to operate under the direction of local bishops. Mitty responded by asking Donohoe to create a month-long San Francisco school, which was the fourth in the nation, after Toledo, Milwaukee, and Los Angeles. Designed to provide local priests an opportunity for "the serious study of the Social Encyclicals and of their practical application to the American condition," the SASP enrolled twenty-eight priests for the four-week course in June 1937. In residence at St. Patrick's Seminary, the priests divided their work into five courses: Principles of Social and Distributive Justice; Catholic Social Philosophy; the Labor Problem; History of the American Labor Movement; and the Agricultural Problem. Donohoe taught the Labor Problem course.[9]

In his 1937 course on labor Donohoe drew on his studies with Ryan (who was popularly known as "The Right Reverend New Dealer") and the research for his doctoral dissertation. A study of collective bargaining under the 1933 National Industrial Recovery Act (NIRA), the work assessed the record of the New Deal law's operation in the light of Catholic labor relations scholarship. Section 7(a) of the NIRA was of particular interest to Catholic social justice advocates because its language put the force of government policy in service of a central principle of Pope Leo XIII's "Rerum Novarum": "Employees shall have the right to organize and bargain collectively through representatives of their own choosing, and shall be free from the interference, restraint or coercion of employers of labor, or their agents, in the designation of such representatives or in self-organization or in other activities for the purpose of collective bargaining or other mutual aid or protection." Donohoe concluded that while the law's collective bargaining provision did "make concrete that right which all employees possess and should exercise," in practice "enforcement of Section 7(a) has been a complete failure." The dissertation included an analysis of then-pending legislation introduced by Senator Robert Wagner of New York, legislation that was intended to replace the NIRA (which the Supreme Court declared unconstitutional in the spring of 1935) with a more effective National Labor Relations Act.[10]

President Franklin D. Roosevelt signed the Wagner Act, which established the National Labor Relations Board, into law on July 5, 1935, and three years later signed the Fair Labor Standards Act (FLSA). These New Deal measures established federally sanctioned and enforceable collective bargaining rights for unions, contained federal rules for a minimum wage and a maximum work week, and banned products of child labor from interstate commerce. Donohoe's vigorous defense of the Wagner Act and the FLSA in years to come derived from his conviction that they conformed to "the Catholic approach to the labor question," which he located in "the doctrine of natural rights." "The specific rights include the right of private ownership, the right of reasonable access to the goods of the earth, and the right of a living wage. The processes are two in number: group action that aims at promoting individual welfare and the assistance of the State to effect the same purpose."[11]

Donohoe's assessment in his dissertation of the extent to which federal labor relations policy succeeded in meeting the requirements of "Rerum Novarum" and "Quadragesimo Anno" was a prologue to his monitoring of labor relations practice in his communications with Bay Area Catholics. He condemned laissez-faire business practice, preached to workers about their moral obligation to join unions, condemned both unionists and employers when they appeared to him to lose sight of the general good as they struggled for the interests of their groups, and insisted on carefully calibrated state participation in the economy while condemning "ruthless State intervention."[12]

While still at St. Patrick's, Donohoe defended labor's gains from attacks by employers who still hoped to turn the clock back to pre–New Deal conditions. In the wake of the 1938 congressional elections, conservative business organizations began a coordinated assault on labor and the liberal legislation of the New Deal. The National Association of Manufacturers (NAM) was especially notable in this regard because it fostered a campaign to establish open-shop conditions by means of "right to work" state legislation. One of the NAM's tactics was to win Catholic clergy over to the side of the open shop by means of a Clergy-Industry Education Program designed to convince Catholic priests that American conditions were so superior to those of Europe that "Rerum Novarum" and "Quadragesimo Anno" should not guide Catholic social policy in the United States. When the archbishop received an invitation to send Bay Area priests to one such program in November 1941, Donohoe agreed to attend with ten other priests in order to speak out about the need for local employers to adopt a "broad social conscience" on labor relations. One year later, writing from the editor's desk of the *Monitor,* Donohoe countered the NAM's complaint that business enjoyed no federal support of the kind the Wagner Act provided labor by pointing out that business organizations did not need legal protection because the right of association by employers "is not under attack."[13]

Donohoe also represented the archbishop at California's Conference of Social Workers. In his address, "The Church and Labor Unions," he called for a "united front of organized employees led by men who think in terms of the general welfare."[14] The archbishop himself often invoked the labor encyclicals and consistently called for the application of Christian principles to everyday life when speaking at meetings of various Catholic lay organizations. Mitty liked to point out that a "religion is worthless unless it has a message for human beings in every phase of human life." He repeatedly exhorted the members of lay organizations, such as parish Holy Name societies, the San Francisco Academy, and the local chapter of the NCCW, to heed the call of Pius XI and bring Christian principles "into industrial and economic matters, into legislative problems, and into political questions."[15]

Archbishop Mitty used the anniversaries of the publication of papal encyclicals to stage public lectures and occasionally radio broadcasts and to encourage lay organizations to host luncheons and discussion groups. These events always received extensive coverage in the *Monitor* and often attracted the attention of the major daily papers as well. In 1936 and 1941—years that marked major jubilees of "Rerum Novarum" and "Quadragesimo Anno"—the church sponsored elaborate events that not only publicized the principles of the encyclicals but also brought leaders of business, labor, and government together to discuss labor relations policy questions.[16]

Publicity went only so far, hence Mitty's work to put the principles of the labor encyclicals into practice by involving the church in activities that fostered cooperation among business, labor, and government. Between 1935 and America's entry into World War II, the formative years of the evolving business-labor partnership in San Francisco, the church sponsored three major programs intended to bring together leaders of business, labor, and government. Two of those programs were designed to provide a forum for discussion that would lead to the creation of a cooperative system of local labor relations modeled on the recommendations of Pope Pius XI.[17]

Father Donohoe's Social Action School for Priests was one of these programs, intended as it was to provide priests with training that would enable them to better aid their parishioners in contending with social and economic problems. The San Francisco school fit nicely with the archbishop's overall strategy in connection with Pius XI's promotion of Catholic Action, as well as his concern with local conflicts between labor and capital. The church-sponsored program aimed to influence future industrial relations activities involving leaders of organized labor and business, as well as representatives of government, academia, and the clergy.[18]

The character of the program indicates the level of importance the church placed on labor relations and expressed the papal doctrine that the resolution of such problems required the cooperation of all affected parties. Donohoe engaged sixteen outside experts from organized labor, business, government, and academia to join the clerical faculty. The lecturers included Burton Edises, regional attorney of the National Labor Relations Board; Almon Roth, president of the San Francisco Waterfront Employers Association; and John Brophy, national director of the Congress of Industrial Organizations.[19]

The church also sponsored programs that were explicitly designed to foster cooperation between various elements of society, especially organized labor and business. In 1936 and again in 1941 (the years marking jubilees of the labor encyclicals), San Francisco hosted Regional Catholic Conferences on Industrial Problems to publicize the principles of the encyclicals. These two-day conferences were open to the public and featured a dozen different sessions focusing on issues related to labor and industry. Speakers were drawn from government, academia, the church, business, and organized labor, and the validity of each perspective was emphasized. Chamber of Commerce president Frederick J. Koster, a convert to Catholicism, made one of the keynote addresses at the 1936 conference, but labor leaders and church officials constituted the majority of speakers and their contributions received the most extensive coverage in the *Monitor.* In his opening address at the 1936 gathering, Archbishop Mitty explained,

> This is a conference to discuss, to learn. We have the highest respect for the principles of other people. We feel that they are holding them in good faith and that they have a right to present their point of view. We do not deal with personalities. We are merely dealing with issues and with principles. We teach that man has certain God-given rights that no government and no group of individuals, no corporations can take away. If industry tends to take them away, or if the social order tends to do it, then it is trespassing on God-given rights. If in industry people are not given a living wage, if they have to live under conditions that destroy morality, then they are touching upon moral principles. It is the duty of [the] Church to speak up in defense of the individual because of her duty as the teacher of mankind.[20]

The conferences represented a deliberate attempt to make Catholic unionism the model for the practice of labor relations in San Francisco. Mitty was determined to bring together the representatives of the city's various interest groups to, as he put it in his address to the 1941 conference, "examine economic maladjustments which are obstacles to a social order based on Christian principles."[21]

The high priority placed on Catholic unionism as a feature of the social apostolate was exemplified in the establishment of the San Francisco branch of the Association of Catholic Trade Unionists (ACTU). The ACTU was founded in New York in March 1937 by several former members of the Catholic Worker Movement who had grown dissatisfied with what they saw as the utopian character of that organization. Their new group proposed to promote unionization and to increase the practice of Catholic principles within the labor movement. The organization conducted labor schools, sponsored public lectures, published pamphlets and newspapers, supported strikes, provided legal assistance for the rank-and-file, and solicited church support for union activities. By 1940 Catholic unionists had established eight regional chapters in cities across the nation. While modeled after the New York organization, each chapter emerged under local conditions and remained essentially autonomous. Jack Henning, a recent St. Mary's College graduate and protégé of Professor James Hagerty, and Laura Smith, of the retail clerks' union, asked Father Donohoe to serve as chaplain, and Archbishop Mitty approved the organization. Its membership was restricted to Catholics, and its constitution declared its purpose in language that Henning had used in a speech at his alma mater: "To foster and spread . . . sound trade unionism built on Christian principles." The ACTU program drew on Catholic labor teachings and stressed both the rights and duties of workers. The rights included job security, an income high enough to allow a family to live a decent life, collective bargaining through independent and democratic unions, a decent share in employer profits, and the right to strike and picket for a just cause, a just price, and decent hours and working conditions. Duties included performing an honest day's work, joining a union, striking only for a just cause, refraining from violence, respecting property rights, living up to agreements freely made, enforcing honesty and democracy in the union, and cooperating with employers in establishing industry councils and producer cooperatives.[22]

San Francisco ACTU members self-consciously worked to build Catholic Action into a force within the San Francisco labor movement, particularly on the waterfront. The most dramatic success of the ACTU's work occurred in Local 10 of the longshoremen's union, where ACTU members successfully competed with Communist Party candidates for local union offices from its founding into the years of World War II.[23]

Although American involvement in the Second World War understandably diverted church interests, energies, and resources away from elaborate labor-related events and programs, Archbishop Mitty continued to involve the church in activities designed to promote cooperation between labor and business for the good of the community. Mitty and Donohoe gave active and outspoken support to a number of war-related programs. They endorsed the war labor boards and the voluntary labor-management committees encouraged by the War Production Board. Because these organizations included equal representation of both labor and capital, the church viewed them not only as necessary for the war effort but also as excellent examples of the kind of cooperative associations that Pius XI had endorsed in "Quadragesimo Anno." The Salvage for Victory and the War Chest campaigns were premised on cooperation between business and labor, and the AFL and CIO county councils regarded the programs as a means to promote union respectability. These wartime efforts fit within the social apostolate because Catholic union leaders would be defining their roles in a broad fashion that would encompass the needs of the community as well as the demands of their constituents. Patriotic service activities could both dramatize Catholic loyalty to the American nation and further the construction of a local Catholic Christian commonwealth.[24]

7

The Catholic Action Educational and Moral Apostolates

Catholic Action opens up a new world for the zeal of the faithful, a new world wherein they can share in the Apostolate of the Church and cooperate with their pastors and priests in spreading the Kingdom of Christ in individual souls, in families and in society.

—Sylvester Andriano, "The Program of Catholic Action in the Archdiocese of San Francisco," September 13, 1938

Sylvester Andriano returned from his trip to Italy in the summer of 1938 after obtaining Cardinal Pizzardo's approval of the San Francisco Catholic Action program, and on September 13 he outlined the new campaign to the assembled priests of the archdiocese at a two-day Diocesan Theological Conference organized by Archbishop Mitty at St. Mary's Cathedral. Andriano described his feelings when the "supernatural significance" of Catholic Action became more vivid after two meetings in the Vatican with the cardinal by quoting the English Romantic poet John Keats: "felt I like some watcher of the skies when a new planet swims into his ken." He asked his audience to think about the new archdiocesan program in the context of world history:

> *Dieu le vault*—God wills it, cried the crusaders of old with Pope Urban II and Peter the Hermit when it was a matter of rescuing the Holy Sepulchre and the Holy Places from the hands of the infidels. *Dieu le vault*—we can repeat today in unison with our pastors and priests in answer to the clarion call of our Holy Father and of our own Archbishop

> when it is a matter of rescuing individual souls, the home, the school, public morals and Christian civilization itself from the blight of the new paganism and the frightful chaos of Communism.[1]

One of Cardinal Pizzardo's calls to action concerned "the apostolate of education involving the maintenance of Catholic schools," something that Andriano had actively pursued years before his Vatican meetings with the cardinal. His speeches at St. Mary's College and at a variety of San Francisco Catholic high school events, combined with Archbishop Mitty's own proselytizing, influenced teachers to use the model of the Catholic men's organization at their own (boys') institutions. Students at St. Mary's High School in Berkeley were the first to organize, creating a Knights of Catholic Action club at their own campus, followed by a Bay Area–wide group called the Student Catholic Action Council. The council and an associated Federation of Catholic High School Religious Organizations of the Archdiocese of San Francisco published a *Student Catholic Action* newsletter and a *Student's Handbook of Catholic Action.* The students based their work on Pope Pius XI's urging that "centers of Catholic Action should be formed in universities and in secondary schools," and their newsletter quoted the Vatican's apostolic delegate to the United States, Archbishop Amleto Cicognani, about the importance among Catholic youth of "unity of action, harmony of purpose, and union of minds." Because Catholic high school students were segregated, with boys and girls attending separate institutions, the federation hoped to use its publications "to help united Catholic girls and boys in our Catholic high schools to do the great things they can do TOGETHER for Christ and his Church."[2]

Catholic Action work with youth played an important role in the agendas of San Francisco's Catholic women's organizations, as well as in the program of the Catholic Men. (Catholic tradition required separate men's and women's organizations.) San Francisco Catholic women had organized a Young Ladies' Institute (YLI) in 1887, and in 1920 they established the city's Archdiocesan Council of the NCCW. By 1936 the YLI claimed a membership of "11,000 strong" in the thirteen counties of the archdiocese, and they celebrated their Golden Jubilee the following year with a parade down Market Street, a program at the War Memorial Opera House, and a solemn pontifical mass at the cathedral. Archbishop Mitty had first announced his Catholic Action campaign at a 1932 speech before the women of the NCCW. Now, addressing the YLI members at their fiftieth anniversary banquet, he reminded them:

> Conditions have changed considerably during these fifty years. Progress in material affairs has been well-nigh startling. How about the things of the spirit? The public in general, and perhaps, too, some of our own Catholic people, are not putting the same emphasis on spiritual values as our forebearers [*sic*] did fifty years ago. Throughout the nation there has been a lessening of the grasp on spiritual truth, on religious belief, on moral principles. There is not that same strong recognition of God as our Creator, as our Ruler, as our Judge. The Ten Commandments are regarded as being worn out—a mediaeval idea; moral principles have been thrust in the background. This condition has a tendency to affect many of our own Catholic people who have seen their most sacred traditions supplanted by a new code of morality which is not the code of Christ.

Mitty closed by exhorting the women to "stand out as the right arm of the Church in your parishes . . . participating in the apostolate of Christ himself."[3]

While both women's organizations participated in the Catholic Action crusade during the middle to late 1930s, the women of the NCCW showed themselves the more active, possibly on account of the close working relationship between Archbishop Mitty and Agnes G. Regan. As a board member of the NCCW from the time of its organizational meeting in Washington, D.C., in 1920, and then as executive secretary shortly thereafter, Regan developed effective communications with all the U.S. bishops. But she was especially close to the San Francisco scene because she grew up in one of the city's wealthiest and most distinguished Irish Catholic families. Her father was a banker who also served for a decade as the personal secretary to the city's first archbishop, Joseph S. Alemany; two of her three sisters became Catholic nuns (there were nine children in the family); she graduated from a Catholic grammar school and St. Rose high school; and she graduated from the San Francisco State Normal School (today's San Francisco State University) and taught in the San Francisco public schools for several decades, eventually serving as a member and president of the city's Board of Education. It was Archbishop Edward Hanna who sent her as a delegate to the first meeting of the NCCW, and she kept close watch on San Francisco affairs from her office in the nation's capital all through her twenty-year tenure as executive secretary.[4]

Archbishop Mitty made no secret of his determination to increase the local influence of the women's groups, writing to one local activist, "You are aware of the fact of how interested I am in the development of the National Council of Catholic Women in this Archdiocese." Mitty appointed Father Eugene J. Shea, a priest assigned to the Catholic Charities office, to work with local Catholic women to implement the youth-oriented programs coordinated by the Washington, D.C., headquarters of the NCCW. Father Shea and Margaret McGuire, president of the Archdiocesan Council, organized a series of leadership conferences in the spring of 1937 designed to train "young women who would be interested and helpful in developing activities for girls of high school and college age." By the late summer of 1939 Father Shea had learned that "parish organizations for high school girls are the most difficult to organize and yet most necessary since most of the public high school youngsters have only an elementary knowledge of their religion." All the more reason, then, for participating in the NCCW's strategy of using radio broadcasts to reach women who might be persuaded to join their local Catholic Action activities. Archbishop Mitty endorsed and publicized Agnes Regan's "A Call to Youth" radio programs, which were broadcast on NBC over seventeen weeks during the winter and spring each year from 1937 to 1940, programs Regan characterized as "a leaders' training school for diocesan, deanery and parish youth chairmen, youth leaders and youth officers throughout the country."[5]

In October 1936 Margaret McGuire answered Mitty's call "to develop a program for girls." Her organization now had eleven councils and one hundred fifty affiliated organizations that were operating in the archdiocese as "an official part of the Program of the Catholic Church in the United States." "Every organization, parish and inter-parish, is a distinct unit yet a very definite part of the great Catholic Federation. In this affiliation no individual organization loses its identity or autonomy. It continues to function for the purpose for which it was founded but through the Federation it promotes a united Catholic Action on a wider scale." McGuire asked the archbishop to approve a plan to hold the 1939 national conference of the NCCW in San Francisco, the meeting to coincide with the Golden Gate International Exposition, scheduled to be held on Treasure Island that year. Mitty endorsed the proposal, and the following May he congratulated the NCCW women "for the work you are accomplishing. I feel that with Catholic Action, with earnest effort, with self-sacrificing zeal, we can begin to accomplish some of the things the Holy Father is asking of the laity to do. We can help to bring the spirit of Christ into the environment in which we live and where we function."[6]

On March 9, 1938, McGuire visited the Chancery office and reported that the city's Tourist and Convention Bureau had donated two thousand dollars to help defray the expense of holding the NCCW's national convention in San Francisco and that she had booked accommodations and meeting rooms in the stately Fairmont Hotel high atop Nob Hill. Preparations for the convention continued through the year, and by the following January, Maude Fay Symington, president of the Marin County unit of the organization, reported on the progress of what promised to be "in every way an exceptional convention; not only the first time the N.C.C.W. is meeting in the West, but holding a convention during the great Golden Gate Exposition year. California, so very Catholic, must lead the World Council of Catholic women in its public avowal of united, triumphant, and militant Catholicism; a challenge to the subversive influences and anti-God activities saturating the entire world today." In May, Archbishop Mitty reiterated his alarm that "we are surrounded by an atmosphere of secularism and worldliness" and his determination to present "the Catholic point of view, in showing forth the Catholic principles and Catholic philosophy of life." "I really want you to realize," he continued, "the amount of dependence that I put upon lay cooperation. The clergy cannot do everything, and the bishop can accomplish only as his clergy and laymen and lay women are willing to do with him . . . the problems of the future, the great things that confront us must be solved by the action of our laity, under the direction of the hierarchy."[7]

During the five-day conference in September 1939, at sessions held in the Fairmont Hotel and at a special Catholic Women's Day in the San Francisco Building at the Golden Gate Exposition grounds on Treasure Island, the importance of establishing Catholic standards of morality was a recurring theme. Hitler's troops had invaded Poland on the first day of the month, triggering declarations of war against Germany by England and its allies, and on the ninth, the opening day of the conference, the Battle of the Bzura began; ten days later a German victory here foreshadowed the Polish defeat at the end of the month. Sylvester Andriano addressed the compelling importance of Christian morality in the face of such events during his speech on the last day of the conference, echoing Cardinal Pizzardo's insistence that Catholic Action included "the moral apostolate concerned with the defense of Christian morality wherever threatened." And so did Pope Pius XII when he spoke to the delegates who attended the annual congress of the International Union of Catholic Women's Leagues in Rome in April. The newly installed pontiff, who took up his duties on March 2, announced his intention to continue his predecessor's "all-embracing program" of "the training and preparation of the Catholic woman in her various fields of apostolate, for the Christian restoration of modern society." He reminded the delegates of "the golden rules outlined by the Pontiff of happy memory who was the great promoter of Catholic Action and who is still its invisible inspiration." And he exhorted Catholics to unify and work against "the absolute denial of invisible realities, of the noble moral values, and of every supernatural ideal."[8]

When Cardinal Pizzardo announced in mid-1938 that "Catholic Action is essentially an apostolate," he included in "the moral apostolate" work aimed at ensuring that the values communicated "in the press, over the radio, in the theater, motion pictures" were ones compatible with Christian teachings. In San Francisco the Archdiocesan Council of Catholic Women took action in defense of "decent literature" by launching a "Clean Reading Campaign" focused on magazines for sale in public places. The city's efforts on this front were not unique, linked as they were to both international and national Catholic faith-based activism on behalf of the moral apostolate. In January 1938 Bishop John F. Noll, of the Fort Wayne, Indiana, diocese, published an article describing his city's League for Clean Reading. Noll was the publisher of a nationally distributed newspaper called *Our Sunday Visitor: The National Catholic Action Weekly*. He was also a National Catholic Welfare Council (NCWC) official, and his article appeared in the NCWC's magazine *Catholic Action*. In February, Father William G. Butler, assigned by Archbishop Mitty as the official adviser to the city's Catholic women, suggested to Margaret McGuire and her colleagues that the Archdiocesan Council "work out a diocesan scheme" modeled on the Fort Wayne campaign. The council's purpose was clear; it would "assist the law enforcement agencies of this jurisdiction to suppress literature and pictures" and "eliminate from magazine sales racks and tables publications which 1. Glorify crime and criminals; 2. Contain matter which is predominantly sexy; 3. Feature illicit love; 4. Print indecent or sexy pictures; and 5. Carry disreputable advertising."[9]

Archbishop Mitty asked Andriano and James Hagerty to take action on this issue in concert with the Archdiocesan Council of Catholic Women, and they established a Committee on Indecent Literature. Members of the committee and volunteers then contacted the city's major news and magazine distributors, only to discover that "the profit motive is much stronger than any moral urge in all too many retail outlets to guarantee any success from such an approach." Another joint working group made a survey of "legislation on pornographic literature, of postal regulations, law enforcement, the honor system, direct censorship, and the boycott." Three months later the committee reported that the laws were adequate and the postal regulations were sufficient, "but law enforcement is impractical because of the laxity of some jurists and juries in returning convictions." And "the element of goodwill [on the part of vendors] is obviously lacking, thus reducing our means of attack to some sort of public boycott." "If a boycott were to be started as an exclusively Catholic undertaking, there would be the danger of an unfavorable public reaction; therefore it is *absolutely essential* that all representative groups be interested in any public action, and further that all are made to feel themselves as an *initial* and *important part* of the forces that are to be employed."[10]

The lay men and women urged Archbishop Mitty to enlist the support of "the Protestant and Jewish church councils" as well as the assistance of city newspapers, city officials, and "all other groups who should be interested in decency." Mitty followed up in June with official instructions to the priests of every parish in the archdiocese to read his official letter condemning "magazines and other periodical literature which are detrimental to the morals of our people, and particularly to the morals of our growing boys and girls." On Sunday June 12 the archbishop's letter was read at every mass in all thirteen counties of the archdiocese, and it was repeated the next Sunday, June 19, after which, at every mass, the congregations repeated the Clean Literature Pledge after the priests.

> I pledge myself to refrain from purchasing, reading or spreading such literature and to endeavor to restrain those under my jurisdiction or influence from so doing;
>
> I pledge myself to refuse patronage in any form to those places of business which persist in displaying, offering for sale or selling such literature, or providing it for the entertainment of patrons who are waiting to be served;

I pledge myself to refuse patronage in any form to those firms which use such literature as an advertising medium;
I pledge myself to patronize those places of business which cooperate in the campaign.[11]

During the summer the clean reading pledge was taken by thousands of San Franciscans, some of whom presumably boycotted the purveyors of "pernicious literature" filled with "pagan manifestations" of "flagrant evil." But the Catholic Action activists in the clean reading campaign were hampered in their efforts because, as Florentine Schage, one of the lay activists, complained to the assistant chancellor, they found "it very difficult to ask retailers to remove literature we consider objectionable when they have no list to use as a check." Archbishop Mitty had such a list, and he invited Miss Schage and several colleagues to pick up a copy at the Chancery Office. In November, Bishop Noll and his like-minded colleagues established a National Organization for Decent Literature, which drew up what it called "our black-list" for use in dioceses across the nation. Noll's organization issued a *Catechism Dealing with Lewd Literature,* which announced its purpose on the title page: "A Comprehensive Treatise for Use by Men and Women Engaged in the Drive against Indecent Literature and for Radio Broadcasts." The *Catechism* took pains to remind its readers, "There would be a danger if we designated 'indecent' the magazines on our black list. We have adopted a Code in keeping with that adopted by the Legion of Decency in relation to Motion Pictures, and we charge the magazines with violation of that Code." Noll urged readers to "understand" that "we do not attach the 'immoral' charge to all these magazines. They are on our banned list because they offend against one or more of a five point Code adopted by the N.O.D.L." Among the magazines on the black list, in addition to *French Night Life, Illustrated Japanese Sex Relations,* and *Savage Arts of Love Illustrated,* were *The Facts of Life* and *Your Body.*[12]

San Francisco neighborhood theaters were screening a short film called *The Birth of a Baby* in November 1938. First Lady Eleanor

Roosevelt recommended the movie for its public health benefits, but the Catholic Men "made a spirited protest" against this and other "indecent pictures" by complaining directly to the nation's official movie censors in Hollywood. This was four years after the founding of the Catholic Legion of Decency and eight years after the adoption of a motion picture production code by the film industry trade association, which remained in effect for nearly forty years. The production code is often associated with the president of the Motion Picture Producers and Distributors of America, Will H. Hays, or with the head of the Production Code Administration, which did the actual work of vetting films, Joseph I. Breen. But the code itself was written by a Jesuit priest, Daniel A. Lord, S.J., with input from Catholic Action advocate Martin J. Quigley and the archbishop of Chicago, George Cardinal Mundelein. Breen was himself an active Catholic, and Hagerty and Andriano confided to him that they hoped for a sympathetic response from Breen's office to their complaint rather than, as in the clean reading campaign, the necessity of making "endless protest to parties who may be helpless to improve the situation or uninterested or irresponsible."[13]

The downbeat assessment of the clean reading campaign by the San Francisco Catholic Men's organization matched that of Archbishop Mitty, who provided his own evaluation of the campaign to the Vatican's apostolic delegate, Archbishop Cicognani. Writing in March 1939, Mitty reported that he was "happy to say that the results were quite satisfactory in the residential districts. A great deal of difficulty was encountered, however, in the business sections." Mitty's report was prompted by Cicognani's official notice that "the Supreme S[acred] Congregation of the Holy Office, in keeping with the competence conferred upon it by the Code of Canon Law (can. 247, #4), feels the need of reminding the Most Reverend Ordinaries of their obligation to censure pernicious writings (cf. can. 1395, #1) and to denounce them to the Holy See (cf. can. 1397)." The Vatican official's concern was prompted by "the continuous and constantly increasing diffusion of all kinds of publications which spread erroneous doctrines, deprave the mind and pervert morals, [imposing] an obligation upon the Shepherds of Souls to be ever more watchful and prompt in keeping the Faithful from such poisoned sources and so 'to defend sound and orthodox doctrine and to defend good morals' (can. 343, #1)."[14]

Mitty and his men's and women's Catholic Action organizations continued the decent literature campaign "with greater zeal and thoroughness" by developing closer working relationships with the city's police department and by joining forces with their counterparts in Los Angeles. This strategy benefited from the fact that Sylvester Andriano was now a member of the Police Commission, having been appointed by Mayor Rossi in July 1937. Andriano, whose reputation for probity had been acknowledged by the president of the Board of Supervisors during the July 1934 strike crisis, and former Chamber of Commerce president J. Ward Mailliard Jr. replaced two members of the commission who had been discredited in a grand jury investigation into police corruption in the city. The report of the investigation by former FBI agent Edwin Atherton laid bare a variety of malfeasance (including abortions, gambling, and prostitution) that netted sixty-seven crooked police officers and two dozen city officials an estimated million dollars per year. The post–grand jury Police Commission set out to demonstrate its trustworthiness with two Catholic Action stalwarts on board: Sylvester Andriano and Police Chief William J. Quinn. Quinn was not in the Atherton Report, and he had been a member of Andriano's organizing committee that established the new Catholic men's organization.[15]

The cooperative relationship between Catholic Action moral apostolate activists and the city police department had been under way for several years when the archdiocesan chancellor Thomas A. Connolly received a tip from Joseph J. Truxaw, the chairman of the Los Angeles Campaign for Decent Literature. Truxaw's source, an L.A. municipal judge, passed on information about a printing firm in San Francisco that was allegedly "the 'HOME' on the Pacific Coast of pornographic cartoons and pictures. Distributions from that place are made by trucks to all parts of California, Nevada, Oregon and Washington." Connolly informed Chief Quinn that "it certainly would be an excellent move for public morals" to close down the firm, and replied to Truxaw that he could "rest assured that the police will not involve the Catholic Church in this matter in any way whatsoever." Three months later Chief Charles W. Dullea (who succeeded Quinn when he retired) informed the Chancery Office that the department's "surveillance and investigation" had yielded arrests that he expected would close down "the source of the printing of indecent literatures, pictures and booklets, distributed throughout this city and the bay counties." Dullea assured the assistant chancellor, Father Edwin J. Kennedy, that the San Francisco Police Department was "pledging to you our fullest support in the suppression of lascivious literature and other immoral booklets."[16]

The moral apostolate won another victory when the Catholic Men of San Francisco persuaded the administration of the Golden Gate International Exposition to cancel an exhibit in the Hall of Science sponsored by the Birth Control Federation of America. Margaret Sanger happened to be speaking to the League of Women Voters of San Francisco the same week that the exposition announced the cancellation of the birth control exhibit. Sanger expressed her disappointment to a reporter for the *People's World,* the local Communist Party newspaper: "Wherever I go I meet the same opposition—and I must say that it is most insidious and effective." Perhaps Anna E. McCaughey of Los Angeles, national chairman of the NCCW, had that victory in mind when she assured Archbishop Mitty that the members of her organization "look upon San Francisco as a focal point where East meets West in developing national service for God, Church, and Country."[17]

8

Catholic Action and Communism

Communism, totalitarianism, and national socialism have made many conquests in recent years. They are now the accepted political philosophy of several states. They have passed from the region of speculation into the field of fact. In so doing they have revealed all their innate contradictions and hideousness.

—Father Hugh A. Donohoe, Memorandum for Archbishop Mitty, September 2, 1937

Sylvester Andriano and his Catholic Action colleagues followed the lead of both the Vatican and the Chancery Office, believing that their work "includes within its sphere the whole field over which Christian principles should penetrate and be applied." Their determination to base public policy on Catholic moral principles put them on a collision course with the leaders of San Francisco's Communist Party (CP). If Catholic Action work evolved in response to Vatican policy, archdiocesan direction, and lay activism, Communist Party work developed in response to Comintern policy, district leadership, and local initiative. The party developed a growing presence in the Golden State at the very time that Catholic Action was moving from theory to practice, and the local Catholic campaign against Communism, which reflected a long-established Vatican policy, underwent revitalization during the 1934 waterfront and general strikes. While CP activists helped to shape the dockworkers' strategy and tactics, Archbishop Hanna, Mayor Rossi, Andriano, and other Catholic activists, especially attorney John Francis Neylan, planned the city's strategy and participated in the strike settlement. In the aftermath Harry Bridges, who denied charges that he was a member of the Communist Party, and CP activists who openly admitted their party affiliation became particular targets of the Catholic Action mobilization.[1]

The CP made things more difficult for its Catholic critics in the five years after the waterfront strike by closing down its separate Red unions and moving toward selective cooperation with, rather than repudiation of, the new CIO unions, some AFL unions, and the Democratic Party. The new "popular front" strategy saw CP publicists praising "progressive Catholics" while condemning those lay Catholics and clergy who were "reactionary" or "fascist." Catholic Action activists, such as Father Raymond T. Feely, S.J., a professor at the University of San Francisco, were now required to take pains to educate members of their faith who might be tempted to believe the assertions of CP members they worked alongside, or cooperated with in political campaigns, "that there is probably some part of the Soviet system that is 'worth a try.'" Catholics in contact with CP members "might be misled by the denials of any concerted religious persecution [in the Soviet Union] and the assertion that 'religion is a private matter' and no concern of the Soviet government." That being the case, "it really should be counted as a duty . . . as a part of Catholic Action" to understand "that the very essence of Communism is violent atheism, and consequently no part of the Soviet philosophy can be tenable for an American citizen."[2]

A summary of Father Feely's pamphlet series titled *The Case against Communism* appeared on the front page of the May 4, 1935, issue of the *Monitor,* announcing, "This Is the May Day Celebration We Want"—a straightforward call for using the day to honor the Catholic moral economy approach to labor relations. In the accompanying three-column-wide cartoon, the figure of the worker towers over the representative of the capitalists. This iconography mirrored the point of view of Andriano and his Catholic Action colleagues. They drew explicitly on the encyclical of Pope Leo XIII and insisted that those whose labor made economic growth possible deserved equal, or perhaps even primary, consideration when the well-being of the community was at stake. The *Monitor* cartoon expressed an equally unambiguous rejection of the Communist and socialist May Day celebration of working-class solidarity against capitalist oppression. It was almost exactly fourteen months since the beginning of the West Coast maritime strike, and while a truce existed between the longshoremen's union and the employers which would last until the autumn of 1936, a cold war of considerable scope was taking place between Catholic Action activists and their CP enemies.

The origins of the Catholic and Communist hostilities went back to 1934, when Mayor Rossi wrote to Governor Merriam requesting additional National Guard troops in anticipation of the general strike, informing the governor, "I am advised by the chief of police that it is feared they will be unable longer to compel obedience to the law" and "[I am] convinced that the situation . . . is largely due to the efforts and activities of Communists who have no regard for our American form of government and are desirous of breaking down and destroying law observance. Due to the activity of this particular class of persons, unlawful and riotous assembly exists in the city and county of San Francisco with intent to offer violence to persons and property therein." Three days later, on the second day of the general strike, vigilantes carried out a series of "red raids" on the *Western Worker* office, the headquarters of the CP, and other alleged nests of radical activity; carloads of leather-jacketed men drove up to the buildings, broke the windows, and trashed the offices, and then moved on to the next site to repeat the exercise. City police followed the vigilantes and arrested the presumed "public enemies" who happened to be present, filling the city jail with several hundred men and women arrested for vagrancy. Characterized by historian David Selvin as "a violent exercise in self-induced hysteria" brought on by "the instigators' perceptions of 'radicals' and 'revolution,'" the raids of July 17 prompted another statement by Mayor Rossi: "I pledge to you that as Chief Executive in San Francisco I will, to the full extent of my authority, run out of San Francisco every Communist agitator, and this is going to be a continuing policy in San Francisco."[3]

Rossi exaggerated the role of CP members in the waterfront and general strikes, but he was not alone in his estimate of their influence, which was shared by Archbishop Mitty and his Catholic Action activists. They included Police Chief William J. Quinn, vice president of a newly formed statewide anti-Communist police officers' association, who believed that communists were "the greatest propagandists that ever cursed the earth. They put out propaganda [during the strike] that influenced the conservative men—and the majority of them in that strike were conservative labor men, desirous of bettering their positions, insofar as their hours of work and earning capacity were concerned. But unfortunately for them, when they got out on strike they found in some instances at least that their organizations were controlled by Communistic leaders and they were powerless to do anything but follow."[4]

Chief Quinn and Mayor Rossi may have been innocent of charges that they ordered the violent raids on July 17, but other San Franciscans shared their sentiments about the dangers posed by the CP to the city's well-being, and they used a variety of tactics to monitor Communist activity and influence. Hugh Gallagher, operations manager for the Matson Navigation Company and chairman of the Pacific American Shipowners Association, hired private investigators to spy on CP members, as did the American Legion; both shared their investigators' reports with the Chancery Office and enlisted the archbishop's support in following up on the results of their investigations. Archbishop Mitty's opposition to the CP had both faith-based and nationalist-inspired foundations. A World War I chaplain-veteran, Mitty secured membership in the American Legion soon after its founding in 1919; in 1935 he was chaplain of the California chapter; in 1936 he participated in planning a "United Front" for "combating Radical and Communistic Activities" made up of the Legion and representatives of the Knights of Columbus, the Ancient Order of Hibernians, and the Young Men's Institute (in which Andriano had served as "Grand President").[5]

Archbishop Mitty kept himself informed about the investigation of several CP members, including Oleta O'Connor, a twenty-five-year-old native San Franciscan who had been raised a Catholic but was now described in a surveillance report as "one of the most radical firebrands among local Communists." By 1935 O'Connor had been a member of the CP for two years, following a year in the Socialist Party, and she was serving as the part-time organizational secretary for the San Francisco party. Her early life mirrored that of many children born into Irish Catholic families of modest means. Her father was a twenty-six-year-old shoe salesman and her mother a twenty-year-old housewife when she was born, and they were living in the South of Market working-class district in a basement apartment on a street no bigger than most city alleyways. As their fortunes improved, they moved to Eureka Valley (today's Castro neighborhood), where Oleta enrolled in Douglas School (now the Harvey Milk Civil Rights Academy) and then transferred to Convent of the Sacred Heart grammar school, run by the nuns of the Religious of the Sacred Heart. After finishing Girls' High School, she attended the University of California in Berkeley, where she was president of the Women's Debating Club. She graduated in 1931, earned a master's degree in Slavic languages in the following year, and then joined the Socialist Party, which she left after a year in favor of the CP. Twenty years later she described how "those things that I believed the Socialist Party should be doing and was not doing were being done by the Communist Party; that the Communist Party, so far as I could see then, was really earnestly and sincerely fighting to help improve conditions within the framework of the existing social system; and that in addition to this and growing out of these struggles, they were educating the people to understand the need ultimately of moving toward a socialist society."[6]

In her busy first two years in the CP, O'Connor worked with the American League Against War and Fascism, a CP front organization, and then on the staff of the *Western Worker.* Next she was put in charge of neighborhood organizing in the Marina and Fillmore neighborhoods before being designated citywide organizational secretary. At the time of the general strike she helped put out the *Western Worker,* and after the vigilantes wrecked its 37 Grove Street office near city hall, she "carried typewriters and paper up and down Telegraph Hill to the private residence where work was being done to prepare the material so that the paper could be put out, despite the destruction of the headquarters and despite the fact that the printing shop had been told not to publish it any more." At the same time, O'Connor was teaching a class on "Americanism" at a Catholic orphanage in the city's Bayview district under the auspices of the Emergency Education Project, a public relief program that was part of the State of California Emergency Relief Administration (SERA).[7]

According to an American Legion investigator, O'Connor "had no legitimate need for relief but was placed on the rolls in one of the many Red plots and obtained a position." Instead of communicating "the patriotic ideas she was supposed to teach" students, she proceeded "to feed them Communist doctrines, glorifying Russia and her leaders." The director of the Emergency Education Project fired O'Connor after following her and discovering that "she had been visiting Communist headquarters at the *Western Worker* offices in the Civic Center." O'Connor landed other jobs, first as a typist in one of the departments of the SERA office itself and then as a writer in the federal Works Progress Administration (WPA) writers' project, and the surveillance continued. By November 1936 an agent reported—more than a year after her first firing—that "although this woman is on the WPA payroll and receives the regular weekly stipend from the government, she spends her entire day, with the exception of checking in in the morning and at night at WPA headquarters, at 121 Haight Street [CP headquarters]," where "she is a teacher at the Communist worker's school on the subject of atheism and Catholicism (as applied to Communist policies)." There is no indication in the report that the agent knew that O'Connor was now serving in the position of CP county educational director.[8]

While Oleta O'Connor was critiquing Catholicism at the CP school, Archbishop Mitty was teaching his own lesson about Americanism in the 1936 Washington's Birthday edition of the *Monitor.* On the front page, over a picture of Washington, readers found a banner filled with tiny American flags and the headline "Communism, a Monstrous Evil," plus an article detailing Pope Leo XIII's 1878 denunciation of "that sect of men who, under various and almost barbarous names, are called socialists, communists, or nihilists, and who, spread over all the world, and bound together by the closest ties in a wicked confederacy, no longer seek the shelter of secret meetings, but, openly and boldly marching forth in the light of day, strive to bring to a head what they have long been planning—the overthrow of all civil society whatsoever." In the same issue of the paper, the archbishop also reprinted his January speech at the golden jubilee dinner of the St. Vincent De Paul Society, "Condemning the Totalitarian State," in which he cited with approval the 1922 Supreme Court decision that invalidated an Oregon law requiring attendance at public schools, thereby preserving parents' rights to send their children to Catholic schools. Mitty asserted that the "inalienable rights" of Americans "are given to us not by the State but they are given to each individual soul by God Himself, and no group of people and **no State has any right to take these inalienable rights away from any individual**" [boldface in original]. Mitty decried the fact that "in other nations these principles ["the State the supreme arbiter in matters of education and in matters of human relations"] are being put into practice."[9]

Archbishop Mitty did not specify which countries deserved the appellation "totalitarian," but three months later Pope Pius XI singled out several regimes for criticism in a speech that was reprinted on the front page of the *Monitor.* Germany, he said, was "known to be particularly dear to Us," but he criticized the Nazi government because it had decided "in violation of all justice and through an effort artificially to identify religion with politics, [that] the Catholic press is not wanted." But the pope especially condemned the Soviet regime, "where a real hatred of God is destroying all that belongs to religion and particularly all that belongs to the Catholic Religion." The pope informed the audience that "he spoke not only as the head of the Church . . . but also as a 'son of our times,' and with solicitude especially for 'human, earthly institutions' which are also menaced by communism." The times are perilous, and

> the first, the greatest and the most general peril is certainly Communism in all its forms and degrees. It threatens openly and assails individual dignity, the sanctity of the family, the safety of civil life and, above all religion. It resorts even to

> open and organized negation of and assault against God, and especially assault against the Catholic religion. An immense amount of literature has been widely circulated putting into full and definite light this program which is already in practice or is being attempted in Russia, Mexico, Spain, Uruguay and Brazil. It is a great and universal danger which threatens the entire world.

Making reference to the Comintern's official adoption of the popular front strategy in the summer of 1935, the pope argued that Communist "propaganda is the more dangerous when, as in recent days, it assumes an attitude less violent in appearance, less impious in its aim to penetrate into places which would be less accessible were that violence continued. And, alas, it obtains in places incredible success, or, at least, is met with the silence of tolerance, an inestimable advantage for the cause of evil and one of the unhappiest consequences for the cause of good."[10]

In San Francisco the new CP strategy arrived at the same time as a new district organizer, William Schneiderman. After attending the Seventh World Congress of the Comintern in Moscow in July and August, Schneiderman returned to the United States and in October moved to California. He explained to readers of the *Western Worker* that the new approach meant the CP should make coalitions with "the poor and middle farmers and the city middle class, the professionals, intellectuals, etc.," and the result would be "a broad People's Front." "We must change our sectarian methods of work which are an obstacle to winning the masses." By the beginning of 1936 the new approach was making a difference; the CP newspaper advertised non-CP events by organizations such as the American Civil Liberties Union, and its own "United Front" activities included labor leaders and politicians who qualified as progressives but were not party members. By the election campaign period in the summer and early fall, the CP was fielding candidates for political office who claimed their program promised a more attractive alternative for beating back conservative Republican and right-wing candidates than the policies offered by liberal Democrats.[11]

The perceived threat of the new policy of the popular front, combined with the party's determination to compete for political office, galvanized the Catholic Action activists into renewed militancy in the summer and fall of 1936. Hugh Gallagher kept the Chancery Office up-to-date with his various investigations, sometimes meeting with the archbishop in the company of "my informant." It was likely Gallagher who supplied the archbishop with a five-page "Special Memorandum in Re: Harry Bridges," containing a chronological report detailing "beyond the question of any doubt the direct contact between Harry Bridges and the Communist Party, as well as the affiliation of Harry Bridges with members of that party who are primarily identified with subversive tactics as relate to labor organizations along the Pacific Coast." Several others, who in contrast to Bridges made no bones about their CP membership, received special scrutiny from the Chancery Office, including Oleta O'Connor, William Schneiderman, and Archie Brown, a Young Communist League organizer who would soon travel to Spain and fight on the Republican side in the International Brigades. The archbishop established regular communication with the American League Against Communism, which had recently opened its office in the city; its executive director boasted that the increasing number of memberships required him to double the office space after the first nine months. And the Chancery Office filed a report from an informant who described a meeting in which the speaker announced that "the Communist Party must make 1936 their objective to gain control in California. He stated that the whole United States is watching the west coast and that if the party is successful in controlling California, the rest of the States will be forced to follow. When these remarks were made every one almost went crazy from happiness."[12]

The informant's account of the meeting may or may not have been accurate, but there is no denying that as the 1936 election campaigns were moving into high gear, Bay Area waterfront labor relations once again attracted national attention, this time in connection with the expiration of the 1934 agreements between the waterfront employers and the maritime workers' unions. Archbishop Mitty called on the two sides "to submit disputed points to an impartial board of arbitration. When conciliation and mediation have failed, this appears to be the only justice and equity, rather than on the basis of the economic power of the employers or the numerical strength and organization of the employees." Mitty quoted Pope Leo XIII's encyclical on capital and labor in support of "the work of arbitration . . . a function that is proper to government." Mitty insisted that "San Francisco wants not a temporary truce but a permanent peace."[13]

Mitty's assumption that a San Francisco community interest existed above and apart from the interests of particular factions, and that the interest of the community as a whole required employers and unions to submit to government arbitration, was shared by neither party to the dispute. The maritime unions were now represented by the Maritime Federation of the Pacific, a coalition of seven unions organized in 1935; its slogan was "An Injury to One Is an Injury to All." Some American Federation of Labor leaders regarded the federation as "a Communist conspiracy" out of keeping with the limited "hours, wages, and working conditions" goals of their craft-centered tradition. The waterfront employers were now party to a campaign to deport Bridges, an effort that had support from a variety of anti-Communist organizations, on the grounds that he was a CP member and not a citizen of the United States. The financial editor of the *San Francisco Chronicle* stormed out of one meeting of employers in outrage after getting the distinct impression that the employers were seriously considering assassinating the Australian. Edward F. McGrady, troubleshooter for the Department of Labor, visited the Bay Area in early September and reported to President Franklin Roosevelt that "after two years of bickering and violations of the contracts on the part of both sides, hatred has developed, and there is a determination on the part of each side to smash the other."[14]

The 1936 Pacific Coast waterfront strike began on October 29 and lasted ninety-eight days—fifteen days longer than the 1934 strike—and neither the employers nor the workers achieved an unqualified victory. In the weeks leading up to the strike, during the strike, and after the resumption of shipping on February 4, 1937, CP activists and Catholic Action militants raised the temperature of the local cold war that had been going on between them since 1934. In August some nine thousand people turned out for the San Francisco appearance of Earl Browder, the CP candidate for president. In October nearly fifty thousand attended the annual observance of the Feast of Christ the King at Kezar Stadium. Pius XI had established this liturgical event eleven years earlier, dedicating the last Sunday of October to services intended to remind all persons, not just Catholics, that Christ was their rightful ruler in things of the spirit. "The annual and universal celebration of the feast of the Kingship of Christ will draw attention to the evils which anticlericalism has brought upon society in drawing men away from Christ, and will also do much to remedy them. While nations insult the beloved name of our Redeemer by suppressing all mention of it in their conferences and parliaments, we must all the more loudly proclaim his kingly dignity and power, all the more universally affirm his rights."[15]

San Francisco Catholics had celebrated the Feast of Christ the King since 1925, first at the San Francisco Seals baseball stadium and then at Kezar Stadium, adjacent to Golden Gate Park. But Archbishop Mitty broke with tradition in 1936 when he announced, in a message carried in the San Francisco daily papers, that the October 25 observance would be dedicated not only to the cause of world peace but also to the campaign against the Communist Party. A week before the Kezar Stadium event, Mitty used the pages of the *San Francisco News* to denounce the new CP slogan that equated Communism with patriotic Americanism. Mitty insisted that backers of the CP were "false prophets" who would "reduce man to the state of slavery by denying the noblest quality of his nature. He becomes a mere puppet, his individuality being entirely submerged in the totalitarian state. Russia, Mexico and Spain speak eloquently of the evils of such a philosophy of government." Communism was not Americanism at all, but rather un-Americanism: "No citizen worthy of the name can subscribe to those false and destructive principles of government which have been imported from Russia." Communism jeopardized the church as well as the state: "The teachings of Stalin are in direct opposition to the doctrine of Christ, our King, and it is our sacred duty to endeavor by all the power at our command to stem the tide of this pernicious system, which if allowed to spread, will destroy Christianity. No quarter can be given." In the *San Francisco Sunday Chronicle* on the day of the observance, the keynote speaker of the day, Father Richard Hammond, invited Protestants to join with Catholics in protesting both "the great sums being spent on armaments throughout the world" and "appeals to class warfare." Father James McHugh, spiritual adviser to the Holy Name Societies in the archdiocese, criticized the CP for "the spread of harmful propaganda" and assured readers, "No Holy Name man can countenance for a moment a philosophy that at once blasphemes Christ and aims to destroy our Government."[16]

The archbishop's call for an anti-Communist crusade brought an immediate response from the CP, which ever since the adoption of the popular front strategy had been advertising itself as the essence of patriotism; the party had scrapped its old "class against class" slogan in favor of the new "Communism Is the Americanism of the Twentieth Century." The CP printed "An Appeal to Catholic People: A Reply to Archbishop Mitty." The broadside, which was widely distributed by party members, presented a three-part argument designed to counter what "you have read about Communism in the Hearst papers." First,

> your enemy is not the Communist Party, which puts forward a program growing directly from your daily needs. Your enemy is the Liberty League—the Mellon-Morgan-Du Pont clique working through the Republican Party—which would smash our living standards and destroy every vestige of liberty and democracy, freedom of press, and religious worship. . . . We Communists are men and women seeking to eliminate the crying injustices perpetuated against the people by a handful of industrialists and bankers. Jobs, social security for all, freedom of speech, press and worship, the preservation of democratic liberties—these are the things we stand for.[17]

Second, readers needed to appreciate the CP viewpoint on "Hitler Germany and Spain Today." In Germany

> fascism has been victorious. Catholics as well as Jews have been thrown into concentration camps, imprisoned, tortured and murdered. Today German Catholics are joining with Communists in an underground movement to smash Hitler's reign of terror. In Spain the common people—mainly of Catholic faith—are fighting desperately to defend their democratically-elected government. While the wealthy Church hierarchy in Spain are supporting the fascists—who have been financed and armed by Hitler and Mussolini—hundreds of propertyless priests are fighting shoulder to shoulder with the people against reaction.[18]

The final point urged readers to acknowledge and reject Archbishop Mitty's erroneous and dangerous views. In his call for the Christ the King rally, the archbishop presented the CP as an alien force whose message was contrary to church teachings and inimical to the public interest. But the truth was that "because the Communist Party is recognized as the steadfast champion of the people," now "the Communist Party is the main target of fascist attacks in the United States."

> When Archbishop Mitty calls for a drive against Communism, he is lining himself up with the reactionary enemies of the people: the Wall Street group, the Republican Party which sponsors Black Legionism and its program of extermination of Catholics, Communists and Jews! There is a way to defeat American fascism. That way is the independent political action of trade unionists, Communists, Socialists, workers, and middle-class people of all religions, united in a People's Front.[19]

One of the People's Front candidates in the 1936 state election followed up on the CP's print attack on Archbishop Mitty by delivering a speech critiquing him on KGO radio the day before the Kezar Stadium rally. Vernon Dennis Healy, a construction worker and member of the pile drivers' union, had first run for office on the CP ticket in the 1934 election for State Senate District 12; he received 4.6 percent of the vote, attracting 1,134 votes (compared with the 23,312 earned by the incumbent, a Democrat named Herbert W. Slater). Now Healy was the CP candidate for Congressional District 1, and he would lose again (and later in 1938 when he ran for a seat in the state assembly), this time garnering a mere 1.1 percent of the vote and losing to Clarence F. Lea, a Democrat and former district attorney of Sonoma County.[20]

Healy adopted a "guilt by association" rhetorical strategy in his radio address on October 24, arguing that Mitty had aligned himself with the "Radio Priest" Father Charles Coughlin, a notorious anti-Semite who broadcast from Royal Oak, Michigan; with "William Randolph Hearst—the enemy of all lovers of peace and freedom, the enemy of every person who stands for the democratic rights for which our forefathers fought and died 160 years ago"; and with "the Wall Street reactionaries." According to Healy, the archbishop had added his voice to "those who shout Communism the loudest [and] who are trying to bring about in this country a fascist dictatorship . . . and are preparing, together with the Hitlers and Mussolinis, to plunge the world into another imperialist war." Whereas Mitty criticized the Soviet Union, the Republican government in Spain, and the Cárdenas regime in Mexico on the grounds that "our Church can accept no system of government that enslaves men," Healy defended them as "democratically elected governments" that were "anti-fascist, dedicated to the preservation of the democratic rights of the people." Healy concluded his broadcast with a call to "Fellow Catholic people" to understand that "there is nothing in our program that is un-American, un-Christian or contradictory with the needs of the Catholic people. We are sure that you will agree with us now that Communism is really the Americanism of the Twentieth Century."[21]

In fact, very few Californians agreed with Healy, judging by the small number who registered to vote as Communists or who voted for CP candidates in November (not all of whom were party members), and while Franklin D. Roosevelt won reelection by a landslide of historic proportions, Earl Browder garnered only 10,877 votes in the Golden State, a mere 0.4 percent of the total. Five months later Archbishop Mitty, unfazed by CP charges that he was helping to prepare the way for a Fascist America, considered making his relationship with the American League Against Communism official. The organization had received "criticisms and suggestions that we add the word 'Fascism' to our title," but instead of explicitly indicating in its name that it opposed Fascism as well as Communism, the group renamed itself the National Americanism Foundation. But after contacting colleagues in New York City and getting "the dope on them," Mitty decided that the foundation was "just another organization against Communism, of which there are so many."[22]

9

Catholic Action, European Crises, and San Francisco Politics

It is a matter of rescuing individual souls, the home, the school, public morals and Christian civilization itself from the blight of the new paganism and the frightful chaos of Communism.

—Sylvester Andriano, "The Program of Catholic Action in the Archdiocese of San Francisco," September 13, 1938

Sylvester Andriano . . . is the "cover" for Mussolini's fascist schools in California. He is the "front man" behind which the Italian government teaches California born school children to "Believe, Obey, Fight" for Mussolini and be disloyal to democracy and America.

—*People's World,* October 26, 1938

On March 19, 1937, the local fuel that had fired the Catholic Action anti-Communist campaign since the 1934 maritime and general strikes received a powerful assist from the Vatican when Pope Pius XI published his encyclical "Divini Redemptoris" (On Atheistic Communism). A scathing indictment of "bolshevistic and atheistic Communism, which aims at upsetting the social order and at undermining the very foundations of Christian civilization," the pope's message also contained a reassertion of the importance of grassroots Catholic Action workers throughout the world—"Our beloved sons among the laity who are doing battle in the ranks of Catholic Action." According to the pope, the "task" is "now more urgent and indispensable than ever," and "militant leaders of Catholic Action . . . must organize propaganda on a large scale to disseminate knowledge of the fundamental principles on which, according to the Pontifical documents, a Christian Social Order must build."[1]

On April 27 the San Francisco county sheriff, Daniel C. Murphy, joined Los Angeles attorney Joseph Scott and Oakland's former postmaster Joseph J. Rosborough at the podium during a rally against Communism at the Civic Auditorium. Sponsored by the Knights of Columbus and the Catholic Daughters of America, the Catholic Action "mass meeting" drew thousands to the Civic Center, where they heard Scott declaim about the incompatibility of Communism and Christianity. Scott was a popular figure in Knights of Columbus circles who in the mid-1920s had appeared with Sylvester Andriano on programs critical of the Calles government in Mexico. Sheriff Murphy reminded the audience that Catholic Action required agitation for social justice as well as vigilant anti-Communism: "Every man that works is entitled to security for himself and his family." Postmaster Rosborough deplored the anticlericalism and atheism of the Republican government in Spain and its Soviet and Soviet-sponsored volunteer allies in the civil war, but he also stressed, "If the ruling class in Spain hadn't been so selfish and ruthless with the human multitude, violence and death wouldn't now be stalking through that tragic land." John D. Barry, a local newspaper columnist known for his skeptical, free-thinking views, initially feared that the mass meeting would "play communism up as far more important than it really was [and] make it better known." But he concluded that "the meeting will do good. It's making communism serve as a challenge to our own short-sightedness and inhumanity."[2]

Barry served as the moderator of another "mass meeting" the following evening at the Dreamland Auditorium, this one sponsored not by Catholic organizations but by the American Friends of the Soviet Union. The warm-up address came from Beatrice Kincaid, who used her time to ridicule the Catholic event the previous evening, which she described as "dull and sluggish." The audience "had such a bewildered look on their faces. The speakers knew nothing at all about Communism." Kincaid was a veteran of a Soviet Union program that recruited volunteers to move to Russia and devote a year or two to help build socialism under Stalin. She insisted that "there is no such thing as persecution in Russia. And they told last night that there is." Archbishop Mitty's informant, a professional stenographer named Carmel Gannon, could not resist a touch of retaliatory ridicule: "And the cut of the people at Dreamland: Many of the men before the meeting opened sat with their hats on and thought nothing of it. And the women chewed gum. The man just ahead of me had hair that looked as if he cut it himself, and never combed it." The main speaker was Victor A. Yakhontoff, a political exile who had served as a major general in the czarist army and assistant secretary of war in the Kerensky social democratic government prior to the Bolshevik victory in the Russian Revolution. Yakhontoff lectured the audience about the need to befriend the Russian people in the hopes that rivalry between Japan and the Soviet Union would turn Stalin toward the United States, which would lead to a defensive alliance and eventual liberalization of the Soviet regime.[3]

For Archbishop Mitty and his Catholic Action leaders, just then preparing the ground for two new San Francisco organizations, the Catholic Men of San Francisco and the St. Thomas More Society, the notion that an eventual convergence of values could develop as a consequence of future mutual diplomatic interests was anathema, given Pius XI's March 1937 encyclical. National CP secretary Earl Browder discovered this after he received no takers among militant Catholic Action activists for his offer, made during a speech to the tenth national convention of the CPUSA, to extend "the hand of brotherly cooperation to Catholics." And San Francisco's new daily CP newspaper, the *People's World,* merely played up the exception to the rule when it quoted approvingly the speech of liberal Catholic Father James M. Gilles, who criticized "red baiting" and urged greater attention to social justice matters, including the "fight for Tom Mooney's freedom" (Mooney and Warren Billings were serving long sentences for trumped-up charges that they had been the "Preparedness Day Parade Bombers" responsible for killing nine people and injuring three dozen more in San Francisco on July 16, 1916). Archbishop Mitty informed shipping company executive Hugh Gallagher, "I cannot see that there is any possibility of comradeship between the Communists and the Catholics. Their teachings are both atheistic and immoral." And the Knights of Columbus Supreme Knight Martin H. Carmody, whose organization stressed its commitment to "a Crusade for Social Justice as well as a Crusade Against Atheistic Communism," told Archbishop Mitty that he was pleased that San Francisco had hosted one of the six thousand meetings across the country dedicated to "a correct presentation of this menace to Christianity and Christian civilization."[4]

Supreme Knight Carmody boasted to the archbishop that his organization had also made progress in thwarting the activities of the CP front called Friends of Spanish Democracy, the purpose of which, he argued, was "primarily to spread Communistic propaganda." "The real purpose of this subversive movement," according to Carmody, was to support the anticlerical socialist Republican regime in Spain, which in his view was an enemy, not a friend, to democracy in that country, and he was proud that his group had been responsible for having the permits for more than fifty meetings canceled by local authorities. The Knights of Columbus, and Archbishop Mitty, also supported the national Catholic campaign to get the U.S. government to honor the arms embargo by Britain and France against the Spanish Republic. The embargo drove the Republican side closer to Stalin's USSR, which alone provided weapons to the Republicans, while Hitler and Mussolini supplied arms to the rebel forces under General Franco. A relative handful of American Catholics worried about what they regarded as the moral dilemma of choosing either the anticlerical Republicans or the Fascist-backed rebels. But most American Catholics followed the lead of their bishops and chose the latter, seeing the conflict as a simple choice between godless Communists and courageous defenders of the church. The National Catholic Welfare Conference established a "Keep the Spanish Embargo Committee" in Washington, D.C.; Mitty's confidant Agnes G. Regan was active in the committee and kept Mitty abreast of its work. And when the committee decided to establish a national network of Catholic Action laymen to create grassroots support for its lobbying work, Mitty appointed Sylvester Andriano as the San Francisco "contact man."[5]

Andriano and the archbishop followed the lead of the vast majority of Catholic Action activists in the United States, clerical and lay alike, who interpreted the Second Republic's attitude to the church to be as hostile as Mexico's in the previous decade. They then rejected the Second Republic's claims to be the legitimate government of Spain. Historian Stanley G. Payne has recently concluded, "The character and extent of the breakdown of public order under the left Republican government in 1936 had no historical precedent of such proportions in western Europe, being equaled (and in fact exceeded) only by the situation in 1917 in Russia, where there was no effective government at all." Father Hugh Donohoe, in a six-page, single-spaced memorandum on Communism prepared for Archbishop Mitty in September 1937, made a related argument when he wrote, "Ten years ago it would have appeared incredible that the religion and civilization of Spain rested on insecure foundations. Now Spain is passing through the dark night of a civil war in which the supporters of Sovietism and Communism are striving to drag it down to the irreligious, unmoral, and barbarous condition of Russia."[6]

American Catholics were appalled by the social chaos under the republic, which included the takeover of churches and church property, the closing of Catholic schools, and the expulsion of priests, and they were outraged by the republic's treatment of the Spanish church. Critics of the republic reasoned that in a genuine democracy, James Madison's and Thomas Jefferson's concept of freedom of religious worship would have a hallowed place and its practice would be ensured, but the Spanish Republic failed to provide such guarantees to Catholicism. Worse, the critics argued, the republic had made public pronouncements that the Catholic Church no longer existed in Spain, which went well beyond disestablishment, and it allowed if not encouraged murders of thousands of priests and nuns and the desecration and destruction of churches. In fact, between July and December 1936, in what one historian of the subject has characterized as "the greatest anticlerical bloodletting Europe has ever seen," the Republicans killed almost seven thousand clergy, representing about 10 percent of all deaths attributable to Republican action during the Civil War and some 12 percent of Spain's Catholic personnel. Most Catholics at the time took the position that the defenders of the republic had been deluded by phony democrats and that both the Madrid government and its defenders' claim to be the true democrats was simply a mendacious and fraudulent assertion of no value whatsoever.[7]

A relative handful of dissenting American Catholics defended the legitimacy of the republic while criticizing its anticlericalism and its failure to check the leftist violence against the church and its clergy, at the same time denouncing the Fascist support for and the violent excesses of Franco's rebellion. But they were few and far between during the nearly three years of bloody and often vicious fighting between July 1936 and April 1939. Archbishop Mitty denounced the dissenters as naive and dangerous, as did his Catholic Action associates Bishop John F. Noll of Fort Wayne and Monsignor Michael J. Ready, executive secretary of the National Catholic Welfare Conference in Washington, D.C. Noll accused the dissenters of "collaborating beautifully, even if unwittingly," with the forces of Satan, and Ready announced that they had bought into the "Red game" of confusing the issue. Donohoe, writing for Mitty, criticized "those who profess to see in the present conflict a struggle between a legitimate and democratic government on the one hand and a party of self-seeking Fascists on the other."[8]

By the time the Vatican recognized Franco in August 1937, Catholic Action stalwarts in San Francisco had already established their own anti–Spanish Republic front in the form of a Spanish Relief Committee (SRC) headed by Monsignor Charles A. Ramm. A convert to Catholicism whose Lutheran parents were immigrants to San Francisco, Ramm graduated Phi Beta Kappa from the University of California at Berkeley. He served as secretary to Archbishop Patrick William Riordan (archbishop from 1884 to 1914). And he was assistant pastor of St. Mary's Cathedral under Mitty, served on the state Board of Charities, and then served for more than thirty years on the Board of Regents of the University of California. Ramm was thirty years senior to Sylvester Andriano in 1937, as was Richard M. Tobin, the San Francisco banker who served as treasurer of the SRC and who was a member of the national Keep the Spanish Embargo Committee. Tobin came from the city's Irish Catholic "old money" crowd with close ties to the national Republican Party (he was minister to the Netherlands in both the Coolidge and Hoover administrations) whereas Andriano and Ramm were Democrats and Andriano had roots in Little Italy rather than Nob Hill. But their ethnic and partisan differences did not interfere with solidarity on the question of the illegitimacy of the Spanish Republic and the lack of credibility of the Communist Party's defense of that government.[9]

Three months after the Spanish civil war began, CP presidential candidate Earl Browder criticized the arms blockade of Spain in a radio broadcast on one of the NBC networks; he urged Americans to lobby for the repeal of the embargo, and he insisted that the Spanish Republican government was democratic and the Franco rebels were Fascists. Four days later William F. Montavon, the director of the National Catholic Welfare Conference's legal department and a member of the Knights of St. Gregory, a prestigious lay Catholic honorary society, answered Browder on the same radio network with a point-by-point rebuttal. Montavon recited "a record of mob violence, marchings of Marxist militia, arson, robbery, [and] assassination," which he insisted proved that the republic was "a government in political bankruptcy." Where Browder had "denounced the upper Hierarchy as big land owners, cruel exploiters of the peasants, fighting with the rebels," Montavon asserted, "There is no scrap of evidence to warrant even a suspicion that any member of the Hierarchy in Spain is a big land owner, an exploiter of peasants or is fighting with rebels."[10]

The San Francisco Spanish Relief Committee set out to answer the CP argument that Americans had a duty to defend the Spanish Republic, a democracy, and a duty to oppose the Franco rebels, who were Fascists. The committee announced its purpose as "to present to those who will read them the facts and the causes of the present struggle in Spain," and it published several pamphlets by local scholars. Aurelio M. Espinosa, chairman of the Stanford University Department of Romance Languages and Literature, contributed *The Second Spanish Republic and the Causes of the Counter-Revolution,* an anti-Republican recounting of events from the time of the republic's proclamation by Alcalá Zamora on April 14, 1931, to the aftermath of the army uprising four days later by Generals Miguel Cabanellas and Francisco Franco—"not a revolution," he concluded, "but a counter-revolution." The second publication of the SRC came from one of the committee members, Umberto Olivieri, who presented an exposé intended to demonstrate that it was Joseph Stalin's rather than Thomas Jefferson's "brand" of democracy that was practiced by the Madrid regime. Olivieri was another of the Catholic anti-Fascist *fuorusciti* active in the Bay Area. The Santa Clara University professor had earned a law degree from the University of Rome and then served as a captain in the Italian army during World War I. He left Italy for San Francisco in 1921, after the defeat of the Catholic Popular Party in the jockeying for political power that eventuated in Mussolini's success the following year. Olivieri's first position was in the Bank of Italy's legal department, where he worked with James A. Bacigalupi, Sylvester Andriano's first law partner, and where he met Andriano, whose offices were upstairs from the bank's lobby. Olivieri, possibly in collaboration with Andriano, organized the seventh centenary of St. Francis of Assisi, the patron of San Francisco, and later left the Bank of Italy for a position as professor of romance languages at Santa Clara.[11]

Andriano wrote the preface to Olivieri's *Democracy! Which Brand, Stalin's or Jefferson's?* Andriano began with a statement that matched those of the CP, which asserted that "the historic soil of that country has become once more the battleground for the clashing ideals of the world. Upon the outcome of the cruel struggle now raging in the land of Cervantes, Calderon, Murillo, Balmes and Isabella, the future of civilization depends. Whether or not we realize it; whether or not we will it, the truth is, we are all involved in that struggle. The issues at stake are too fundamental, too vital, too universal for anyone to remain neutral." But while the CP chose the Republican side, Andriano opted for the Nationalists. "Order or Chaos; Christianity or Communism; Civilization or Barbarism; God or No-God—that is the one and only issue involved in this titanic struggle.

On one side or the other of that single issue each must align himself." "Order," for Andriano, required a foundation of Catholic Christian moral authority; both the Spanish Republic and the Soviet state represented moral chaos.[12]

In his pamphlet Olivieri presented a list of the "faults of the Spanish government," favorably compared Franco to George Washington, and characterized the "tenets of the Third International of Moscow" as "the false pretenses of a hypocritical democracy . . . for whom democracy is the Trojan Horse for the establishment of communism." Olivieri concluded by warning readers who shared his and his committee's views to be prepared to defend themselves against anti-Catholic and even personal attacks, because "if we speak in favor of the Nationalists—or rebels—we run the risk of being accused of being fascists because every opponent to communism, right or wrong, is in the current conception a contemptible fascist."[13]

In fact, anti-Catholic attacks by the CP were already under way in 1937, and they would intensify as San Franciscans felt more and more obliged to take sides when the conflicts in Europe spread beyond Spain to involve Germany, Austria, and Czechoslovakia. The local attackers zeroed in on a variety of alleged Catholic shortcomings, including "the great scandal of silence"—the failure of Catholics to condemn the bloody purges and reprisals carried out against the Republicans in Spain by the Catholic Franco. One critic dispatched letters to Archbishop Mitty and Father Raymond Feely of the University of San Francisco, arguing that "the Pope blessed Franco, who is using Mohammedan Moors in his war against Spanish Catholics, and also blessed Mussolini (the Supreme Fascist), in his rape of Ethiopia." F. R. Fuller maintained that there was more to fear from "the Catholic Octopus (the Hierarchy) with its tentacles spread all over the earth" than from the "Red Octopus." "'Roman Catholicism' is a foreign 'Ism' run by a foreigner,—the Pope." And if one asked "Why all this Knights of Columbus Crusade against communism?" the answer was to distract the public from Catholic malfeasance. "Can it be possible that the flare-up (temporary or otherwise) caused by the present 'Graft Investigation' has threatened to expose those Catholics who are in the majority as the rulers of our fair city (both civil and industrial)?"[14]

Fuller ended his litany of the "train of abominable machinations and terrorism as practiced by the 'Catholic Hierarchy' all down the centuries" with the exhortation "Read the 'People's World'!!" Three weeks after it published its first issue, the official CP newspaper *People's World* editorialized that "Pete [McDonough] was not the Fountainhead." The press had popularized the phrase "Fountainhead of Corruption" to describe the bail bondsman who was the chief target of the Atherton graft investigation in 1937. The *People's World* now argued that the phrase fit "the corrupt Rossi administration," of which Andriano was a member, better than it did McDonough. And nine months later the *People's World* wrote, "Unkind critics of Rossi call Mr. Andriano the Mayor of San Francisco," a statement that was part of an exposé pillorying Andriano as "the 'front man' behind which the Italian government teaches California born school children to 'Believe, Obey, Fight' for Mussolini and be disloyal to democracy and America."[15]

The targeting of Sylvester Andriano and Mayor Rossi from January to October 1938 took place amid both the continuing attempts of the CP to elect their candidates to local offices and the deepening political crises in Europe. Germany annexed Austria on March 11, and on September 29 Hitler and Chamberlain signed the Munich Agreement, followed by German occupation of the Czech Sudetenland on October 5. And then came the night of November 9, *Kristallnacht* (the night of broken glass), when Nazis attacked Jews and their homes, businesses, and synagogues throughout Germany. Oleta O'Connor, who married a San Francisco plumber in 1937 and changed her name to Yates, now served as the CP's state election campaign manager. After the 1936 elections she and her colleagues faced a more formidable Catholic Action competition because Archbishop Mitty and his lay activists now drew strength from Vatican actions that called into question the CP's argument that Catholicism equaled Fascism. That CP argument had already become tenuous for those San Franciscans well informed enough to know that the Lateran Accords with Italy were a pragmatic accommodation to the fact of Mussolini's regime, not a principled endorsement of the theory of Fascism. But the equation of Catholicism with Fascism faced an even more daunting challenge after Pope Pius XI issued his robust repudiation of Nazism on March 14, 1937, in the encyclical "Mit Brennender Sorge" (On the Church and the German Reich).[16]

Sent by special Vatican envoys rather than by public post in order to frustrate Nazi censorship, written in German rather than Latin for maximum effect in that country, and read to congregations by bishops instead of their delegates, the encyclical created consternation among Nazi officialdom. The pope condemned the "aggressive paganism" of the Third Reich because it "exalts race, or the people, or the State . . . above their standard value and divinizes them to an idolatrous level, [and] distorts and perverts an order of the world planned and created by God." "None but superficial minds could stumble into concepts of a national God, of a national religion; or attempt to lock within the frontiers of a single people, within the narrow limits of a single race, God, the Creator of the universe, King and Legislator of all nations before whose immensity they are 'as a drop of a bucket.'" Nazi secret police confiscated all the copies they could find, and Hitler's government did what it could to minimize the impact of the encyclical in Germany. Overseas it was widely distributed and favorably received, especially in the United States, where the German ambassador complained that twenty-five million Catholics "stand united and determined behind their Church."[17]

Nowhere was that assessment more accurate than in San Francisco, where for decades the Jewish population had lived relatively free of the anti-Semitism that plagued their coreligionists in most American cities. In 1930 Archbishop Edward Hanna put Catholics officially on the side of American Jewish well-being by making an archdiocesan donation of five hundred dollars to the campaign for a Jewish Community Center. In 1931 Hanna received an American Hebrew Medal, given each year to those who "achieved most in the promotion of better understanding between Christians and Jews in our country." And in 1936, in order to advance "justice, amity, and understanding among American Catholics, Jews, and Protestants," Archbishop Mitty supported a "Good Will Tour" around the country by Jesuit Father Michael J. Ahern, Presbyterian minister Dr. Everett Clinchy, and Rabbi Morris Lazaron. This effort aimed at "combating and diminishing religious and racial bigotry," and it reached more than fifty thousand people in twenty-seven cities in ten different states.[18]

On New Year's Day, 1938, the archdiocesan newspaper published an article condemning "Anti-Semitism" as "contrary to Catholic Doctrine," along with an editorial called "The West Coast." "We are really a different people. We do not need to follow as the East leads. We should lead because we are still free to express our principles, to admit the truth and to follow where it leads." In November, Archbishop Mitty participated in a twenty-seven-minute radio address condemning *Kristallnacht.* The CBS broadcast, sponsored by the Catholic University in Washington, D.C., went out on the evening of November 16, and Mitty was one of five Catholic clergy and laymen, including former governor Alfred E. Smith of New York, who denounced the Nazi attacks. Father Maurice S. Sheehy, chairman of the university's Religious Education Department, opened the broadcast, saying that "the world is witnessing a great tragedy in Europe today" and that Catholics were determined "to raise their voices, not in mad hysteria, but in firm indignation against the atrocities visited upon the Jews in Germany." Mitty was the first to speak after the introduction. "As Catholics we have a deep and immediate sympathy with the Jewish men and women who are being lashed by the cruelty of a fierce persecution, especially in Germany. They for racial reasons and we for our religion are writhing there under the same intolerant power."[19]

Mitty's call for solidarity between Catholics and Jews fit nicely with San Francisco traditions, but it was a bold tactic since many Catholics still opposed expressions of amity with Jews as an unacceptable admission that their religion was equal to Catholicism in God's eyes. "Thank God," Mitty continued, "that at last a careless world has waked up, and knowing what is going on across the waters, denounces persecution of race or religion everywhere with one vast united voice that rings around the earth. It is the voice of a better humanity, whose latent sense of justice, freedom and fellowship has at last been aroused by a fundamental appeal." Mitty ended his call for Catholic solidarity with the Jewish people with a familiar denunciation of "all class feeling" because it "has in it the dangerous element that sets one man against another. It may be hostile feeling against race or religion or economic conditions. Let us honestly search our own hearts and if we find this evil thing there, do our best in all our dealings with our fellow-men, in all the relations of life, to root it out of our being."[20]

The *People's World* did not provide coverage of Archbishop Mitty's radio broadcast denouncing *Kristallnacht.* Nor did the CP official newspaper carry the story of Pius XI's formal protest to the Italian state condemning the Nazi-inspired anti-Semitic racial laws adopted by Mussolini's government on November 10. But throughout the winter, summer, and early fall of 1938 the CP hammered away at the alleged corruption of the Rossi city administration, explicitly asserting a nefarious community of interest that joined city officials, Catholic Action, Fascism, and Nazism. In January, as we have seen, the *People's World* exposed what it considered to be the true character of Mayor Rossi's administration; Rossi and his minions, not Pete McDonough, deserved the title "Fountainhead of Corruption." In February the paper rejected the argument in the London *Catholic Herald* that "a worldwide trend [was under way] on the part of the Vatican and the Catholic hierarchy away from the Rome-Berlin-Tokyo axis and toward the democratic powers." The real story, according to the *People's World,* was that San Francisco's Catholic newspaper was "parroting the reactionary cry of 'Communists.'" And the Catholic Action League of Decency raid on the pornography publisher by police chief Quinn was denounced as interference with freedom of speech rather than "a police matter." In March, Sylvester Andriano's friend Amadeo P. Giannini, founder of the Bank of Italy and chairman of the Bank of America, was excoriated in the headline: "Giannini in Plot to Aid Mussolini: Coast Banker wants Billions for Fascism." The news story claimed that by participating in a British-led consortium to invest in an Italian government project, the banker was a Fascist sympathizer. An editorial three days later claimed that Giannini "moved heaven and earth to aid Mussolini," and "the exposure of Giannini shows how expansive and intricate is the network of conspiracy among these plotters for world Fascism."[21]

In May, Rossi's "reactionary government" was accused of colluding with the private corporation Pacific Gas and Electric because Rossi refused to support public ownership of utilities. And "it is not too early to think of a real civic house-cleaning next year, when Mayor Rossi, the real 'fountainhead of corruption,' will come to you seeking reelection." An editorial on May 28 suggested a campaign slogan for the 1939 mayoral race: "Shine in 39: Oust Rossi." In July those leaders in the Italian community who failed to condemn the Mussolini regime's adoption of the Nuremberg racial laws found themselves condemned as "Italian Aryans." And two days after the signing of the Munich agreement, the *People's World* announced that Mayor Rossi's planned appearance at the annual United German Societies meeting, which would also be attended by the German consul general Baron Manfred von Killinger, would take place "under the swastika" and would signify that the mayor was joining the "Nazis in celebrating [the] Czech deal." Rossi did attend, a CP-organized demonstration took place, and city police officers removed and arrested numerous anti-Nazi pickets, including Oleta O'Connor Yates, from the streets surrounding California Hall. According to the CP, "Mayor Rossi is a Fascist" and his participation in the event was an "outrageous insult . . . to the Democratic and Freedom Loving people of San Francisco." It was three weeks later that the *People's World* published a three-part story: "Mussolini Money Subsidizes Fascist Schools in California," in which children were "Told Their Mission in Life is Armed Conquest for Fascism," concluding with "Rossi Police Commissioner [Andriano] 'Front' for Fascist Schools."[22]

Twelve days later Communist Party candidates for state offices met defeat at the hands of California voters; Oleta O'Connor Yates, running for a seat in the state assembly, received only 845 votes

(2.3 percent) compared with 20,379 for the winner, Democrat George D. Collins Jr. But while the CP candidates were rejected all over the state, voters embraced the Democratic Party cause, ending a long period of Republican control by electing Culbert Olson governor, Ellis Patterson lieutenant governor, and Sheridan Downey senator. All three were liberal Democrats, as were a large proportion of the Democrats who captured the majority in the state assembly. The CP, which had thrown most of its assets into the campaigns of liberal Democrats rather than those of its own standard bearers, interpreted the election results as a vindication of the People's Front strategy. An election worker who exulted at a postelection party—"We won!"—was told to calm down by William Schneiderman, the district organizer: "We did not win, comrade. The Democratic Party won." But even Schneiderman could not deny that "a certain euphoria was prevalent in Party ranks." The editor of the *People's World* later recalled, "I was swept up by the same exuberance as the young woman, and was jolted, therefore, by the sudden confrontation with what I knew, of course, was the reality."[23]

The reality that intruded on the comrade's enthusiasm included the daunting spectacle that had occurred ten days before the election, when Archbishop Mitty's Catholic anti-Communist crusade had once again attracted more than fifty thousand celebrants to the annual Feast of Christ the King rally at Kezar Stadium. The Chancery Office advertised a special feature of the 1938 rally, one that distinguished it from earlier such celebrations: it served as the capstone event in the first weekend conference of Sylvester Andriano's new Catholic Men of San Francisco organization. And the archbishop presented his audience with the strongest-yet exhortation to join "the Crusade to which Pope Pius XI summons you—to a Crusade of Catholic Action . . . in order that we might do something to save Christian civilization and Christian principles." Mitty bemoaned the "loss of faith on the part of so many people"; "we have seen since the World War the rise of the Totalitarian state. . . . We see what has happened in Russia, what was attempted in Mexico. We see what has happened in Germany, what is happening in Spain." "Throughout the world there is this vast avalanche coming upon humanity which threatens to wipe out Christian civilization, which threatens to destroy nineteen centuries of Christianity." "We have developed a certain double conscience: Do not bring your religion outside of the four walls of the Church. They say they do not want political churchmen without defining what "political" means. If religion has nothing to do with the things of human life it is not worth much. Christ wants us to bring our religious principles into our recreation, into our social activities, into industrial and economic matters, into legislative problems, into international relations. We have the fundamental principles that will solve all of these problems."[24]

Two weeks after Mitty's Kezar Stadium address, the *Argonaut,* a local public affairs journal, published Father Donohoe's article "Communism: Anti-Religious and Anti-American." Donohoe, now teaching at the archdiocesan seminary, took aim squarely at the People's Front slogan "Communism Is Twentieth Century Americanism." Donohoe argued that "the high democracy of the founding fathers" was based on the principle that the "state receives its authority from God, not directly but through the medium of the people." Thus, "American democracy means more than the fickle rule of the many; it is something more than simple arithmetic; it means the rule of the majority in harmony with eternal law." Donohoe quoted Earl Browder's own *What Is Communism?* to the effect that "we Communists do not distinguish between good and bad religions, because we think they are all bad for the masses." Donohoe argued that the CP denied "the basic truths that are the essence of the Christian heritage" when it rejected belief in "a Creator, a personal God," and "the belief that marriage is a life-long union between man and woman." The CP call for "complete liberation of women from all inequality" demonstrated that "Christian teaching on woman's place in society is likewise subjected to persistent attack." Referring to the fact that "in Russia today there are political purges because some Communists fail to conform to the new code of 'democratic' principles" as more evidence of CP perfidy, Donohoe concluded that opposing Communism should go hand in hand with "the renewed acceptance of the Christian heritage in private and in public life," and that Americans who joined the crusade against Communism were thereby "serving God and country."[25]

Two months later Pope Pius XI died in Rome, and as Catholics throughout the world mourned his passing, San Franciscans rededicated themselves to his Catholic Action principles as they geared up for another city election season. At the same time, events in Europe moved the world inexorably toward war. In March, Hitler dismembered Czechoslovakia and occupied Bohemia and Moravia. France and England then reconsidered their Munich agreement with Germany, and Prime Minister Chamberlain declared that if Poland was attacked, Britain and France would respond. In April the people of Spain saw their civil war come to an end, but in the United Kingdom men faced a new conscription law, and then Italy invaded Albania. Germany and Italy agreed to aid each other in case of a war involving either country, the so-called Pact of Steel, in May. Then on August 23 the improbable occurred: Germany and the Soviet Union agreed to a nonaggression pact. One week later Hitler invaded Poland, and two weeks after that Stalin attacked Poland as well, thus dividing that country between them and setting off a declaration of war against Germany by Britain and France.

To San Francisco Catholic Action activists, the Nazi-Soviet pact represented yet another instance of Stalin's perfidy and Communism's essential moral bankruptcy. To San Francisco CP activists, the Molotov-Ribbentrop agreement posed a challenge: how could they remain faithful to the sharp turn in Moscow's strategy and at the same time continue their search for political power in local government? Catholic Action leader Sylvester Andriano worked to reelect his friend and client Mayor Angelo Rossi, while the CP backed a candidate whose credentials met its revised standards of anticapitalist commitment. The CP's choice for mayor was Franck Havenner, a transplanted easterner who had lived in Arizona before coming to the Bay Area. Havenner had impeccable progressive credentials: secretary to Senator Hiram Johnson; California manager of the LaFollette Progressive Party campaign in 1924; a decade of progressive activism on the city Board of Supervisors marked by steady criticism of the Pacific Gas and Electric Corporation and staunch support for public utilities. Havenner's public power stance matched that of the CP, and the party endorsed his record in Congress, where he had won election in 1936 on the Progressive and Democratic tickets.[26]

Havenner entered the mayoral race with the official backing of the Democratic Party county committee and the promise of support from the moderately liberal *San Francisco News*. But the friendly editor at the *News* died before the campaign, and the paper's promised endorsement never materialized. Havenner's chances probably were hurt even more by the unsolicited endorsement he received from longshoremen's leader Harry Bridges. Havenner was neither a Communist nor a puppet of radical unionism, but he did not aggressively repudiate the Bridges endorsement and found himself the target of red-baiting that portrayed him as a tool of international Communism. Rossi's supporters, including the city's Catholic Action stalwarts, scattered billboards throughout the city that showed the city hall, after a Havenner victory, with red paint covering its French Renaissance dome. When a Havenner campaign march up Market Street was led by a brass band wearing longshoremen's caps and dockworkers' shirts, pro-Rossi newspapers took it as proof that Havenner would be the mayor of radical San Francisco rather than—in the phrase originated by Rossi's predecessor, James Rolph Jr.—"the mayor of all of the people." Voters returned Rossi to office with a plurality of more than twenty thousand votes (48 percent in a six-person race). Voters also rejected the three CP candidates for city office—Oleta O'Connor Yates for city assessor and Elaine Black and Archie Brown for Board of Supervisors. Andriano and his Catholic Action activists were pleased by the election results, giving little thought to a feature of the Rossi campaign that would come back to haunt Andriano: one of Rossi's supporters was the Italian consul general.[27]

10

Andriano's Ordeal

The Loyalty Hearings

Sylvester Andriano. This man is indubitably the fountain head of all Fascist activities on the Pacific Coast. He is Mayor Rossi's legal adviser and Rossi is said not to make any important moves without consulting Andriano.

—Myron B. Goldsmith, "Testimony to the Dies Committee," August 19, 1940

It is high time that the Fascist agent Sylvester Andriano should be booted out of the draft board, where to the shame of San Francisco, he has been allowed to remain all this time in spite of bitter protests by labor and other anti-Fascists.

—*People's World,* May 29, 1942

Criticism of Catholic leaders such as Sylvester Andriano, who had participated in the Italian government's outreach programs during the Fascist regime and who had never made public condemnations of Mussolini, increased in volume and reached a crescendo pitch in late 1939 and 1940. Following the Nazi-Soviet pact in August 1939 and Germany's attack on Poland in September, more Italian political exiles, *fuorusciti,* arrived in the United States determined to fight Fascism from a distance. Gaetano Salvameni, Max Ascoli, and other anti-Communist opponents of Mussolini founded the Mazzini Society, a national organization with local branches aimed at expanding and intensifying the critique of alleged Fascist sympathizers in Italian American communities. In November, J. Edgar Hoover instituted a Federal Bureau of Investigation (FBI) file of possible suspects with Italian, German, or Japanese backgrounds who would be "potentially dangerous" to national security in the event of war with the Axis powers. Then, on June 10,

1940, President Franklin Roosevelt added to the discourse on Italian American propensity to disloyalty when he enlisted a hoary anti-Italian stereotype to condemn Italy's invasion of France: "the hand that held the dagger has struck it into the back of its neighbor."[1]

In San Francisco, charges of Catholic complicity with Fascism were nothing new, but they increased in volume and intensity. The CP's accusations, cloaked in its rhetoric of being the genuine voice of "labor," became commonplace after the 1934 strikes; attacks on Mayor Rossi and his administration intensified after 1936; and Andriano was targeted in 1938. Italian Masons and Italian socialists critiqued Italian Catholics before World War I and during the 1920s. They accelerated their invective in the 1930s partly because of the signing of the Lateran Accords in 1929 and partly because Archbishops Hanna and Mitty were making progress in their campaign to rekindle the practice of Catholicism among the city's Italian population, a project that had involved Andriano from the beginning. The increase of devotional piety was evident in the thriving character of Corpus Christi and Immaculate Conception, the two Italian churches outside North Beach. And in Little Italy the Salesian fathers' Americanization School boasted that it had been able "to bring back to their faith hundreds of Italian boys who had been spiritually neglected." At Sts. Peter and Paul Church, "the Italian Cathedral," the community's embrace of Catholicism could be seen in the establishment of five new statues and images in the three chapels in the back of the church between 1922 and 1940, each one devoted to a Madonna representing a specific locale in Italy. The well-attended public feasts associated with Madonna della Guardia, Madonna dei Miracoli, Madonna della Misericordia, Madonna del Lume, and Madonna delle Grazie provided dramatic testimony to the fact that Italian Catholic devotional piety was growing, not decreasing, in San Francisco.[2]

The anti-Catholic reaction never flagged. Pierino Pedretti, the anticlerical editor of the newspaper *Il Corriere del Popolo,* condemned Pope Pius XI for blessing Mussolini and castigated Archbishop Hanna for proselytizing the city's Italians. Pedretti singled out Andriano for particular scorn in 1930 as a "Catholic-Roman" who slavishly followed the Vatican despite its Lateran Accords. Now, however, the local competition became caught up in the national debates about whether the United States should participate in the European war and whether the officials of Italian and German ethnic organizations threatened American national security. Anti-Fascists, including Masons, anti-Catholic *fuorusciti,* and Communist Party members alike, assuming the role of seasoned fighters against clerico-fascist dictatorship, volunteered for service against Catholic *prominenti* whom they regarded as Mussolini sympathizers in the nation's Italian communities.[3]

Sylvester Andriano's socialist, Communist, and Masonic political rivals accused him of serving Mussolini's government as a Fascist agent at three sets of hearings called by two subversive-hunting government agencies. The U.S. House of Representatives Committee on Un-American Activities (HUAC) held hearing in August 1940 and December 1941; and the California legislature's Joint Fact-Finding Committee on Un-American Activities (Tenney Committee) held hearings in May 1942. Congress had established HUAC in mid-1938 as a temporary investigating committee consisting of seven members charged with tracking "un-American" individuals, organizations, and publications and reporting the findings to Congress and the nation. Martin Dies, a Texas Democrat, the committee's first chairman, served until it became a permanent standing committee of the House in January 1945. Dies devoted most of the committee's efforts during 1939 and 1940 to monitoring those charged with Communist and Nazi fifth-column activities, which he castigated in his 1940 book *Trojan Horse in America.* Dies had only one fifteen-page chapter on Mussolini's regime in his book, but he insisted that the regime's sympathizers had to be included in his investigations because "Italian consular officials and secret Fascist agents are spreading Fascist propaganda throughout the ranks of many Italian-American organizations in the United States."[4]

In July 1940, as German forces occupied the Channel Islands and the Luftwaffe expanded its bombing of Britain, Dies and his investigator, James Stedman, held executive hearings in Tennessee, Texas, and California. On August 16 and 17, as Germany announced its total blockade of the British Isles, they took testimony in Los Angeles about Communist activities. Two days later they came to San Francisco in search of Fascist subversion and heard from Myron B. Goldsmith, a freelance writer and public accountant, and Antonio M. Cogliandro, a former president of the Speranza Italiana Masonic lodge.

At the time of the hearings Myron Beauregard Goldsmith was a forty-seven-year-old transplanted Virginian, an army reserve officer and World War I veteran who had volunteered to collect information about suspicious persons for the American Legion. In January 1942 the army sent him to the South Pacific, where he earned a promotion to major, and after the war he coauthored a book, *Manila Espionage,* which was made into a 1951 movie called *I Was an American Spy*. In 1940 Goldsmith was living in an apartment on Telegraph Hill only a few blocks from Sts. Peter and Paul Church, and he freely admitted that his testimony derived from two informants in the Italian community, Antonio Cogliandro and Carmelo Zito, both of whom were anything but friendly to the Catholic Church. Cogliandro's testimony to HUAC followed Goldsmith's, and Zito would later testify against Andriano at the Tenney Committee hearings. Goldsmith asserted that Andriano's leadership in the Italian Chamber of Commerce and in the Italian language classes for children held after school hours constituted prima facie evidence that the lawyer served Mussolini.[5]

Goldsmith claimed that "within the past few years Andriano spent 18 months in Italy" when in fact his trips in 1931 and 1938 took him away for weeks, not months; he identified Andriano as the president of the Italian Catholic Federation when in fact he would not serve in that capacity until 1946; he labeled Andriano "the attorney for the Italian consulate general" when in fact he handled only certain types of cases for Italian citizens referred to him by the consulate but received no retainer; he asserted that Andriano spoke at "all Fascist gatherings" without identifying even one such event. And Goldsmith maintained that "the Italian Catholic Federation . . . is tied up with the Fascist movement" when in fact its founder and executive officer, Luigi Providenza, lived in San Francisco because he was a Catholic Party political exile who had left Italy to avoid bodily injury from both Mussolini's Fascists and members of the Italian Communist Party. Goldsmith boldly proclaimed: "Sylvester Andriano. This man is indubitably the fountain head of all Fascist activities on the Pacific Coast. He is a former supervisor and was an appointee of Mayor Rossi as police commissioner, a post which he resigned several years ago. He is Mayor Rossi's legal adviser and Rossi is said not to make any important moves without consulting Andriano. He is always one of the principal speakers at all Fascist gatherings where his reiterated theme is 'Our Light Comes from Rome.'"[6]

Goldsmith wrapped up his testimony by repeating the charges made by the *People's World* two years previously about Mayor Rossi's participation at the California Hall meeting of the United German Societies: "Rossi *is said* [emphasis added] at that time to have raised his arm in the Nazi salute." "I regard Rossi only potentially dangerous as a fellow traveler," Goldsmith testified, but he added that during Rossi's tenure as mayor the city's Columbus Day celebrations "have been, *according to reports* [emphasis added], nothing more than Fascist manifestations at which the speakers have always been the Italian consul, Rossi, Andriano, and Father Galli [of Sts. Peter and Paul Church]."[7]

Antonio M. Cogliandro testified after Goldsmith. Cogliandro was a veteran of the San Francisco competition between Catholics and Masons since World War I. He identified himself to the committee as "a thirty-third degree Mason; past master of my lodge and past grand representative," and boasted "that his father was called a 'conspirator' [by the Vatican] during the war for Italian Independence [1866–1870] because he had worked with [Giuseppe] Mazzini and [Giuseppe] Garibaldi, 'the liberators.' He stated that Mussolini had destroyed all this (Socialist) work." A native of Calabria, Cogliandro had attended a seminary but dropped out and left the church. By 1940 he was as disaffected as Andriano was devout, and he was no doubt chagrined by the fact that in the time since the First World War, the Italian Catholic Federation's missionary work had succeeded in persuading many of the southern Italian and Sicilian members of Speranza Italiana to become active Catholics and raise their children in the church. Cogliandro joined Goldsmith in singling out both Andriano and Father Joseph Galli, a priest at Sts. Peter and Paul Church, as Fascist leaders. Galli came under attack for, among other things, his sponsorship of an alleged Fascist organization, the Gruppo Giovanile Italo-Americani, a North Beach ethnic pride drill team and marching band that Andriano also supported. Neither Goldsmith nor Cogliandro offered evidence proving the Fascist provenance of the group, nor did they volunteer the information that the banner carried by the group in parades featured both the American flag and the Italian national colors.[8]

As part of his testimony, Cogliandro submitted a report on organizations "engaged in Fascist propaganda" in San Francisco which he had originally drafted for his friend and fellow Republican Party activist Earl Warren, then serving as the California state attorney general. This report became part of the committee record and was subsequently printed as part of the transcript of the hearings. Chairman Dies did not ask Cogliandro to comment on the fact that he had a conflict of interest when it came to analyzing the record of Sylvester Andriano. Like A. P. Giannini of the Bank of America, Andriano was a lifelong Democratic Party activist who had campaigned for Democrat Culbert Olson for governor in 1939, and he was expected to do so again in 1943. But Cogliandro was a friend of Earl Warren, and Warren was in the midst of an increasingly bitter series of public conflicts with Governor Olson that would eventually lead him to declare his own candidacy for the office.[9]

When the Tenney Committee came to San Francisco five months later, Cogliandro testified again and used the same tactics of guilt by association and misleading half-truths when he repeated his belief that Andriano deserved exposure as a leading Fascist fifth-columnist. The Tenney Committee, like similar "little HUACs" established by state legislatures before 1945 in Massachusetts, New York, and Oklahoma, was the product of state and national partisan rivalries, in addition to concerns about the impact of international affairs on national security. Born in early 1940 as a temporary committee of the state assembly to ferret out potential Communists in the State

Relief Administration, it grew into a permanent joint assembly and senate committee of seven members in January 1941. Jack B. Tenney, a Los Angeles musician, chaired the committee until mid-1949, first as a Democratic assemblyman and later as a Republican state senator. The legislature authorized Tenney's committee to continue searching for subversives in state government agencies. It also expanded the committee's powers to include subpoenaing witnesses and gathering information about any activities that could be construed as threatening coastal defense, jeopardizing the Golden State's economy, or weakening citizens' patriotic devotion to the nation. The committee received explicit approval to investigate "Communist Party, Fascist, and Nazi Bund" activities and individuals, as well as organizations "controlled by a foreign power."[10]

At executive sessions in November and early December 1941, the Tenney Committee heard from Cogliandro and Carmelo Zito and from Andriano himself. On December 4 Cogliandro introduced a touch of drama to the proceedings when he claimed to have been the subject of a foiled assassination attempt: "shot from ambush, the assassin's bullet passed through Cogliandro's coat, without injuring him." The committee did not request any evidence for this claim nor did it seek corroboration of its veracity. Sylvester Andriano denied his critics' allegations; he had never attended Fascist meetings, and when he orated that "our light comes from Rome," it was because he was "very enthusiastic over 'Christian Rome' when he visited there." And he was referring to the church as the source of light, not Mussolini's Fascist regime, while speaking at Catholic events, not Fascist gatherings. But Tenney decided to accept Cogliandro's and Zito's assertions, concluding that "considerable Fascist activities" and "Fascist propaganda and indoctrination" existed in "the Italian colony in San Francisco," and he scheduled four public hearings for the following spring.[11]

On Sunday morning December 7, three days after Andriano testified to the Tenney Committee, Japan attacked Pearl Harbor, and in a week's time the United States was at war with the Axis powers. National security issues acquired a sudden urgency, and in the Bay Area, Italian Americans, both noncitizen "enemy aliens" and naturalized citizens, faced a barrage of questions about the strength of their loyalty to the United States. In the weeks following Pearl Harbor the mastheads of local newspapers told readers what to do in case of an attack on the Bay Area: "Air Raid Signals: Blackout—Fluctuating blasts for two minutes. All Clear—Steady blasts for two minutes." On January 29 Attorney General Francis Biddle began declaring California coastal areas off limits to Italian-, German-, and Japanese-born noncitizens, and on February 19 President Roosevelt issued Executive Order 9066. The order authorized the military to exclude and intern "any or all persons" whose evacuation was deemed necessary for national security. Some three hundred Italians and five thousand Germans were interned in addition to the one hundred twenty thousand Japanese-born residents and their American-born children.[12]

When the attorney general expanded the number of the off-limits communities along the coast, Archbishop Mitty asked Andriano to visit the Chancery Office for a discussion of how to respond to the concerns voiced by pastors who ministered to Italian-born parishioners in the designated areas. One such pastor, Father John S. Owens, of St. Peter's Church in Pittsburg, an industrial city on the shores of the San Joaquin River forty-two miles from San Francisco, described the crisis facing the Italians in his congregation.

> Most of them came here many years ago, when this place was quite small, and was called New York Landing. Unfortunately they lived as a colony, and did not learn to speak English, and so could not pass the examination for citizenship. But they were law-abiding people, worked very hard, and built up the town. Many of them, the men especially, were not model Catholics; but they had the faith, and an extraordinary respect for married life and the home. Now they have to move out of this district; and needless to say, it will be very hard on the older people, some of whom have lived in the same home for fifty years. Perhaps your Excellency could say a word to the proper authorities in favor of these poor people, and so prevent unnecessary harshness.[13]

Andriano urged Archbishop Mitty to contact United States Attorney Frank S. Hennessy or Attorney General Francis Biddle in order to discuss the possibility of amending what he considered "the recent drastic measures against enemy-aliens." According to Andriano,

> the great majority of non-citizens in these affected areas is made up of elderly men and women who in reality make up the most industrious, the most peaceful and law-abiding element of the Italian-American community. This is especially true of the women who following the Catholic tradition took care of their homes and their children and since they took no interest in politics never bothered about becoming citizens. Most of them have native born children. Many of them have sons in the armed forces. While no statistics are available, it can be safely affirmed that the Italians in this area have furnished and are furnishing a larger percentage of men to the armed forces than any other racial group among the more recent immigrants.
>
> It is the well considered opinion of those who are in the best position to know that the Italian people here are entirely loyal to this country; that there is not the remotest danger of any acts of disloyalty, fifth column activities or sabotage among them and that the drastic measures adopted as far as the Italian aliens are concerned have no foundation in fact. These measures have caused widespread consternation not only among the aliens but also among the citizens of Italian birth or origin and there is a general feeling among the entire Italian-American community that such measures instead of making for national solidarity and unity of effort in this emergency are causing dissatisfaction and resentment especially among the native born children of the aliens and are prejudicial to the best interests of this country.[14]

Following his meeting with Andriano, Archbishop Mitty contacted Monsignor Michael Ready at the National Catholic Welfare

Conference about the "rather pitiable situation" with regard to "the Italians and Italian-Americans" who "make up a very large percentage of this diocese." Mitty reiterated Andriano's arguments in favor of amending the attorney general's evacuation orders: "The situation with regard to the Italians is totally different from that with regard to the Japanese and Germans," and "we feel that the attention of the proper authorities should be called to the fact that the carrying out of this regulation, without any discrimination, would seriously affect the morale of the sons and grandsons of those who are affected. Even Joe Di Maggio's father is in the group!" The archbishop explained, "We are presenting this as a picture of the situation for the sake of enlightenment and not in the nature of a protest against the Government." Monsignor Ready showed Mitty's letter to Attorney General Biddle, who "liked the tone and reasonableness," and Biddle "assured me that our Sisters and Priests would be considered especially in whatever regulations had to be issued regarding aliens in the district." The attorney general added that he had "already taken this matter up with the War Department with the view to obtaining a reconsideration of their recommendation that all alien enemies, without exception, be evacuated from certain prohibited areas." Ready assured Mitty that "Mr. Biddle said there was no disposition in the Government to act arbitrarily."[15]

Biddle's reassurances notwithstanding, the evacuation of Italian "enemy aliens" continued, as did FBI arrests of persons deemed "potentially dangerous" to national security. By November 1942 there were 2,262 persons of Italian ancestry under arrest and much larger numbers of Japanese (5,534) and Germans (4,769). Pollsters discovered that Americans were more fearful of secret loyalties to the Axis powers by German Americans (82 percent) than by Italian Americans (29 percent) or Japanese Americans (24 percent). But for a variety of reasons, including the president's own racial prejudices and those of Lieutenant General John De Witt, head of the Western Defense Command ("The Japanese race is an enemy race"), the White House and the U.S. Army dismissed objections from the FBI director and the attorney general and treated the mainland Japanese as a suspect group, not as a group that might include suspect individuals. Some 120,000 were forcibly removed to hastily assembled camps run by the War Relocation Authority in barren sections of the West and Southwest. With the Japanese accounted for, President Roosevelt quipped to Biddle, "I don't care so much about the Italians. They are a lot of opera singers, but the Germans are different, they might be dangerous." Roosevelt removed Italian citizens from the enemy alien list effective Columbus Day, 1942. But in the meantime, "potentially dangerous" Germans and Italians were made subject to an Individual Exclusion Program (IEP) established in August, which ultimately excluded 563 persons from designated coastal areas nationwide, 174 of them in the Western Defense Command, which included the San Francisco Bay Area.[16]

Sylvester Andriano found himself designated a "potentially dangerous person" in 1942 when the Tenney Committee subpoenaed him on its return to San Francisco on May 25. This time, the committee held public hearings in the Borgia Room of the St. Francis Hotel, and the proceedings turned into something of a dress rehearsal for the anti-Communist show trial hearings of the 1950s: political circuses marked by publicity-seeking and self-aggrandizing showmanship by the committee members. The room was crowded with newspaper reporters and press photographers, who eagerly recorded the finger-pointing charges against alleged traitors and the arm-waving protestations against "star chamber proceedings." On the first day Chairman Tenney caused a sensation when he began the proceedings by announcing that the committee's private investigator, who "did practically all the actual work and research in preparing for this hearing" and who worked "entirely at his own expense, simply because he believes it the proper thing to do," was "very brutally beaten up" by three men on a street near the hotel. The audience was left with the impression that the attack was retaliation by parties upset with the investigation of pro-Fascist activities in the city. But another explanation seems equally plausible, especially since Tenney put into the record the fact that the victim had not made a police report and since he claimed the attack took place several blocks down the hill from the hotel in the Tenderloin district of bars and nightclubs—a neighborhood notorious at the time for muggings and robberies of unwary customers of the prostitutes who worked out of the numerous bars. On the second day the audience erupted in laughter when Mayor Rossi balked theatrically before taking an oath to tell the truth and announced that he was worried someone would take his photograph and claim he was giving the Fascist salute.[17]

On May 25, the first day, Carmelo Zito, a member of the *fuorusciti* who along with Cogliandro had supplied the information that Myron B. Goldsmith used in his testimony at the HUAC hearings, now launched his own attack against Andriano. Zito offered a striking contrast to the Catholic *fuorusciti* involved in Andriano's Catholic Action work, such as Luigi Providenza. Providenza had left Italy during the political infighting leading up to Mussolini's victory in 1922, and Zito had fled Italy after the Fascist victory, with a law degree from the Royal University of Messina in 1921. Zito arrived in New York City in December 1923, and two years later, at the age of twenty-six, he married Armida, a woman from his boyhood town of Oppido Mamertina in Reggio Calabria. After arriving in San Francisco, Providenza founded the Italian Catholic Federation and published the Catholic Action newspaper *Il Bollettino,* but Zito found work as an associate editor for two New York City Italian-language socialist newspapers, *Il Veltro* and *Il Nuovo Mondo.* Zito's boss at *Il Veltro,* Arturo Giovannitti, organized the Anti-Fascist Association of North America and became its secretary-general; the two men were actively involved in the lobbying campaign to release Sacco and Vanzetti, and they remained close friends.[18]

In 1931 Zito left his wife in Manhattan and moved to Boston with his mistress, Marie Nocito, and their three-year-old daughter. When Armida followed them to Boston, they decamped for San Francisco, where Zito sold insurance until he found work in 1935 as the editor, and then editor and publisher, of the socialist newspaper *Il Corriere del Popolo.* He also resumed the anti-Fascist work he had begun with Giovannitti ten years before in New York City. Andriano found himself in Zito's sights in January 1937 because one of Andriano's pet projects for years was the Italian language school, which offered after-school lessons for children in six neighborhood locations in the city. In a bold headline Zito argued that the school should be exposed because it was not an Italian school but rather "the Fascist school": "THE FASCIST SCHOOL IS ANTI-AMERICAN SCHOOL." According to Zito, since the textbooks came from the Italian government, they were tainted by Fascist ideology, despite the fact that the school dated to 1886 and was supported by various local Italian American organizations and local businesses, including the Bank of America and the Transamerica Corporation, in addition to the Italian government. Zito collected copies of the textbooks used at the school, and he began monitoring the extracurricular activities that accompanied the language lessons, including athletic and musical groups that were modeled on those sponsored by the Fascist government in Italy; he regarded all such activities as Fascist front organizations. Zito's efforts were rewarded when the city's major daily newspapers followed up on his stories and the local American Legion added investigation of possible Fascist subversion to its existing anti-Communist subversion agenda.[19]

After the *People's World* began publishing in January 1938, *Il Corriere del Popolo* and the CP paper both covered Italian and Italian American events, and both papers printed news articles and editorials with strong anti-Rossi and anticlerical perspectives. On October 13, ten days after Zito became a United States citizen, Girolamo Valenti made the news in both papers. Valenti was the former editor of *Il Nuovo Mondo,* the New York City newspaper that Zito had worked on, and currently edited the official paper of the Socialist Party's Italian Federation, *La Parola del Popolo.* Valenti testified that Italian consulates in American cities were hotbeds of Fascist propagandizing, all of it designed to undercut the loyalty of the nation's Italian-born and Italian-ancestry residents. Twelve days later the *People's World* attacked Sylvester Andriano for his association with the Italian language schools, and the illustrations accompanying the three-part story were the very textbooks and photographs of extracurricular activities collected by Carmelo Zito.[20]

Immediately after Italy entered World War II on the side of Germany on June 10, 1940, Zito held a press conference to once again expose Andriano and "a dozen or more prominent Italians as leaders of an alleged Fascist movement here [engaged in] fifth column activities." Zito was also interviewed for an NBC program, where he claimed that "75 percent of the Italian-Americans were against Fascism, 15 percent had no interest in the issue due to educational limitations, and 10 percent remained pro-Fascist despite Mussolini's alliance with Hitler and Italy's declaration of war on France and England." Later that year he provided information to Goldsmith for his testimony before HUAC, and on May 25, 1942, he gave public testimony to the Tenney Committee about Sylvester Andriano's alleged un-American activities.[21]

After identifying himself to the committee, Zito explained that when he became editor of *Il Corriere del Popolo,* "I increased the tone of the anti-Fascism in the paper, sometimes going to the excess in the fight on fifth columnists and people that is [*sic*] in the United States to spread Fascist propaganda." Asked if he had "made any independent study or investigation of the Italian Fascist situation in San Francisco," Zito replied, "I was constantly on the watch for anything that to my judgment was action to spread anti-democratic ideals or anything that was to support dictatorship." According to Zito, the Italian-language newspaper *L'Unione* was one of four "vicious" newspapers "instrumental to drug the public opinion among the Italian Americans to the point they are not capable any more to understand the benefits of democracy and the blessings of the land in the country of their adoption." Zito claimed that *L'Unione* was the weekly paper of the Italian Catholic Federation, but in fact it was being published in 1942 by the San Francisco Catholic archdiocese, having originally been the weekly of the Italian Catholic Union, founded in 1919 by Andriano and Bacigalupi. Zito's misstatement was either a mistake or, more likely, an indirect attack on Providenza's Italian Catholic Federation organization, which was involved in anti-socialist and anti-Communist political work, in contrast to the Italian Catholic Union, which limited itself to Catholic devotional activities.[22]

Zito's direct attacks on Andriano came when the editor characterized the Catholic Action leader's participation in several Italian American organizations as deliberate attempts to foster fealty to

Mussolini and loyalty to his Fascist state. Asked about the Italian language school, Zito replied, "The Fascistic school I think is the proper name—the Fascistic school. They aim to teach no language whatsoever—they have the aim to teach that Mussolini is God, that he is the man sent by Providence, and Il Duce, he is all the time right, and his moral is to belief, to obey, to fight." Zito told the committee how Andriano had successfully lobbied to stall in committee a proposed law that Zito had supported for passage in the state senate. The bill would have placed the Italian language school under the control of the California State Board of Education. By opposing such legislative oversight, Andriano deserved to be considered a Fascist sympathizer, Zito argued, even though, as he himself admitted to the committee, Andriano (and Archbishop Mitty) opposed the bill because such a law had the potential of "hurting the Parochial schools."[23]

Zito alleged that Andriano deserved exposure as a Fascist sympathizer because "Mr. Andriano was honorary president" of "this Scavengers Association of San Francisco" that "collected the scrap iron free . . . because we must send to Mussolini the necessary iron to fight the war [in Ethiopia in 1936]." When committee chairman Tenney asked Zito, "Mr. Andriano made the policy for the collection of scrap iron and tin?" Zito answered, "I can't tell you that." Zito also attacked Andriano for his association with Mayor Rossi and with Father Galli. According to Zito, "I saw often Rossi rendering the Fascist salute in public demonstrations," and as for Father Galli, he allowed the "display on the right side of the altar in the church the Italian colors, with the Italian color flag, the Fascist insignia. In the church on the other side, of course, was the American flag, to justify it."[24]

Zito insisted that "Fascism has the blessing of our mayor, Andriano, Mr. [Ettore] Patrizi, the Grand Master of the Sons of Italy [who all] make the Fascist salute." Andriano was one of the Fascist "ring leaders, who took the oath of allegiance to the United States with mental reservations, who in becoming citizens said they renounced allegiance to all potentates of a foreign country." They "took this oath, and they violated the oath, so strip them out from the citizenship and treat them as enemy aliens." Zito also praised the committee for its work and urged the establishment of "a committee like this in every State, not, understand, just for the duration of the war, but always, to discourage any out of the United States activity; in other words any infiltration of isms in the United States." He added, "I hope you will go to the extreme in exposing the fifth column here and redeeming the California Italian workers from this pawn of Fascism."[25]

Zito's solicitude for the well-being of the state's Italian workers earned him a laudatory article, illustrated with his portrait, in the *People's World* the next day, but on the afternoon of May 25 the proceedings continued and the committee heard from Andriano. Andriano was the second to testify, following Renzo Turco, another attorney, who along with Andriano and *L'Italia* editor Ettore Patrizi would be forced by the army to leave the city in September under the auspices of the Individual Exclusion Program. Turco ended his testimony by challenging the veracity of Zito's accusations:

> TURCO: I mean all that stuff he said. I am surprised so much time is even wasted to listen to that stuff.
>
> CHAIRMAN TENNEY: Do you have any evidence to refute the material given to the Committee?
>
> TURCO: My God—it is just a question of looking around; to begin with did he produce any evidence?
>
> MR. COMBS: Oh, we have a great deal of evidence.
>
> TURCO: How in the world, for instance—
>
> CHAIRMAN TENNEY: (Interrupting) Mr. Turco, we are not going to go into any discussion of the matter. The evidence will have to speak for itself.
>
> MR. COMBS: You are excused, Mr. Turco.[26]

Andriano challenged Zito's testimony and questioned the reliability of the committee's information from the very start of the session, when he corrected assertions about his public service ("I think you have the dates all mixed up") and the Italian language school ("That is not the fact"). Andriano explained that his role as a board member and later as president of the school did not include the actual management of the institution, that is, "participation in the supervision of the type of instruction that was disseminated at the schools." In response to Zito's claims that in 1937 Andriano had colluded with the Italian consul general, who tried to exercise control over the operation of the school, Andriano pointed out that in reality he had participated in the "general objection to the aggressiveness of Mr. Rensetti in conducting the Italian Schools." Andriano added that when that consul general "sought to inject himself, intrude in the celebration and control the appointment of committees [for planning the annual Columbus Day celebration] we simply took the thing out of his hands."[27]

After a lengthy series of questions about the curriculum and instruction at the school, which as he had already explained were outside the scope of his role as a member of the board and president, Andriano tested the committee's patience with a lecture about how they should be doing their job: "I respectfully suggest, Mr. Chairman, if you desire to investigate the Italian Schools you send for the teachers that taught the children that go through the schools, and there are a legion of boys and girls, hundreds and thousands of boys and girls, who have gone through the school in San Francisco; many are in the armed forces; and I am sure they will be able to tell you what they were taught in the schools."[28]

Then Assemblyman James Phillips began a new line of questioning, demanding to know why, since the children attended the city public schools in regular hours, "was it felt necessary for some reason to have them attend some other schools besides the American schools?" When Andriano answered that "since I have been in Italian-American activities, and that dates back thirty years—we have always felt it was a good thing to have the children of Italian-born parents learn a little bit about the language of their fathers." Phillips then asked if some of the children were American citizens, and when Andriano answered that they *all* were, Phillips wanted to know, "Why was it necessary to teach them about a foreign country if they were American citizens?"

PHILLIPS: And on which do you think the greatest emphasis should be laid for the American children, that they should study the language of a foreign country or the language of the country of which they were citizens?

ANDRIANO: I think there was equal emphasis placed on both. The Americanization schools have been conducted for many years in San Francisco, both by the Salesian fathers and others.

PHILLIPS: You consider it just as important to know as much about a foreign country as their parents should know about the country of the children of which they are parents?

ANDRIANO: My experience has been a child who knows something about the language of his parents makes a better American citizen.

CHAIRMAN TENNEY: That is the same statement made by the Japanese.

ANDRIANO: That may be, but I think I know something about the Italian-American situation in San Francisco.

CHAIRMAN TENNEY: I merely reiterate, the Japanese say the same thing.

ANDRIANO: That doesn't detract from the truth of the statement I am making.

ASSEMBLYMAN JESSE KELLEMS: Don't you feel, Mr. Andriano, that probably America would be stronger all the way around if we would forget to call them, let's say, Franco Americans and Italian Americans, and talk about just Americans?

ANDRIANO: I, frankly, avoided that, and have always used the term Americans of Italian origin.[29]

When the questioning moved on to his role in the Italian Chamber of Commerce and his travel to Italy in 1938, the committee accused Andriano of disseminating propaganda, praising the achievements of the Fascist regime, and boasting about the widespread popular support for Mussolini. Andriano explained that the "propaganda" referred to in a brochure displayed by the committee was tourist information supplied by the tourist agency connected to the Chamber of Commerce, not political propaganda on behalf of Fascism. And he pointed out that Zito's charge that he had enthusiastically praised Mussolini in an interview with *L'Italia* was false. He explained that on his return from Italy he had lunched with the editor of the paper, Ettore Patrizi, and in the course of the lunch made anecdotal comments pertaining to some of his impressions while in Italy. There had been no interview, and Patrizi had exaggerated what Andriano had said about the high morale of some of the people he had met during his visit. And when the committee displayed a document that purported to be a photostatic copy of the minutes of a Fascist organization with his name listed as one of the attendees, Andriano replied that he "certainly never attended any of its meetings, so, consequently, as far as I am concerned it is a damnable lie."[30]

After two and a half hours of testimony the committee concluded by asking Andriano whether he had served in World War I (he had not) and whether he was still serving on one of San Francisco's draft boards (he was). The committee also wanted to know whether he had followed the example of New York City mayor Fiorello La Guardia and had his decorations from the Italian government "melted and made into bullets." Andriano replied that he would not "turn them into bullets or anything else" and he would wait for instructions from "competent authorities in Washington."[31]

On May 26 and 27 the Tenney Committee heard from several other critics of Rossi and Andriano. Charles H. Tutt considered the Catholic Church an accomplice to Mussolini's regime; he was director of the local branch of the anti-Fascist Mazzini Society and served as the committee's translator. Harry Bridges and CP member Archie Brown used the hearings to even the score with their Catholic Action opponents; their testimony focused primarily on Mayor Rossi's Catholic Action–inspired labor relations practices. Chairman Tenney, who typically demonstrated considerable skepticism about the veracity of a CP member's testimony, now asked Bridges to serve as an expert witness concerning the mayor's political philosophy. The moment was captured by a newspaper reporter: "Bridges smiled. He was permitted to put this unsupported statement on record: 'I always thought Rossi was a Fascist. I was always sure of it, in my own mind—politics aside. I am glad people are waking up to it.'" Rossi condemned "the damnable lies of irresponsible people, which are creating religious and racial bigotry in a city world famed for its tolerance," and the "deep, treacherous and selfish motives" of "those who prompted my presence here" in what "is a smear campaign, pure and simple." And Rossi blasted the committee as "a glaring example of government by poisoned platitudes and scandalous generalities . . . a star chamber inquisition that is most un-American." The very next day, Bridges received an order from Attorney General Biddle that he be deported to Australia for violation of the federal law that made it a crime to belong to an organization that advocated the overthrow of the United States government by force.[32]

The Tenney Committee was unfazed by the biased character of the testimony against Andriano; like the HUAC hearings, and contrary to its own self-serving description of its work, the Tenney proceedings yielded only assertions, not evidence, concerning Sylvester Andriano. No evidence was offered supporting the claims that Andriano served as an agent of the Fascist government of Italy and participated in Fascist propagandizing among the Italian-ancestry population of the Bay Area. The Tenney Committee heard from a total of thirty-three witnesses in the executive sessions of November and December 1941 and the public meetings in May 1942. Only eight witnesses referred to Andriano at all, and five of them merely acknowledged that they knew of his work with the Italian language school. Mayor Rossi affirmed Andriano's patriotism, denied charges that Andriano was a Fascist agent, and testified that he had never seen Andriano give the Fascist salute. Three witnesses, Goldsmith, Zito, and Cogliandro, claimed that Andriano stood at the apex of a San Francisco Fascist triumvirate whose other members were Turco and Patrizi. Goldsmith's information came from Zito and Cogliandro, and none of the three accusers provided evidence that any of Andriano's extensive activities involved attempts to influence public opinion on behalf of the Italian government. Nor did they present evidence that Andriano lobbied on behalf of Mussolini's regime to shape government policy in ways that would help Italy and harm the United States.[33]

Research in the Archivio Storico Diplomatico del Ministero degli Affari Esteri, the archives in Rome that contain the declassified files relating to the overseas activities of the Italian Fascist government, confirms what Andriano freely admitted in the hearings: his presidency and membership on the boards of the Italian language school and the Italian Chamber of Commerce. But there is no record that the attorney received instructions from the Fascist government, cooperated in creating or distributing political propaganda for the Fascist regime, or operated as an undercover agent. Nor has such evidence been discovered in the archives of the San Francisco Catholic Archdiocese, the archives of St. Mary's College of California, or, as discussed in the next chapter, Andriano's FBI file.[34]

The two witnesses who asserted that Andriano was a security risk pointed to his long-time participation in the Italian Catholic Federation and his other Catholic Action activities as proof of his affiliation with the Fascist state. They reasoned that because the Vatican, which had accommodated itself to Mussolini's regime, had officially sanctioned Andriano's organization, Andriano himself was therefore complicit with Fascism. In addition, according to his detractors, his legal business through the Italian consulate, his service on the boards of directors of the Italian language school and Italian Chamber of Commerce, and his presidency of the school and the chamber also qualified as Fascist leadership because the school and the chamber were outreach activities of the Italian government. Cogliandro and Zito omitted from their testimony the fact that Andriano had been involved with the school since before the Fascist regime, and the chamber accepted nominations for the office of chamber president only at the request of members, who correctly expected that they could block a genuinely pro-Fascist candidate from winning the election if a Catholic Action leader were on the ballot.[35]

Why did Andriano fail to explain his reasons for accepting the Italian Chamber of Commerce presidency, and why did he refuse to discuss the importance of faith and ethnic pride in his motivations for his work in the Italian language school? Part of the answer surely lies in his personal style, which in contrast to the "hail fellow well met" persona of his friend Rossi seems to have tended toward the aesthetic and even the austere. This silence suggests unwillingness on his part to accept the Tenney Committee's legitimacy. Like Mayor Rossi, who denounced the committee for conducting "a star chamber inquisition that is most un-American," Andriano lectured the committee about its process, challenged its right to question his activities, and denounced the charges as "a pack of lies."[36]

After the hearings his Catholic Action colleague James Hagerty suggested that Andriano should protect Catholic Action from possible guilt by association by making a public announcement explaining the nature of his relationship with the Italian consulate and detailing the reasons that his work with the Italian language school and Italian Chamber of Commerce did not constitute disloyalty. Andriano reviewed his promotion of Italian culture, which began while he was a student, continued after his graduation in 1911, expanded when he began his law business, and persisted after he became a city supervisor, police commissioner, draft board chairman, and president of the Catholic Men of San Francisco. "Because we are at war with Italy must I now apologize if for thirty years and more I have striven with what little talent god [*sic*] has given me to keep alive and foster in the hearts and minds and wills of my people the faith, the culture and the traditions which earned for Italy the proud title of mother of civilization?" He explained to Hagerty that he had always promoted American patriotism as well as Italian pride; through all his cultural work with members of the Italian community he intended to communicate one "dominant thought: To be true to the faith of their fathers; to glory in and live up to their moral and cultural heritage; to be faithful, loyal and devoted to this their country to which they were so greatly indebted." "If on two or three occasions I said a good word about Mussolini it was always in connection with some specific thing that he had done, such as restoring order, setting up vocational groups as advocated in the Pope's encyclicals, introducing the teaching of religion in the public schools or signing the Vatican Treaty."[37]

Andriano insisted, "I never had any sympathy with Fascism as such although I did approve some of the things done by it, but I have always strongly disapproved of some of its principal tenets such as its totalitarian philosophy, its claim to monopoly in education; its regimentation of youth and its militarism." He reminded Hagerty that after he returned from his European trip in 1938, he had expressed even stronger objections because of "Mussolini's tie-up with Hitler." Finally, Andriano told Hagerty that he had refused to cooperate with the Tenney Committee because he was modeling himself on "the example of St. Thomas More." More had rejected Parliament's politically inspired "reformation" of English legal tradition, including the new law used by the court to convict him of treason. Andriano rejected the committee's right to convene a pseudo court and label him a Fascist on the basis of hearsay and politically motivated denunciations. He refused to acknowledge the legitimacy of a show trial where there was no presumption of innocence, where he had no opportunity to present witnesses on his own behalf, and where the rules of evidence were virtually nonexistent. "By standing on my civil rights, far from doing a disservice to that cause, I am actually rendering a service to it, for surely no one can be censured for upholding the dignity of the law by insisting upon not being stigmatized as a dangerous or potentially dangerous citizen without due process of law, or for not countenancing any abuse of authority in violation of constitutional rights."[38]

The Tenney Committee accepted its witnesses' condemnations of Andriano rather than his denials of the charges and labeled the attorney a security risk. The committee then sent a telegram to President Roosevelt presenting the politically motivated assertions of Zito and Cogliandro as proven facts, falsely stating that Andriano was an "official representative of a nation with which the United States no longer has diplomatic relations," and urging that Roosevelt remove him from his position as chairman of San Francisco Draft Board 100.[39]

11

Andriano's Ordeal

Exclusion and Exile

As you know, this case has attracted a great deal of attention and the Bureau may be subjected to criticism should we fail to fulfill our investigative responsibilities in connection with it.

—J. Edgar Hoover to Special Agent in Charge Nat J. L. Pieper, November 21, 1942

The Andriano exclusion order was issued by General DeWitt, in charge of the Western Defense Command. The quality of his judgment may be gauged by his recent statement: "A Jap's a Jap. It makes no difference whether he is an American citizen or not."

—Attorney General Francis Biddle, "Memorandum for the President," April 17, 1943

Readers of the May 27, 1942, *New York Times* article on the Tenney Committee hearings discovered that in response to Carmelo Zito's testimony, Mayor Angelo Rossi "denied ever having given the Fascist salute," and that the mayor condemned both Zito ("he is editor of a paper that is always attacking me") and Antonio Cogliandro ("a political rogue"). The *Times* coverage dramatized to a national readership the long-time political and religious rivalries between Catholics and anti-Catholics in the Italian American community and between Catholic anti-Communists and their Communist Party competitors which had been a fact of life in San Francisco political culture for decades, especially since 1934. The hearings did not bring these rivalries to an end but merely signaled the beginning of an even more dramatic phase of the contest, marked by heightened concerns about national security in a time of war.[1]

One theme in the statement that Mayor Rossi made at the Tenney hearings pertained to "the damnable lies of irresponsible people, which are creating religious and racial bigotry in a city world famed for its tolerance" and "creating discord and suspicion among the people of this seaport." Archbishop Mitty developed this theme further the day after the mayor's appearance, in a letter to Monsignor Michael J. Ready of the National Catholic Welfare Conference, a letter in which Mitty asked Ready to "use your good offices, should it be possible for you to do so, in preventing the dismissal of Mr. Andriano from his draft board." Mitty described how Rossi and Andriano "were subjected to a 'smear' campaign on the part of the members of the committee" and described "the principal witness against them" as "an anti-clerical, a Mason, and probably a Communist."[2]

The archbishop described to Ready how members of the local Mazzini Society ("who are for the most part anti-clerical and Communistic") had successfully lobbied the committee to return to San Francisco, this time for highly publicized public hearings. Mitty filled in the background:

> For the past few years this Society has been trying to get the rank and file of the Italian people here in San Francisco, of whom there are forty thousand or more, to affiliate themselves with the Society. They have had little success, since the character of the Society is known to the Italian population. This hearing apparently is an attempt to intimidate and terrify the Italian element into following the lead of the Society, on the grounds that they will be judged un-American and pro-Fascist should they not do so. Should credence be given to any report of this State Committee, it will cause a rift here that will take years to heal.[3]

According to Mitty, "The decent element of the city of San Francisco all realize that the hearings constitute an attempt to smear some of our prominent Catholics, that they are motivated by un-American, anti-Catholic and Communistic prejudices." In the case of Andriano, "Mr. Andriano is known as a fearless, intelligent and completely honest gentleman and has been entirely impartial in his Draft Board decisions; otherwise the F.B.I. would have had him dismissed many months ago. Should the President act on this telegram, it appears to me that it will discredit the F.B.I. here, as well as give some substance to the findings of this committee, which would be fraught with grave consequences."[4]

While Mitty was appealing to Monsignor Ready to do what he could to discredit the Tenney Committee's legitimacy and block its call for Andriano's removal from the draft board, the editors of the *People's World* and *Il Corriere del Popolo* were gloating over the apparent success of their offensive against Andriano and Rossi. The CP paper ran a news story, once again referring to Andriano as "the power behind Rossi," and a column by regular contributor Mike Quin (Paul William Ryan). Quin characterized the mayor as "an artful dodger" even while admitting that both Rossi and Andriano explicitly denied sympathy with Fascism, and he interpreted the two men's evident discomfort during their testimony as proof of the truth of the pro-Fascist charges against them. "Sylvester Andriano," Quin wrote, "took a fearful frying at the hearing, but it all seemed well deserved."[5]

The next day, Charles Tutt of the Mazzini Society, a frequent contributor to Zito's newspaper, renewed his criticism of "Fascist Propaganda in California" in *Il Corriere del Popolo.* Tutt had testified at the Tenney hearings and served as the committee's translator. Now he drew on his training as a professor of the Italian language to present a tendentious deconstruction of a story in Ettore Patrizi's *L'Italia,* claiming to demonstrate that Patrizi had positively welcomed the Japanese conquest of Bataan rather than neutrally recounting its occurrence. And both papers, joined by *San Francisco Chronicle,* called for Andriano's ouster from Draft Board 100. The *People's World* also condemned the deportation order of Harry Bridges ("America's Friend, Fascism's Foe") and praised him for his testimony exposing the alleged "Fascist activities and associations of high public officials in San Francisco," the "Fascist agents who have ruled and intimidated the Italian population of San Francisco" and who must "be brought to account."[6]

Archbishop Mitty now decided it was high time that the archdiocese "took a crack at some of the testimony" of Zito and Cogliandro during the Tenney hearings, and on May 30 the *Monitor* published a front-page editorial condemning "one Zito, the editor of an Italian anti-clerical sheet in this city," whose accusations constituted "a new low in smear campaigns." Cogliandro was also singled out by name, and both men were accused of aiding and abetting a practice inimical to "the unity of America."

> Before the United States entered the war, Americans were divided. There were interventionists and non-interventionists. The division even extended into the government itself. As a matter of fact, even administration officials endorsed the sending of scrap iron and other war materials which are now being used as weapons against our brave soldiers and sailors. The men and women on both sides of the pre-war arguments were sincere. They argued over what was best for our nation. However, since Pearl Harbor all ranks have been closed; no longer are there interventionists and non-interventionists. True Americans have rallied as a man to defend our country. Victory, and complete victory, over Hitler, Hirohito and Mussolini is the objective.
>
> However, within the past few weeks there has arisen on the home front a threat to the unity of America, [a "scandal mongering" campaign singling out particular individuals "for a public tarring and feathering"]. The most offensive trick in the campaign to stir up civil discontent is to search out something the person wrote or said years ago, under circumstances totally different from those of the present time, and to reprint it now in order to stimulate hatred. In bringing these matters up, the object of the slanderer is apparent, for he is not consistent. He does not, for instance, mention his own ideology bed-fellows who also gave voice as recently as within the past year, when they were defending and endorsing the Hitler-Stalin pact.[7]

The *Monitor* editorial concluded by describing "a religious angle, for frequently Catholics are made the victims in a manner and method suggestive of the unspeakable Hitler purges—purges made possible by cruel misrepresentation and emotionalism." Zito perhaps "wishes the government to suspend the publication of every Italian paper here but his own, which would give a free hand in propagandizing the Italian people to their ultimate destruction. Underlying the testimony so far adduced, is the antagonism of a certain few ex-Catholics toward the Catholic Church—an antagonism that is prostituting one of the most noble of all virtues—patriotism and love of country—for its own ends."[8]

Similar sentiments were voiced by twenty-two San Francisco attorneys and public officials, who sent their own telegram to President Roosevelt: "we condemn and oppose the recommendation of the committee in this case" because "to remove a person from office after eighteen months of service on the basis of an accusation by an investigating committee rather than by an impartial finding violates the most elementary justice." Whether moved by their personal loyalty to Andriano, galvanized by the editorial in the *Monitor,* or angered by the *People's World* generalizations about "Fascist" city officials, the signatories condemned the Tenney Committee recommendation because "such unfairness would conflict with fundamental American principles [and be] destructive of unity in a time of crisis." The signers included Sheriff Daniel C. Murphy, a former state senator and county labor council president, future district attorney Edmund G. "Pat" Brown (whose tenure from 1944 to 1952 would be marked by aggressive implementation of the Catholic Action moral apostolate), the city's Chief of Civil Defense Eugene Broderick, Professor James L. Hagerty from the Catholic Men organization, and eighteen others, most of them participants in the Catholic Action campaign.[9]

Ten days after Zito accused Rossi of Fascist sympathies, the city Board of Supervisors unanimously expressed its confidence in the mayor, and in mid-June at the annual commencement exercises of the city's Catholic high schools at the Civic Auditorium, Archbishop Mitty offered a personal defense of Sylvester Andriano. Mitty encouraged the graduates and their families to take heart and be confident that the United States would vanquish the Axis powers. "We need only fear the enemy within, the people who will strive to stir up disunity, unknown nobodies who will attempt to smear the reputations of decent people who have lived all their lives among us serving their fellow men." On June 17 Monsignor Ready notified the archbishop, "I did what I could prudently and was told here that no notice would be given to the protests [by the Tenney Committee and the Mazzini Society against Andriano's remaining on the draft board] since the agitation concerned California and the elements were very well identified." Mitty replied, "I do not think that they [Zito and Cogliandro] succeeded very much." But Andriano thought differently, writing to Hagerty on June 22 that "the politicians, Masons and Mazzinians and their confederates in the papers have ceased their clamor for my scalp for the time being, but it's just a lull. At the opportune moment they will resume their antics."[10]

Andriano did not have to wait long for a resumption of hostilities, for Zito attacked "the powerful Andriano" in an editorial in his July 9 issue, this time mocking him for a lifetime spent as a sycophant Catholic. Andriano, according to Zito, came to San Francisco from Italy and "having reached the nearest Church knelt down, confessed himself, received communion, mumbled ejaculations, intoned Gregorian hymns, crossed himself with compunction, dipping his whole fist in the holy water font and became a lawyer." Zito then conjured up a version of the classic anti-Catholic charge that the church represented an ominous threat to American liberty.

> A month has gone by [since the Tenney hearings]. What does public opinion, so appropriately referred to by the Tenney Committee, matter? Governor Olson (no one will accuse Olson of being a Fascist) was afraid to trifle with the Catholic dynamite and in answer to a protest of the Mazzini Society he confessed with seraphic ingenuousness that Andriano had been recommended to him by the higher clergy. The Queen of the Pacific is pinnacled with a hundred church towers and deafened by the sound of a thousand bells.

> Do the protections of the high clergy reach as far as Washington and are they so powerful as to cover up the moral and judicial responsibility of a servant of the Fascist tyranny while the entire people, the generous American people, bars the way with its bleeding breast to the troglodyte monster marching through the world?[11]

Two weeks later Zito attacked again. This time Andriano was condemned not for being "powerful" but for cutting a poor figure (La Figuraccia), thereby tainting the community "like the smell of ammonia in an old toilet" (come il puzzo di ammonica al vecchio vespasiano). Andriano was a Fascist agent because he had served as the president of the Italian school and the Italian Chamber of Commerce, which were "the center for the moral sabotage of fifth columnism" (il centro di sabotaggio morale del quinto colonnismo erano le istituzioni delle quali Andriano era il Presidente). Andriano was a "Fascist agent" (agente fascista) who put "the sons of immigrants, since they were baptized, under the wings of the Fascist bat" (sotto le ali di pipistrello del fascismo i figli degli immigranti fin dal fonte battesimalae). "San Francisco is an extremely beautiful city adorned with steeples and resounding with the echo of a thousand bells. Are those in Washington too afraid to play with the Catholic dynamite?" (Hanno pauro anche Washington di scherzate con la dinamite cattolica?).[12]

When Andriano wrote to the membership of the Catholic Men of San Francisco on July 25, two days after Zito published his latest attack, he had just submitted to a post-hearings interview at the San Francisco FBI office. Andriano did not mention the meeting to his colleagues, but he admitted that because "we are all called to do our part in the defense of our country, it is difficult to maintain the purpose, the organization, and the program of Catholic Action. Changing circumstances . . . make necessary the adapting of our methods and activities to carry out our purposes in this emergency period." In a private letter to Hagerty, Andriano confessed to his weariness at "the ever more vicious onslaughts of those who are seeking my scalp," unaware that he was about to be subject to the decisions of precisely that "Washington" whose authority Zito wanted to be imposed on him.[13]

On August 19, 1942, the War Department created the Individual Exclusion Program (IEP), which provided for the removal from coastal areas of persons "whose presence was considered dangerous to national security." The authority for this program was Public Law 77-503, a March 21, 1942, statute that provided legislative legitimacy for Roosevelt's Executive Order 9066 and authorized criminal penalties for violating the order. Five days after the IEP began, a panel of army officers of the Western Defense Command met with Andriano for a review of his case file. The file dated from July 18, 1939, when the bureau received its first report from a confidential informant that Andriano was the director of the school where "children of Italian parentage are taught fascist ideology." On December 31, 1940, with four such entries in his file, the FBI classified Sylvester Andriano as "Fascist."[14]

Andriano had thus been a subject of FBI interest for nearly three years when he testified at the Tenney Committee public hearings. By then he had already been caught up in the wartime bureaucratic politics associated with J. Edgar Hoover's expansion of the FBI's intelligence operations, and the Andriano investigation demonstrates the lengths to which the FBI director was prepared to go to advance the bureau's reputation for effectiveness in conducting such work in a time of national emergency. During the summer of 1936 President Roosevelt, Secretary of State Cordell Hull, and Hoover met to discuss how to gather information about potentially "subversive" individuals and organizations. Hoover was given authority to establish a General Intelligence Section, which would identify and monitor persons "engaged in activities of Communism, Nazism, and various forms of foreign espionage." According to Hoover, the president wanted the program to remain secret, insisting that "the matter . . . be handled quite confidentially." In Hoover's words, "the President, the Secretary of State and I should be the ones aware of this" work. By 1938, 2,500 names and addresses were on a secret list of "dangerous" persons. In May 1940 the Justice Department created a Special Defense Unit responsible for aiding U.S. attorneys in prosecuting treason, sedition, espionage, sabotage, "and kindred offenses," and in June 1940 the FBI established a Custodial Detention Program charged with responsibility for the disposition of individuals "who may become potential enemies to our internal security."[15]

President Roosevelt put the FBI's thus far secret intelligence-gathering responsibilities on a formal public footing in September 1940, just three months after Congress passed the Alien Registration Act and the Smith Act, which required all foreign citizens to register and be fingerprinted and which declared it illegal to belong to an organization that advocated "overthrowing or destroying" the United States government. From then on, the FBI worked in concert with Naval Intelligence (ONI) and Army Intelligence (G-2). Sylvester Andriano was a United States citizen, but all three of the intelligence agencies considered "hyphenated Americans" like himself as well as noncitizen residents from potentially hostile countries to be potentially dangerous persons. On March 31, 1941, Hoover sent Andriano's name and address to the Special Defense Unit for custodial detention action "in the event of national emergency." (After Pearl Harbor the War Department put him on the list of individuals "recommended for apprehension by the Federal Bureau of Investigation and internment for the duration of the war because of pro-Axis sympathies and/or activities.") The FBI's recommendation was based on accusations from a confidential informant, charges that were identical to those made at the August 19, 1940, HUAC hearings by Goldsmith, Zito, and Cogliandro. Andriano was allegedly the "spearhead of Italian propaganda in San Francisco" and had said "We must look to Rome for our guidance." He was the attorney "for" the Italian consulate, president of an Italian language school, and president of the Italian Chamber of Commerce. The FBI even included the erroneous statement that Andriano was president of the Italian Catholic Federation as grounds for his detention in case of war.[16]

Andriano thus became a candidate for "custodial detention" in case of national emergency because a confidential informant to the FBI made charges that the bureau accepted at face value and used as the foundation for its future recommendations. The original charges were supplemented with additional material as the investigation developed. From December 1940 on, the bureau operated on the assumption that Andriano's "Fascist" designation was a fact, and in June 1941 San Francisco Special Agent in Charge (SAC) Nat J. L. Pieper declared, with no qualifications, that Andriano was "one of the strongest pro-Fascist sympathizers in the San Francisco area." In August, Pieper went even further when he informed the Washington office that according to his confidential informant, Andriano "is considered by the Italian colony as one of the most ardent and powerful supporters of Mussolini in the United States." Eight months before Pearl Harbor, then, the FBI had established a pattern that would continue throughout the investigation, privileging condemnatory material from one confidential informant that buttressed the original charges, and dismissing information sympathetic to Andriano that challenged the credibility of the accusations.[17]

After Pearl Harbor, unbeknownst to Andriano, the FBI's investigation immediately attracted scrutiny by top officials in the Justice Department due to the questionable character of the charges and the possible bias of the confidential informant. Wendell Berge, assistant attorney general, informed Hoover on December 24 that there was "not sufficient evidence" to warrant criminal proceedings, and in any case Andriano did not fall under the auspices of the Special Defense Unit because he was an American citizen. Berge also wanted "the information contained in the Bureau dossier [on Andriano] to be verified." Hoover then turned to Edward J. Ennis, director of the Alien Enemy Control Unit, and asked whether Ennis wanted the FBI's help in the "apprehension of subject Andriano." But Ennis replied that Andriano was not an "alien enemy" and did not fall within the jurisdiction of his agency. San Francisco SAC Pieper believed that "the most that can be expected from this case is to obtain a Custodial Detention [and] in no event will it be possible to prove espionage on the part of Subject or that he is the Agent of a foreign principal." Hoover responded in March that "with regard to Mr. Andriano and in view of his civic prominence, I want you to see to it personally that this case is handled carefully and discreetly by experienced Agents attached to your office."[18]

After the Tenney Committee hearings, which received national publicity, Hoover and Berge continued to debate the merits of the Andriano case. Did Andriano's service on the board of the Italian language school mean that he "was acting as the agent of a foreign principal"? Hoover thought so, and sent Major General Lewis B. Hershey, director of the Selective Service Commission, a memorandum summarizing the FBI's file on Andriano and newspaper clippings with the Tenney Committee's recommendation to remove him from Draft Board 100. On June 11 Berge posed several questions to Hoover. Did Andriano's dealings with the Italian consulate mean that he was "an unofficial representative" of the Italian government? "It should be determined whether or not these activities amounted to anything more than merely furnishing information." How credible was the bureau's "confidential source"? Berge also wanted to know the identity of the informant whose statements were the foundation for the case against Andriano. When Hoover asked his San Francisco SAC about the informant, Pieper replied that he "does not speak very good English and does not present a very good appearance." "He does give the impression that he is sincere and certainly he is positive enough in his statements, though again it might be possible to show some bias on the part of the witness [redacted]."[19]

The FBI's confidential informant never testified because Sylvester Andriano never went to trial, but on July 24 he was interviewed by a special agent in San Francisco. On August 14 the agent submitted a forty-eight-page report on the investigation thus far and a transcript of the Andriano interview. His synopsis addressed each of the accusations made in the loyalty hearings and by the bureau's informant, beginning with Andriano's relationship with the Italian consulate: "Investigation fails to show Subject acted in other than attorney and client relationship." The Italian Chamber of Commerce was a non-issue because "its activities [were] practically cleared on revocation of registration as foreign agent in July, 1941." Regarding the Italian language school, "investigation to date reveals only one book which might be construed as containing propaganda which was used during Subject's term as president." "Subject admits being president of above groups and control of Italian government of schools and Fugazi Hall but denies knowledge of any Fascist propaganda."[20]

In his interview Andriano addressed in detail the issues that had come up in the testimony against him during the loyalty hearings. His accusers claimed that Andriano endorsed textbooks supplied by the Italian government to the language school that celebrated Fascism, but "before his term [as president] a set of books had been sent to San Francisco by the Italian Government which had contained material favorable to Fascism and objectionable. He stated, however, that this set was destroyed in the schools." Another charge was that he had accepted "decorations" from the Italian government. Andriano explained that in 1926 or 1927 the government awarded him a Cavallero award and in 1930 a Cavallero Officiale award. In 1937 he received his third and final award, that of Commendatore. In each case these awards "came as a complete surprise to him" and "he did not know what he had done to get them." He did not exhibit them, and "the certificates conferring same were still rolled up in the tube in which they came." His critics accused him of being a Fascist ideologue. Andriano denied even having studied "the Fascist system." He pointed out that he had studied Pope Pius XI's encyclicals on Catholic Action and on the Reconstruction of the Social Order, and he explained that the former papal letter "condemns the Fascist regime [and] specifically condemns the Fascist Party, particularly the blind obedience to Il Duce. Subject cited the above encyclical [on Catholic Action] with the idea that it expressed his views on Fascism." His accusers claimed that Andriano had frequently spoken at public events where he praised the accomplishments of Mussolini and his regime.

> He never extolled Fascism and seldom mentioned Mussolini, and then said if he did mention Fascism it was because it was the Italian Government and as such fostered Catholic religion and stated that religion had been almost lost in Italy when the Communists held sway. He reiterated that he never subscribed to the fundamental principles of Fascism

> and criticized the philosophy of "everything in the State." He stated that the world must look to Rome for guidance and inspiration, but he has never said that it should look to Mussolini.

At the very end of the interview Andriano "explained his feelings toward Italy and the United States by comparing Italy with his mother and the United States with his wife and drawing the following analogy: A man marries and takes a vow to remain faithful to his wife. Then as long as his wife and his mother maintain friendly relations the man can keep a love and regard for both, but when the two break off relations, then the man must, in accordance with his vows, remain faithful to his wife."[21]

Hoover did not record his reaction to Andriano's analogy, nor did he let up on the investigation after reading his special agent's report calling into question the truthfulness of the charges. In August the FBI began opening Andriano's mail, checking letters for invisible ink and microdots (they found nothing), making copies of the contents of his religious magazines *English Catholic Newsletter* and *Sword of the Spirit,* and searching the articles for hidden meanings or cryptic messages (none were found). Marine Corps Colonel C. G. Parker Jr., deputy director of the Selective Service System, questioned "the authenticity of the information" used by the Tenney Committee and the FBI against Andriano. His "Local Board No. 100" was "one of the most efficient boards in San Francisco," and Andriano's "removal would place us in the position of discharging a good board member based on an unfounded criticism." Hoover replied on September 6 that "the confidential informant who furnished the information included in my memorandum has furnished this Bureau much information in the past and it has been found to be reliable." Four days later Hoover leaked the details of the investigation to newspaper columnist and radio newscaster Walter Winchell, pointing to the Andriano case as a prime instance of Fascist influence in American communities. Two weeks later Jack Tenney also wrote to Winchell, the letter copied to Hoover, that Andriano's was "the most flagrant case of all" the examples of "Fascist influence in California." Tenney repeated the charges, claims the FBI's own special agent had found to be bogus, concerning the character of Andriano's connections to the language schools and the chamber of commerce, and his decorations from the Italian government, and he ended his comments by complaining that "we have not heard from the President" in response to the committee's demand that Andriano be removed from the draft board. Five days later, on September 28, General De Witt issued an Individual Exclusion Order banning Sylvester Andriano from all coastal areas in the United States.[22]

General De Witt decided to exclude Andriano after the military board met with the attorney on August 24, but Frank J. Hennessy, the U.S. attorney for northern California, and his deputy, Alfonso Zirpoli, disagreed with the exclusion recommendation and appealed the decision. Hennessy and Andriano had been friends for twenty-five years, and Zirpoli considered Andriano "a real patriot," not a pro-Fascist security risk. General DeWitt banished Andriano nonetheless. Mayor Rossi and then Archbishop Mitty met personally with DeWitt and asked him to reconsider, but he treated Rossi with disrespect, displayed minimal civility to Mitty, and refused to rescind the exclusion order. The archbishop, who was traveling to Washington, D.C., for a National Catholic Welfare Conference meeting, tried to intervene with administration officials on Andriano's behalf. He could not see Attorney General Francis Biddle or Secretary of War Henry L. Stimson, but he met with Assistant Secretary of War John J. McCloy. McCloy told Mitty that there was nothing Washington could do since this was a matter that fell solely under the authority of the head of the Western Defense Command, General De Witt.[23]

In response to the exclusion order, Andriano left San Francisco for Chicago on October 10. Zito's editorial five days later in *Il Corriere del Popolo* called on his readers to "Rejoice!" (Gioite, o amici!). Columbus Day had arrived, and Little Italy was free of Sylvester Andriano and Father Galli (non c'erano Andriano o il prete Galli). Zito expected, "When the war is over with our certain victory, you can be sure that you will not see them coming back to North Beach to mock democracy, because all of them—naturalized and non-naturalized—will be sent to Italy." Zito concluded with a cheer for General De Witt (E sia lodao il generale De Witt), and he urged the Department of Justice to "intervene and revoke the citizenship from Mussolini's agents. They are not worthy of it. We should send them to a concentration camp [al campo di concentramento], forcing them to work, for the entire duration of the war, and, at the end, ship them as postal packages to Italy."[24]

Andriano relocated himself to Chicago, where he stayed at the Hotel La Salle in the heart of the Loop district, but he refused to comply with the requirement that he submit himself for photographing and fingerprinting and that he keep the FBI informed of his whereabouts. In late October, Andriano learned that Zito was lobbying the Justice Department to revoke his citizenship, and during the winter months he decided that "if I was not going to be let alone and I must defend myself against denaturalization proceedings I might as well have a showdown in the jurisdiction where I have lived and labored for over forty years." On March 19, 1943, Andriano returned to California, where he stayed in Los Angeles and at his ranch in Los Altos, in Santa Clara County. His Catholic Action colleagues persuaded him to leave California to avoid being accused of violating the army's orders, so Andriano removed himself from the Exclusion Area on May 23. But he refused to return to Chicago, deciding instead to stay in Denver, where he lived in the Sears Hotel until he returned to San Francisco on the Feast of the Immaculate Conception of Mary, December 8. The army rescinded the Exclusion Order effective Christmas Day, 1943.[25]

The FBI continued to gather information about Andriano, adding his refusal to comply with all of the exclusion order's requirements to his alleged Fascist sympathies as grounds for investigation. From October 1942, when he left San Francisco, until he returned to the city after his exclusion order was rescinded, FBI special agents in Chicago, Denver, El Paso, and Los Angeles kept track of his movements. Army Intelligence G-2 operatives conducted surveillance of Andriano, opening his mail and reporting the contents to the FBI. "As you know," the director wrote on November 21 to Special Agent Pieper in San Francisco, "this case has attracted a great deal of attention and the Bureau may be subjected to criticism should we fail to fulfill our investigative responsibilities in connection with it."[26]

If Andriano's case attracted attention, Hoover himself was partly to blame because he had leaked the details of the case to Walter Winchell on September 10. Winchell was probably responsible for the *March of Time* radio broadcast on the CBS network on October 8 that featured the Andriano case. Then, on October 18, *Time* magazine carried an article, "RoBerTo Checked," describing how in San Francisco "Fascists there used to say RoBerTo as a greeting—Ro for Rome, Ber for Berlin, To for Tokyo. Italy sent teachers, books and medals for the Italian schools. Mussolini won a popularity contest hands down over Franklin Roosevelt." Sylvester Andriano alone was identified by name as one of "the ousted Fascistophiles" who were "excluded from the San Francisco military area as dangerous to security—the first such action against white citizens."[27]

Following the pattern that characterized the investigation from the beginning, Hoover continued to disregard testimony reported to him that supported Andriano's denial of the charges. When the San Francisco office interviewed the teacher at the Italian language school whose tenure coincided with Andriano's presidency, she told the agent that "only Italian language and literature were taught in the schools and . . . no attempt was made to teach the children Fascist ideology. She stated that in fact the Italian Consul had specifically forbidden the teaching of Fascism in the school, and the textbooks, though furnished by the Italian Government, contained no Fascist propaganda." According to Pieper and Hoover, however, the use of alphabet books in which "D" stood for "Duce" and textbooks lauding the accomplishments of Mussolini's regime constituted "Fascist teachings."[28]

On February 6, 1943, Pieper interviewed Archbishop Mitty, who insisted that "all of the facts and the true character of Andriano were not known" and that the investigations had not "brought forth all of the facts regarding the man and his character." Mitty maintained "that many political enemies of Andriano have been able to paint him in such a bad light that the true worth of the man, his integrity and patriotism was not known." Mitty relayed a conversation he had had with Andriano over dinner in Chicago, where Mitty had made a stopover while returning from Washington, D.C. Andriano, according to Mitty, "felt that an injustice had been done to him . . . nevertheless he had gained so much from being an American citizen he felt that it was a small price to pay for such a privilege."[29]

Andriano was interviewed again by the FBI while living in the La Salle Hotel in Chicago, this time by Special Agent S. J. Drayton. Andriano told Drayton that while "the Wartime Civil Control Administration had the power to exclude him from the Western Defense Command, they exhausted their power by ordering him to leave and he was not obligated to report to them." He regarded "the compliance to the Wartime Civil Control Administration's instructions to be fingerprinted, a desecration of his rights as an American citizen. . . . He took an oath upon being naturalized not to be desecrated. Outside the restricted areas," Andriano continued, he was "a free American citizen, just like any other citizen," and "he is under no obligation to report his movements." Since "all other American citizens in the area of Chicago were not required to report their movements, therefore it was not necessary that he would report his movements."[30]

Hoover and his assistant director, D. Milton Ladd, were incensed by Andriano's refusal to be photographed and fingerprinted and to report his whereabouts. Andriano regarded the order as "an infringement on his rights as an American citizen." Hoover regarded Andriano's refusal as a flagrant gesture of disrespect toward the government and a personal affront to himself as FBI director. Hoover made several attempts to persuade the attorney general to initiate a criminal prosecution of Andriano for violating Public Law 77-503. That law, dated March 21, 1942, provided legislative legitimacy for Roosevelt's Executive Order 9066 and authorized criminal penalties for violating the order. Hoover and Ladd decided that the Andriano case was an ideal test case.[31]

Secretary of War Stimson and Assistant Secretary McCloy agreed and joined Hoover in urging an indictment. When Attorney

General Biddle refused, Stimson complained on March 31, 1943, to President Roosevelt that Biddle's position "flouts the intent of Congress." On April 17 Biddle replied to Roosevelt that "the Executive Order permitting the exclusions" was "never intended to apply to Italians and Germans. Your order was based on 'protection against espionage and against sabotage.' There is absolutely no evidence in the case of ANDRIANO, who has been a leading citizen of San Francisco for thirty years, that he ever had anything to do either with espionage or sabotage. He was merely pro-Mussolini before the war. He is harmless, and I understand is now living in the country outside of San Francisco." Biddle refused to order a criminal indictment against Andriano, but even he accepted the FBI accusations against the attorney. In his memoirs published nineteen years later, Biddle wrote, "The [exclusion] program was pretty edgy anyway, and this was the hell of a test case to pick." Biddle recalled that "the stupidity of such an indictment might wreck the whole [exclusion] program" because "there was nothing against [Andriano] except that he had been active in the fascist movement like so many successful Italians."[32]

On August 9, 1943, a month after the Allied invasion of Sicily and a month before the armistice between the Allies and the new Pietro Badoglio Italian government, the Justice Department called for an end to Andriano's exclusion after concluding a formal review of his case. Hennessy, the U.S. attorney in San Francisco, had from the beginning objected to the inclusion of Andriano on the list of persons "recommended for apprehension by the Federal Bureau of Investigation and internment for the duration of the war." Andriano returned to San Francisco fifteen months after Biddle's 1942 Columbus Day declaration that Italians were officially no longer America's enemies and the government had canceled all restrictive measures. The *San Francisco Chronicle* and *Il Corriere del Popolo* did not greet the news of the rescinding of Andriano's Individual Exclusion Order as a triumph of justice and civil liberties, nor did they display enthusiasm that the attorney had returned to San Francisco. The *Chronicle* referred to Andriano as "long one of the West's outspoken advocates of Fascism." And Zito enumerated his previous accusations and concluded, "What was the pre-war ordinary activity of the attorney Andriano? It can be summarized in two words: Fascist propaganda." Andriano himself reviewed his San Francisco public career in the light of his ordeal in a letter to his Catholic Action colleague Hagerty one month before he returned to the city.

> I am afraid, however (would that I were mistaken) that some people consider me, or rather not me, but what they associate with me, to wit. Catholic Action, more dangerous than ever. It's one thing to pay lip homage to the Pope, to talk learnedly and lecture on the Encyclicals . . . but it's quite another thing when some "fanatical" individuals fancying they have a mission, begin to take the words of the Pope seriously [and] more intolerable still, actually go about to *organize* [emphasis in original] the laity like the clergy and to carry out the Pope's program for the moral, social, and economic reconstruction of the world. Perhaps I am still potentially dangerous in some quarters.[33]

The FBI continued its investigation of Andriano after he returned to San Francisco. Hoover wanted to indict Andriano on criminal charges, now on the grounds that during his term as president of the Italian Chamber of Commerce he had failed to meet some of the formal requirements of the Registration Act for foreign-sourced organizations. Finally, on April 13, 1944, Assistant Attorney General Tom Clark ordered Hoover to discontinue all investigatory proceedings against Sylvester Andriano.[34]

Epilogue

Perhaps I am still potentially dangerous in some quarters.

—Sylvester Andriano to James Hagerty, November 12, 1943

Catholic Action is a world wide movement, and departments of the National Conference are all represented in San Francisco. We Communists have been negligent in taking this factor into consideration.

—San Francisco Communist Party County Committee, 1948

Writing from Denver a month before his return to San Francisco, Sylvester Andriano shared with Professor Hagerty his suspicion that "perhaps I am still potentially dangerous in some quarters." But he was not referring to the leaders of the San Francisco Catholic Church or the city's Italian Catholic community, and his Catholic Action work did not end when the cold war began but continued in relation to local, national, and international affairs. In 1944 he directed a Sts. Peter and Paul Church program for war relief called Caritate Dei (For the Love of God), which shipped packages of food and clothing to the residents of Italian cities. Andriano's work was rewarded with yet another commendation from Italy, this time from Pope Pius XII. In October 1946 he accepted the presidency of the Italian Catholic Federation, succeeding Father Bandini and Luigi Providenza, who had headed the organization during the war years. In his presidential address he noted that "many of the Italian and Italian-American organizations that flourished here before the war are now either dormant or dead, and social and cultural life among our people has suffered accordingly." He announced an "all-embracing program, the Program of the Three C's: Charity; Citizenship; Catholicism."[1]

The Communist Party *did* consider Sylvester Andriano and Catholic Action still potentially dangerous. In 1944 Oleta O'Connor Yates managed to get an appointment to Mayor Roger D. Lapham's Council for Civic Unity; at the first meeting of the council the chairman stressed that "members should feel free to speak their minds." However, Yates found herself the only radical in a sixteen-member committee dominated by moderates and conservatives. They included Father Thomas F. Burke, Archbishop Mitty's hand-picked delegate for civil rights work, and Catholic Action activist and city controller Harold Boyd. The chairman was attorney Maurice Harrison, a friend of Andriano's since the mid-1920s and fellow Catholic Action stalwart in the St. Thomas More Society. Yates continued her attempts to win public office, running unsuccessfully for a seat on the Board of Supervisors in 1947. (She was later convicted of violating the Smith Act, but the Supreme Court reversed the verdict on First Amendment grounds in 1957 in *Yates v. United States*.)[2]

In the spring of 1948, frustrated by its inability to limit Catholic political power in local elections and in the labor movement, the San Francisco CP's county committee commissioned a research report on "Catholicism in San Francisco." The report went out to all San Francisco party members, along with a recommendation for "our people" to "read LENIN ON RELIGION." "We Communists have been negligent in taking this factor into consideration, and while there has been a token recognition of the importance of Catholicism in our community, we have not given it the attention it merits." Party activists discussed the eight-page single-spaced report at neighborhood branch meetings and then at a day-long conference in September. As they prepared for the 1948 elections, San Francisco Communists did so with the understanding that "Catholicism has a broad mass appeal which has been carefully fostered over the centuries," that "Catholic Action is a world wide movement," and that "the Church through Catholic Action is out to reclaim its lost worlds."[3]

In August 1955, now sixty-six years old, Andriano was inducted into the Knights of Malta, a prestigious Catholic charitable organization with medieval military roots, and a month later he presided at the first postwar meeting of the Italian Chamber of Commerce. He began to cut back in his law practice and his community work, but he agreed to serve as the northern California chairman of the American Conference on Italian Migration, assisting with the national organization's fundraising efforts. In 1956, when Archbishop John J. Mitty celebrated his fiftieth anniversary as a priest and his thirtieth anniversary as a bishop at a Palace Hotel banquet, Andriano sat at his right hand and gave the keynote address. Several months later Oleta O'Connor Yates resigned from the Communist Party. According to her husband, in an interview recounting her career after she died in 1964, she realized when Nikita Khrushchev "detailed the excesses of the Stalin regime, its slave labor camps, and its brutality," that "the Hearst papers, the FBI and others had been saying that for years. But hard core Communists like Oleta wouldn't believe them." "After we made our decisions [to leave the party], we felt truly liberated."[4]

Carmelo Zito remained an ardent socialist, maintaining his connections with his New York socialist colleague Arturo Giovannitti until he died in 1959; Zito wrote the introduction to a 1957 collection of Giovannitti's poetry, *Quando canta il gallo* (When the Cock Crows). Zito was increasingly baffled by the relatively apolitical young cultural radicals who filled the coffeehouses in North Beach. With the readership of *Il Corriere del Popolo* in steady decline, he closed down the paper in 1967. Andriano and Monsignor Luigi Civardi continued their association, begun in 1938 when they met during Andriano's visit to Rome to review the program for the Catholic Men of San Francisco. In 1961, the same year St. Mary's College named him Alumnus of the Year, Andriano published his translation of Civardi's *Christianity and Social Justice,* a work carrying the imprimatur of the bishop of Monterey-Fresno and intended to be "a text for Christian social education and training." During a visit to Italy two years later Sylvester Andriano's heart stopped after a strenuous day working in the orchard of his boyhood home in

Castelnuovo Don Bosco, and on October 9, 1963, he was buried back in San Francisco after a Rosary in North Beach and a Requiem High Mass at Sts. Peter and Paul Church.[5]

The story of Sylvester Andriano's Catholic Action work, the divided character of his city, and the impact of World War II on his life and work suggests several conclusions that shed light on San Francisco, California, and the nation during the period. First, competition between Catholics and Communists for status and power in the second-largest city of California (and the western United States) began in the 1930s and continued into the postwar period. Before, during, and after the war Catholic Action advocates were determined to make room for what might be called applied religion in the making of public policy. Communist Party activists, along with Masonic leaders and anticlerical anti-Fascist *fuorusciti,* were just as determined to stop them. This continuity underscores the importance of both Roger Lotchin's disproof of the generalization that World War II produced a wholesale transformation of the major California cities and Mark Massa's and Philip Jenkins's affirmation of the persistence of anti-Catholicism in American history.[6]

Andriano's Catholic Action derived from his religious faith, and his zealous commitment to that faith coexisted with a deeply felt devotion to Italian language, culture, and history. Andriano would not have been hauled before investigating committees had he not been Italian, but it was two *Italian* anti-Catholic activists who seized the opportunity afforded by the HUAC and Tenney Committee hearings to neutralize a Catholic opponent whose political power was on the ascendant. This finding suggests that the conclusions of Rose Scherini, Gloria Lothrop Ricci, and others, which demonstrate how ethnicity made Italian residents of California vulnerable to un-American activities investigations, need to be revised to take into account the role played by Catholic religious activism and anti-Catholic prejudice among Italians.[7]

Andriano was a prominent Catholic who happened to be Italian. His San Francisco residence placed him in a city where Catholic moral principles enjoyed legitimacy and where Catholic business, labor, and political leaders, irrespective of ethnicity, possessed considerable power, privilege, and prestige. Their ethnicity allowed Angelo Rossi and Sylvester Andriano to avoid being part of a mass roundup and to escape long-lasting damage to their financial assets, reputations, and standing in the community. Stephen Fox, Arnold Kramer, and Tetsuden Kashima have recently documented the degree to which Italian ancestry and German ancestry protected residents of those backgrounds from the more general exclusion, relocation, and imprisonment that proved the fate of Japanese residents. But they have also demonstrated the limits to such ethnicity-related protection. And they have uncovered detailed evidence of the punitive and inhumane approach to his duties adopted by General DeWitt. The Andriano case confirms the importance of these findings and provides additional evidence of DeWitt's disregard of the individual rights of those suspected of and charged with being "potentially dangerous." Andriano's status (along with that of the city's mayor) at the top of the predominantly Irish Catholic social and religious establishment provided him with the backing of the archbishop and two dozen supporters who tried to intervene with the army on his behalf. DeWitt dismissed the entreaties out of hand, ordered Andriano's exclusion to proceed, and fought the later appeal by the U.S. attorney.[8]

The fact that it was the leaders of competing religious and political institutions, and not an uprising of the general public, that originated, developed, and resolved the Andriano case demonstrates the importance of interest group politics in California's un-American activities controversies during World War II. The Andriano case also shows the crucial importance of the strategic choices made by political officials in their relations with the leaders of such interest groups. This can be seen in the contrast between the modus operandi of the Tenney Committee and that of the Tolan Committee (House of Representatives Select Committee Investigating National Defense Migration) in 1942. Assemblyman Jack B. Tenney selected witnesses known to be hostile to Andriano, encouraged them to offer unsubstantiated charges filled with half-truths and falsehoods, and then claimed to have made a vital contribution to Pacific Coast defense by removing Andriano from California. By contrast, Congressman John H. Tolan, as Fox has demonstrated, carefully selected witnesses to facilitate his goal of limiting public anxiety and "deftly extracted their testimony in a way that evoked sympathy for the Italians."[9]

Finally, this book disproves the notion that a generalized hysteria gripped the people of the Pacific Coast in the first six months of the war, to the point that they clamored for government suppression of civil liberties. Andriano's exclusion did not occur because of the eruption in California of mass cultural phenomena such as Richard Hofstader's "paranoid style" or Michael Rogin's "countersubversive tradition" and "American demonology." Instead, the Andriano case demonstrates the importance of studying loyalty investigations during wartime with a methodology that takes account of culture and discourse, to be sure, but is also mindful of the causal influence of biography, religion, society, and politics. This approach, which can be termed critical realism, has also been used to good effect in studies of security investigations such as those by M. J. Heale and by John Sbardellati and Tony Shaw.[10] The un-American activities investigations in wartime California that jeopardized the civil liberties of Sylvester Andriano can best be understood as part of a political process created by the decisions of particular individuals in specific institutions in the context of local conditions and national and international developments.

In the late 1930s and the first years of World War II a number of influential left-wing San Franciscans, including local Communist Party leaders and anti-Catholic Italians, some of whom were left-wing political exiles from Fascist Italy, enlisted the help of un-American activities committees and the FBI to discredit Sylvester Andriano and his Catholic faith-based political program and to limit its influence in the Bay Area. In the late 1940s and 1950s local leftists themselves became the victims of FBI investigations, loyalty hearings, condemnatory insinuations, and "red baiting" charges based on guilt by association. It is no small irony that by mobilizing the witch hunt against Andriano (and Rossi), the left itself contributed to the climate of fear that would poison the political atmosphere of San Francisco in the post–World War II decade.

But Andriano did not leave public life, Archbishop Mitty and his Catholic Action cadre continued their campaign, and by the end of the 1950s, Communism was discredited and San Francisco Catholicism seemed to be enjoying a renaissance of social prestige and political power. In the middle and late 1960s veterans of the Catholic Action crusade of the 1930s might have imagined that the election of their favorite sons, John F. Shelley (1963) and Joseph L. Alioto (1967, 1971), to the mayor's office and John F. Henning as head of the state AFL-CIO (1970) signified the beginning of a golden age of Catholic cultural power.

But it was not to be. Neither the "Old Left" veterans whom Shelley and Alioto appointed to positions in city government nor the younger Catholic Action activists who had participated in the events of the World War II years anticipated the force of the social and cultural changes that occurred during the 1960s. French Surrealism and Zen Buddhism came to North Beach; the impact was evident when Carmelo Zito found himself mystified by the apolitical cultural radicals at Caffe Trieste and the Coexistence Bagel Shop. Rome came to San Francisco again, this time in the form of the Second Vatican Council changes in doctrine, liturgy, and cultural style; the consequences were foreshadowed when in 1960 Andriano wrote in protest to the *Monitor*: "The language is undignified, coarse and irreverent, if not downright scandalous." Catholic residents, their numbers lessened by the massive migration to nearby suburbs, divided into warring factions as never before. And the young "New Left" and "counterculture" advocates who poured into San Francisco during the sixties and seventies had little patience for the moral absolutism and cultural conservatism that they associated, rightly or wrongly, with the Catholic Church.[11]

Today the bust of Mayor Angelo Rossi greets visitors who enter city hall at Van Ness Avenue, and the name of Harry Bridges graces a public plaza at the foot of Market Street. Few San Franciscans recall the name Sylvester Andriano, but his story is important because it serves as a cautionary tale about how easily government officials can make mistakes that lead to the abuse of citizenship rights during wartime. Andriano did not sympathize with Fascism, and he was not an agent of the Mussolini government. He was a devout San Francisco Italian American Catholic attorney and local government official, whose participation in his archbishop's Catholic Action initiative provoked an anti-Catholic campaign against him. Andriano's ordeal illustrates some of the ways that European political and cultural rivalries became part of the urban politics of the American West during the period from World War I to the cold war. The Andriano story also demonstrates the lengths to which J. Edgar Hoover was prepared to go to advance his bureau's reputation as the number-one defender of domestic security during World War II. And it demonstrates Hoover's failure, indeed stubborn refusal, to submit the charges against Andriano to critical scrutiny and corroboration. For that reason, the Andriano case is a reminder of the continuing need for citizen activism in monitoring homeland security policy to protect against such abuses of power.

Notes

CHAPTER 1. SYLVESTER ANDRIANO, A CATHOLIC ATTORNEY IN SAN FRANCISCO

Epigraphs: Sylvester N. Andriano, "Italian Immigrants in America," *Collegian* VII (May 1909), 444–445, and *San Francisco: A Guide to the Bay and Its Cities,* comp. by Workers of the Writers Program of the Works Projects Administration in Northern California (New York: Hastings House, 1940), 238.

1. Biographical information about Sylvester Andriano when not otherwise indicated derives from his fifteen-page, single-spaced, typewritten autobiography contained in a letter to James L. Hagerty (hereafter Andriano autobiography) dated March 10, 1943, and biographical data in letters from Andriano to James Hagerty, all in box 237, James L. Hagerty Papers, Archives of the College of St. Mary's of California, Moraga (hereafter Hagerty Papers), and an interview with David Cicoletti, Sylvester Andriano's grand-nephew, August 21, 2006.

2. Angelo Andriano file, Archives of the Archdiocese of San Francisco, Menlo Park (hereafter AASF). I have been unable to find information about John Andriano and Teresa Novaro, who are listed as siblings of Sylvester in an obituary of Giuseppe in the *Monitor,* the official newspaper of the San Francisco Archdiocese, dated October 24, 1931; U.S. Bureau of the Census, 1910, *San Francisco Assembly District 41, San Francisco, California,* roll T624_101, page 11A, enumeration district 267, image 638.

3. Deanna Paoli Gumina, *The Italians of San Francisco, 1850–1930,* 3rd ed. (New York: Center for Migration Studies, 1999), 29, 33; U.S. Bureau of the

Census, 1930, *San Francisco, San Francisco, California,* roll T626_207, page 12B, enumeration district 344, image 758.0; U.S. Bureau of the Census, 1930, *San Francisco, San Francisco, California,* roll T626_200, page 23A, enumeration district 157, image 540.0; U.S. Bureau of the Census, 1930, *Fremont, Santa Clara, California,* roll T626_219, page 14A, enumeration district 11, image 793.0; Sylvester Andriano to Archbishop Edward Hanna, June 13, 1929, Angelo Andriano file, Chancery Archives; Cicoletti interview.

4. Andriano autobiography; Andriano, *Collegian* VII (May 1909), 440.

5. Sylvester N. Andriano, "An Italian Hill Town," *Collegian* VI (November 1908), 72–73.

6. Sylvester N. Andriano, "The Apostle of the Little Ones," *Collegian* VIII (June 1910), 453–454.

7. Sylvester N. Andriano, "That Old Statue," *Collegian* IX (January 1911), 136–137.

8. Sylvester N. Andriano, "The Italian Dialects," *Collegian* VIII (June 1910), 459–460.

9. Andriano, *Collegian* VII (May 1909), 444–445.

10. Andriano autobiography; *Monitor,* December 11, 1915.

11. *Monitor,* February 10, 1917; U.S. Bureau of the Census, 1920, *San Jose, Santa Clara, California,* roll T625_148, page 10A, enumeration district 181, image 267; U.S. Bureau of the Census, 1920, *San Francisco Assembly District 31, San Francisco, California,* roll T625_136, page 16B, enumeration district 145, image 537; Gumina, *Italians of San Francisco,* 33.

12. California Senate, Fifty-fifth Session, *Report of the Joint Fact-Finding Committee on Un-American Activities in California* (Sacramento: California State Printing Office, 1943), 282–321, at 291 (hereafter *Un-American Activities in California*); Felice Bonadio, *A. P. Giannini: Banker of America* (Berkeley and Los Angeles: University of California Press, 1994), 46–47.

13. William Issel and Robert W. Cherny, *San Francisco, 1865–1932: Politics, Power and Urban Development* (Berkeley and Los Angeles: University of California Press, 1986), 56–57; Rose Scherini, "The Italian American Community of San Francisco: A Descriptive Study" (Ph.D. dissertation, University of California, Berkeley, 1976), 3; Archdiocesan Census file, AASF.

CHAPTER 2. ANTI-CATHOLICISM IN LITTLE ITALY

Epigraphs: Elizabeth Gray Potter, *The San Francisco Skyline* (New York: Dodd, Mead, 1939), 70, and Leonard Austin, *Around the World in San Francisco: Where San Franciscans from All Nations Meet, Eat, Dance, and Get to Know One Another* (San Francisco: Fearon, 1959), 43.

1. Andriano autobiography; Alessandro Baccari Jr., Vincenza Scarpaci, and Rev. Gabriel Zavattaro, S.D.B., eds., *Saints Peter and Paul Church: The Chronicles of the Italian Cathedral of the West, 1884–1984* (San Francisco: Alessandro Baccari, 1985), 44, 63, 96.

2. For a detailed account of the bombings, see Baccari et al., *Saints Peter and Paul Church,* 96–101.

3. For labor unions and their left-wing critics in San Francisco, see Issel and Cherny, *San Francisco, 1865–1932,* 80–100.

4. Rudolph Vecoli, "Galleani, Luigi," in *Encyclopedia of the American Left,* 2nd ed., ed. Mari Jo Buhle, Paul Buhle, and Dan Georgakas (New York: Oxford University Press, 1998), 253–254.

5. Edward R. Kantowicz, *Corporation Sole: Cardinal Mundelein and Chicago Catholicism* (Notre Dame, Ind.: University of Notre Dame Press, 1982), 11–12.

6. Felix Frankfurter, "The Case of Sacco and Vanzetti," *Atlantic Monthly* 139 (March 1927), 409–432.

7. See Issel and Cherny, *San Francisco, 1865–1932,* 73–78, for details on the political culture of the "South of the Slot" district.

8. Luigi Rovaldi, "Nostre Corrispondenze," *La Questione Sociale,* November 3, 1906, 3, quoted in Paola A. Sensi-Isolani, "Italian Radicals and Union Activists in San Francisco, 1900–1920," in *The Lost World of Italian American Radicalism: Politics, Labor, and Culture,* ed. Philip V. Cannistraro and Gerald Meyer (Westport, Conn.: Praeger, 2003), 189–203, at 193.

9. "San Francisco, Cal." *Cronaca Sovversiva,* September 23, 1911, 1, quoted in Sensi-Isolani, "Italian Radicals," 195.

10. Sensi-Isolani, "Italian Radicals," 197; *L'Italia,* September 23, 1911.

11. Peter R. D'Agostino, *Rome in America: Transnational Catholic Ideology from the Risorgimento to Fascism* (Chapel Hill: University of North Carolina Press, 2004), 99 (Hanna quote), 84 (Nathan quote); Andrew M. Canepa, "Profilo della Massoneria di lingua italiana in California (1871–1966)," *Studi Emigrazione* 27 (1990), 87–107.

12. Hanna won the annual award for the promotion of better understanding between Christians and Jews sponsored by the *American Hebrew* magazine in 1931; correspondence relating to Hanna's recruiting of Father Albert Bandini in the Bandini file, Chancery Archives.

13. Andriano autobiography; Baccari et al., *Saints Peter and Paul Church,* 69; Marino De Medici, "The Italian Language Press in the San Francisco Bay Area from 1930 to 1943" (Master's thesis, University of California, Berkeley, 1963), 17–20.

14. Italian Catholic Federation, *The Italian Catholic Federation: The First 50 Years* (San Francisco: Italian Catholic Federation, 1974), 4–11; Richard A. Webster, *The Cross and the Fasces: Christian Democracy and Fascism in Italy* (Stanford, Calif.: Stanford University Press, 1960), 78–106; Roy Palmer Domenico, *Remaking Italy in the Twentieth Century* (Lanham, Md.: Roman and Littlefield, 2002), 37–46; John N. Molony, *The Emergence of Political Catholicism in Italy: Partito Popolare, 1919–1926* (London: Croom Helm, 1977).

15. Italian Catholic Federation, *Italian Catholic Federation,* 5, 7.

16. Iris Origo, *A Need to Testify: Portraits of Lauro de Bosis, Ruth Draper, Gaetano Salvemini, Ignazio Silone, and an Essay on Biography* (London: John Murray, 1984), 40.

17. John A. Ryan, "The Doctrine of Fascism," *Commonweal* (November 17, 1926), 42–44; Ryan, "Fascism in Practice," *Commonweal* (November 24, 1926), 73–76; Albert Bandini, "The Doctrine of Fascism," *Commonweal* (December 15, 1926), 158; Bandini, "The Facts of Fascism," *Commonweal* (January 19, 1927), 300; D'Agostino, *Rome in America,* 187–189; Wilson D. Miscamble, "The Limits of American Catholic Antifascism: The Case of John A. Ryan," *Church History* 59 (1990), 523–538.

CHAPTER 3. CATHOLIC ACTION, FROM ROME TO SAN FRANCISCO

Epigraphs: Pope Leo XIII, "Graves de Communi Re" (On Christian Socialism), 1901; Pope Pius X, "Il Fermo Proposito" (On Catholic Action in Italy), 1905; Pope Pius XI, "Non Abbiamo Bisogno" (On Catholic Action in Italy), 1931; "Sermon on Catholic Action," by Coadjutor Archbishop John J. Mitty to the National Council of Catholic Women, May 7, 1932, Mitty Sermon Collection, Chancery Archives. Full English texts for "Graves de Communi Re" and "Il Fermo Proposito" may be found at the Web sites referenced in Note 6; for "Non Abbiamo Bisogno," see Note 12.

1. Webster, *Cross and the Fasces,* 109–112; Domenico, *Remaking Italy,* 57–59.

2. Sylvester Andriano to Archbishop Hanna, June 13, 1929, Angelo Andriano file, Chancery Archives. In December 1933 Father Angelo wrote to the archbishop requesting permission to return to San Francisco. The archbishop agreed, but the priest's superiors in Turin refused to release him from his new post. Angelo Andriano to Archbishop Hanna, December 8, 1933, and Andriano to Hanna, March 20, 1934, Angelo Andriano file, Chancery Archives.

3. "Attorney Launches Anti-dry Attack," *San Francisco Chronicle,* November 19, 1925.

4. Andriano autobiography; *San Francisco Chronicle,* November 19, 1925; *San Francisco Examiner,* March 15 and May 8, 1928.

5. See Tracy H. Koon, *Believe, Obey, Fight: Political Socialization of Youth in Fascist Italy, 1922–1943* (Chapel Hill: University of North Carolina Press, 1985), 116–142.

6. For the English texts of "Graves de Communi Re" (On Christian Socialism) and "Il Fermo Proposito" (On Catholic Action in Italy), see the Web sites http://www.vatican.va/holy_father/leo_xiii/encyclicals/documents/hf_l-xiii_enc_18011901_graves-de-communi-re_en.html and http://www.vatican.va/holy_father/pius_x/encyclicals/documents/hf_p-x_enc_11061905_il-fermo-proposito_en.html. The Vatican's official English titles of the papal encyclicals are not necessarily verbatim translations of the original Latin or Italian titles.

7. "Ubi Arcano Dei Consilio" (On the Peace of Christ in the Kingdom of Christ) is at the Web site http://www.vatican.va/holy_father/pius_xi/encyclicals/documents/hf_p-xi_enc_23121922_ubi-arcano-dei-consilio_en.html.

8. *San Francisco Examiner,* February 2, 1928; *San Francisco Chronicle,* October 17, 1929. See Richard Gribble, CSC, *An Archbishop for the People: The Life of Edward J. Hanna* (New York: Paulist Press, 2006), chaps. 4, 5, and 6, for a detailed account of Hanna's commitment to Catholic Action activities in San Francisco. Andriano's role as Archbishop Hanna's personal adviser in matters pertaining to the Italian community is evident in the way the attorney handled the Italian consul's angry response to an editorial in the archdiocesan newspaper that contained criticism of the Mussolini regime. Ironically, the *Monitor* editorial criticized an Italian visiting professor for *anticlerical* remarks in a public speech. Nevertheless, the archbishop had the editor retract his comments on the strength of Andriano's concern that the editorial could have an "adverse effect upon the cordial relations existing between your Grace and the Italian people and the official representative of the Italian Government or hindering the progress of our work among our people." Andriano to Hanna, December 7, 1928, *Monitor* file, Chancery Archives.

9. Koon, *Believe, Obey, Fight,* 129–130.

10. Ibid., 130–134.

11. Andriano autobiography; Koon, *Believe, Obey, Fight,* 135–136.

12. "Non Abbiamo Bisogno" (On Catholic Action in Italy) is at the Web site http://www.vatican.va/holy_father/pius_xi/encyclicals/documents/hf_p-xi_enc_29061931_non-abbiamo-bisogno_en.html.

13. Koon, *Believe, Obey, Fight,* 136–137.

14. Webster, *Cross and the Fasces,* 112. For more on these events, see Peter Kent, *The Pope and the Duce: The International Impact of the Lateran Agreements* (New York: St. Martin's Press, 1981), and John Pollard, *The Vatican and Italian Fascism, 1929–1932: A Study in Conflict* (New York: Cambridge University Press, 1981).

15. Andriano autobiography.

16. Jeffrey M. Burns, "Mitty, John Joseph," in *The Encyclopedia of American Catholic History,* ed. Michael Glazier and Thomas J. Shelley (Collegeville, Minn.: Liturgical Press, 1997), 967–968; "Life Summary of Archbishop Mitty," *Monitor,* August 31, 1935.

17. "Quadragesimo Anno" (On Reconstructing the Social Order) is at the Web site http://www.vatican.va/holy_father/pius_xi/encyclicals/documents/hf_p-i_enc_19310515_quadragesimo-anno_en.html.

18. Mitty, "Sermon on Catholic Action."

CHAPTER 4. CATHOLIC ACTION THEORY AND PRACTICE IN SAN FRANCISCO

Epigraphs: Academy of San Francisco Organizing Committee, "Catholic League for Social Justice in the Archdiocese of San Francisco: Plan to Inaugurate Crusade," April 18, 1933, in folder A46.9, Catholic League for Social Justice file, Chancery Archives; *Leader,* July 21, 1934.

1. The role of the National Catholic Welfare Conference (NCWC) in encouraging and monitoring diocesan implementation of papal Catholic Action theory is described in a personal handwritten letter from Rev. John J. Burke, general secretary of the NCWC, to Archbishop Mitty, June 1, 1932, in NCWC 1932–1935 Correspondence file, folder 1 of 2, Chancery Archives; see also excerpt from the minutes of the NCCW, November 16, 1933, quoted in "Department of Catholic Action Study, National Catholic Welfare Conference," in NCWC Catholic Action Study file, folder 3 of 3, Chancery Archives.

2. "Catholic League for Social Justice in the Archdiocese of San Francisco," pamphlet in Chancery Archives; "Report of Progress in the Crusade for Social Justice, Bulletin #6, June 16, 1933," mimeographed newsletter in folder PR118, Crusade for Social Justice file, Chancery Archives.

3. Amleto Giovanni Cicognani to Edward J. Hanna, date illegible, in NCWC Correspondence file, 1933, folder 1 of 2, Chancery Archives.

4. "Program for the Year," August 11, 1933, in folder A46.9, Catholic League for Social Justice file, Chancery Archives; Roy A. Bronson to John J. Mitty, September 28, 1933, in folder A46.9, Catholic League for Social Justice file, Chancery Archives.

5. "A Revolution by Professors," *Monitor,* January 27, 1934.

6. Details concerning events of the 1934 strike unless otherwise indicated are from David F. Selvin, *A Terrible Anger: The 1934 Waterfront and General Strikes in San Francisco* (Detroit: Wayne State University Press, 1996).

7. Robert W. Cherny, "Prelude to the Popular Front: The Communist Party in California, 1931–35," *American Communist History* 1 (June 2002), 11, 19–20.

8. Documentary evidence of Harry Bridges's membership in the CP has been discovered in the archives of the former Soviet Union by historian Robert W. Cherny, who describes the complicated relationship between Bridges and the Communist Party in "Constructing a Radical Identity: History, Memory, and the Seafaring Stories of Harry Bridges," *Pacific Historical Review* 70 (2001), 571–599, and Cherny, "Harry Bridges and the Communist Party: New Evidence, Old Questions; Old Evidence, New Questions," paper delivered at the annual meeting of the Organization of American Historians, April 4, 1998. See also Harvey Klehr and John E. Haynes, "Communists and the CIO: From the Soviet Archives," *Labor History* 35 (1994), 444–446; Harvey Klehr, John Earl Haynes, and Fridrikh Igorevich Firsov, *The Secret World of American Communism* (New Haven, Conn.: Yale University Press, 1995), 104.

9. "The Maritime Strikes," *Monitor,* June 9, 1934.

10. Ibid.

11. Ibid.

12. *San Francisco Chronicle,* June 21, 27, 1934; Andriano autobiography.

13. *Leader,* July 28, 1934; Andriano autobiography.

14. Archbishop Edward J. Hanna's radio broadcast, July 13, 1934, http://www.sfmuseum.org/hist4/maritime9.html.

15. Joint Maritime Strike Committee statement, reprinted in Mike Quin [pseudonym of Paul William Ryan], *The Big Strike* (Olema, Calif.: Olema Publishing Co., 1949), 180.

16. Telegram from T. G. Plant to Frances Perkins, July 23, 1934, Papers of Secretary of Labor Frances Perkins, National Archives, Record Group 174, box 35, Conciliation—Strikes—Longshoremen—1934 file.

17. Andriano autobiography; memorandum of a telephone conversation of July 15, 1934, between Roger Lapham and Frances Perkins, dated July 18, 1934, Papers of Secretary of Labor Frances Perkins, National Archives, Record Group 174, box 42, Conciliation—Strikes—Longshoremen—1934 file; *Leader,* July 28, 1934.

18. *Leader,* July 21, 1934.

19. *Leader,* July 28, 1934; *Monitor,* July 28, 1934.

20. *San Francisco News,* July 23, 1934; Cherny, "Prelude to the Popular Front," 41.

CHAPTER 5. SYLVESTER ANDRIANO AND CATHOLIC ACTION IN SAN FRANCISCO

Epigraphs: Sylvester Andriano to Archbishop John J. Mitty, March 2, 1936, Italy/Italian folder, Correspondence Files, Chancery Archives; Archbishop John J. Mitty, May 29, 1937; Archbishop John J. Mitty, "Address to the Archdiocesan Council of the National Conference of Catholic Women," May 29, 1937, Mitty Sermons and Addresses, Chancery Archives.

1. *Monitor,* May 11, 1935; Andriano to Mitty, March 2, 1936.

2. *Monitor,* April 6, 1935; Msgr. Luigi Civardi, *A Manual of Catholic Action* (New York: Sheed and Ward, 1943), reprint of 1935 English edition.

3. Andriano to Mitty, March 2, 1936.

4. *Monitor,* April 6, 1935.

5. Ibid.; Mitty to Andriano, March 4, 1936, 1936–1937 "A" folder, Correspondence Files, Chancery Archives.

6. "Plan for Catholic Action," Catholic Action 1936–1940 folder, Correspondence Files, Chancery Archives.

7. Ibid. Costantini quotation also in ibid. See also the biography of Costantini at http://www.fiu.edu/~mirandas/bios-c.htm.

8. "Plan for Catholic Action."

9. Archbishop Mitty to Rev. Thomas N. O'Kane, letter marked "Confidential," Catholic Action 1936–1940 folder, Correspondence Files, Chancery Archives.

10. Biography file, Hagerty Papers.

11. Joseph L. Alioto, "The Catholic Internationale," *Moraga Quarterly* 7 (Winter 1936), 68–72.

12. Ibid., 72.

13. Andriano to Mitty, December 22, 1936, Catholic Action 1936–1940 folder; "Catholic Action Group," January 6, 1938, uncorrected draft marked "News item: *The Monitor,*" all in Correspondence Files, Chancery Archives.

14. Mitty to various addressees, December 22, 1937, Catholic Action 1936–1940 folder, Correspondence Files, Chancery Archives; "Catholic Action Group," January 6, 1938, uncorrected draft marked "News item: *The Monitor,*" and attached typewritten notes of January 6, 1938, meeting, Catholic Action 1936–1940 folder, Correspondence Files, Chancery Archives.

15. Archbishop John J. Mitty, "Address on Catholic Action," October 29, 1938, Mitty Sermons and Addresses, Chancery Archives; Andriano to Mitty, May 19, 1938, Catholic Action 1936–1940 folder, Correspondence Files, Chancery Archives; *San Francisco Call Bulletin,* October 27, 1938; *San Francisco News,* October 28, 1938.

16. Hagerty to Mitty, March 28, 1938, Catholic Men folder 1 of 2, 1938–1941, Correspondence Files, Chancery Archives; Andriano autobiography.

17. Various reports and correspondence in Catholic Men folders 1 of 2 and 2 of 2, 1938–1941, Correspondence Files, Chancery Archives.

18. Andriano to Mitty, August 18, 1941, Catholic Action 1938–1941, folder 2 of 2; "Summary of State of Organization Following Spring Series of District Meetings, 1941," Catholic Action 1938–1941, folder 1 of 2, all in Correspondence Files, Chancery Archives; John J. O'Connor, "Emphasis on Action," *St. Anthony Messenger* (February 1942), 3–5, 55–56.

CHAPTER 6. THE CATHOLIC ACTION SOCIAL APOSTOLATE

Epigraph: Stanislaus Riley, "Place of the Laity in Catholic Action," *Monitor,* March 22, 1935.

1. Cardinal Pizzardo, "Catholic Action Aims Are Defined in Letter of Cardinal Pizzardo," National Catholic Welfare Conference News Service, July 4, 1938, copy in Catholic Action, 1936–1940 folder, Chancery Archives.

2. John J. Mitty to Hugh Gallagher, October 6, 1936, in Labor File, 1934–1939, Chancery Archives.

3. William Issel, "Business Power and Political Culture," *Journal of Urban History* 16 (November 1989), 52–77, at 72–73, and William Issel, "New Deal and World War II Origins of San Francisco's Postwar Political Culture: The Case of Growth Politics and Policy," in *The Way We Really Were: The Golden State in the Second Great War,* ed. Roger W. Lotchin (Urbana: University of Illinois Press, 2000), 68–92; *Monitor,* Bay Area Development Edition, May 1, 1937; for representative articles and editorials, see *Monitor,* June 8, 1935; April 17, 1937; and March 23, 1940.

4. *Monitor,* September 7, 1935; September 11, 1943; and May 8, 1937. W. R. Otto to Mitty, March 1, 1938, and Edward D. Vandeleur to Mitty, January 3, 1941, both in Labor File, 1939–1943, Chancery Archives. Labor arbitrator Sam

Kagel, a close friend of Michael Casey, recalled the Teamster president as a regular attendant at Sunday Mass and remembered having to wait until after church services to drive Casey to a union meeting in San Jose. Author's interview with Sam Kagel, June 15, 1998.

5. Donohoe Personal Record, Chancery Archives; the dissertation is titled "Collective Bargaining under the NIRA" (Catholic University of America, Washington, D.C., 1935).

6. *San Francisco Chronicle,* February 7, 1948, 9; August 12, 1958, 12; and August 18, 1987, 22; Donohoe Personal Record, Chancery Archives.

7. Michael Kelly interview with Sister Patrice Donohoe, April 28, 1999, Belmont, California, quoted in Michael Kelly, "Reverend Hugh A. Donohoe" (seminar paper, San Francisco State University, 1999).

8. Correspondence relating to these duties is in box 4, Hugh A. Donohoe Papers, Chancery Archives.

9. Bishop Edwin O'Hara to Mitty, April 8, 1937, in Social Action School for Priests folder, Correspondence Files, Chancery Archives; *Monitor,* June 26, 1937.

10. Donohoe, "Collective Bargaining under the NIRA," 91.

11. Ibid., 93.

12. Ibid., 100.

13. Hugh A. Donohoe, "As the Editor Sees It," *Monitor,* December 19, 1942, 5.

14. *Monitor,* April 20, 1940.

15. Mitty, "Address to Regional Conference on Industrial Problems," June 8, 1936, in Archbishop Mitty's Sermons, Dedications and Talks (hereafter Mitty Sermons), January–June 1936 folder; Mitty, "Address to Archdiocese Council of the National Conference of Catholic Women," May 29, 1937, Mitty Sermons, January–June 1937 folder; Mitty, "Address on Catholic Action," October 29, 1938, Mitty Sermons, July–December 1938 folder, all in Chancery Archives.

16. *San Francisco Examiner,* May 16, 1936; *Monitor,* May 23, 1936; *Monitor,* May 17, 1941.

17. Edward J. Kennedy (assistant chancellor) to Hurford Sharon, June 11, 1937, Labor File, 1934–1939, Chancery Archives. For more about the imprint of Catholic social theory on the public policy debate about the cooperation of business, labor, and government in San Francisco, see Issel, "New Deal and World War II Origins." For Catholic discourse on this topic in a New England setting, see Gary Gerstle, "Catholic Corporatism, French Canadian Workers, and Industrial Unionism in Rhode Island, 1938–1956," in *Labor Divided: Race and Ethnicity in United States Labor Struggles, 1835–1960,* ed. Robert Asher and Charles Stephenson (Albany: State University of New York Press, 1990), 209–225.

18. *Monitor,* April 17, 1937, and June 26, 1937.

19. "Summary Report on the Social Action School for Priests," June 25, 1937, Social Action School file, 1937–1939, Chancery Archives; *San Francisco Chronicle,* June 18, 1937.

20. *Monitor,* June 13, 1936.

21. Mitty's address to the 1941 Regional Catholic Conference on Industrial Problems, quoted in the *Monitor,* October 4, 1941.

22. Jack Henning, "The Catholic College Graduate and Labor," *Moraga Quarterly* 9 (Spring 1939), 165–170; "ACTU Preamble, Constitution, Pledge" and "Proposed Changes . . . San Francisco Chapter 6," mimeographed, July 8, 1948, in the Labor Management School Records/ACTU, Archives of the University of San Francisco.

23. For more on the ACTU and other Catholic labor initiatives, see William Issel, "'A Stern Struggle': Catholic Activism and San Francisco Labor, 1932–1958," in *American Labor and the Cold War: Grassroots Politics and Postwar Political Culture,* ed. Robert W. Cherny, William Issel, and Kieran Taylor (New Brunswick, N.J.: Rutgers University Press, 2004), 154–176.

24. Rev. Hugh Donohoe, "Labor Day Sermon" delivered in St. Mary's Cathedral, *Monitor,* September 2, 1942. Rev. Vincent Breen, "Address to San Francisco Association of Catholic Trade Unionists," June 6, 1943, *Monitor,* June 12, 1943. Rev. Joseph Munier, "Labor Day Sermon" delivered in St. Mary's Cathedral, September 5, 1943, *Monitor,* September 11, 1943.

CHAPTER 7. THE CATHOLIC ACTION EDUCATIONAL AND MORAL APOSTOLATES

Epigraph: Sylvester Andriano, "The Program of Catholic Action in the Archdiocese of San Francisco," paper read at the Diocesan Theological Conference, September 13, 1938, *Moraga Quarterly* 9 (Autumn 1938), 3–6.

1. Andriano, "Program of Catholic Action."

2. Pizzardo, "Catholic Action Aims"; Sylvester Andriano to Brother S. Edward, December 30, 1938; *Student Catholic Action* 1 (November 1941), 2; *Catholic Action for You,* box 170; *Student's Handbook of Catholic Action,* 27, box 346.02, all in History of Catholic Action Collection, Christian Brothers Archives, Mont La Salle, Napa, California.

3. Josephine J. Molloy to Archbishop Mitty, July 10, 1936; Genevieve E. Manning to Archbishop Mitty, July 2, 1937, both in YMI/YLI 1936–1937 folder, Correspondence Files, Chancery Archives; "Y.L.I. Grand Institute," July 18, 1937, Mitty Sermons, Chancery Archives.

4. For more about Agnes G. Regan, see Dorothy A. Mohler, "Agnes Regan as Organizer of the National Council of Catholic Women and the National Catholic School of Social Service," in *Pioneering Women at the Catholic University of America,* ed. E. Catherine Dunn and Dorothy A. Mohler (Washington, D.C.: Catholic University of America Press, 1988), 21–35.

5. Eugene J. Shea to Archbishop Mitty, August 9, 1939; Margaret McGuire to Reverend and Dear Father, March 3, 1937, both in Youth Programs 1937–1941, Correspondence Files, Chancery Archives; the Regan quote is from

Agnes G. Regan to Archbishop Mitty, January 6, 1938, NCCW/NCCM 1938–1939, folder 2 of 2, Correspondence Files, Chancery Archives.

6. Margaret McGuire to Rt. Revered Thomas A. Connolly, October 4, 1936; Memorandum, "Catholic Action," both in NCCW/NCCM 1938–1939, folder 2 of 2, Correspondence Files, Chancery Archives; "NCCW Archdiocesan Council Hold Annual Meet in San Francisco," May 29, 1937, Mitty Sermons.

7. Memorandum from Monsignor Connolly to Archbishop Mitty, March 9, 1938; Maude Fay Symington to Archbishop Mitty, January 14, 1939, both in NCCW/NCCM 1938–1939, folder 2 of 2, Correspondence Files, Chancery Archives; "N.C.C.W. Fifteenth Conference Ends with Luncheon at City Club—Archbishop Mitty," *Monitor,* May 27, 1939.

8. Pizzardo, "Catholic Action Aims"; "Address of His Holiness, Pope Pius XII, to the Congress of the International Union of Catholic Women's Leagues, Rome, April, 1939"; Agnes Regan to Most Rev. Thomas A. Connolly, D.D., November 4, 1939; "Memorandum from Representatives of N.C.W.C. to Congress, I.U.C.W.L. Rome—1939," all in NCCW/NCCM 1938–1939, folder 1 of 2, Correspondence Files, Chancery Archives.

9. Pizzardo, "Catholic Action Aims"; "Proposed Project for San Francisco Archdiocesan Council: Clean Reading Campaign," and "Motions Relative to Magazine Rack Clean-Up Campaign," n.d. but sometime in February 1938, both in NCCW/NCCM 1938–1939, folder 2 of 2, Correspondence Files, Chancery Archives.

10. Italics in original. "Report of the Committee on Indecent Literature," May 5, 1938, Catholic Men of San Francisco 1938–1941, folder 1 of 2; James Hagerty to Archbishop Mitty, May 18, 1938, Catholic Men of San Francisco 1938–1941, folder 1 of 2; Margaret McGuire to Archbishop Mitty, June 11, 1938, NCCW/NCCM 1938–1939, folder 1 of 2, all in Correspondence Files, Chancery Archives.

11. Archbishop Mitty to Reverend and Dear Father, June 10, 1938, letter marked "Official," in Mitty Sermons, Chancery Archives.

12. Florentine Schage to Rev. Harold E. Collins, February 28, 1939, Correspondence Files, NCCW/NCCM 1938–1939, folder 2 of 2; Rev. John Francis Noll, *Catechism Dealing with Lewd Literature* (Huntington, Ind.: Our Sunday Visitor Press, 1939), 8; "Magazines Banned by the National Organization for Decent Literature," October 12, 1939, Correspondence Files, National Catholic Welfare Conference Catholic Action Study folder, 1939, all in Chancery Archives.

13. James L. Hagerty to Joseph Breen, Esq., November 18, 1938; James L. Hagerty to Archbishop Mitty, November 18, 1938; Rt. Rev. Thomas A. Connolly to James L. Hagerty, November 19, 1938; all in Catholic Men of San Francisco 1938–1941, folder 1 of 2, Correspondence Files, Chancery Archives. For more on the production code and Breen's role, see Thomas Doherty, *Hollywood's Censor: Joseph I. Breen and the Production Code Administration* (New York: Columbia University Press, 2007), and Gregory D. Black, *Hollywood Censored:*

Morality Codes, Catholics, and the Movies (New York: Cambridge University Press, 1994).

14. Archbishop Mitty to Most Reverend Amleto G. Cicognani, D.D., March 30, 1939; A. G. Cicognani to Your Excellency, March 19, 1939, both in National Catholic Welfare Conference, Catholic Action Study folder, 1939, Correspondence Files, Chancery Archives.

15. The text of the Atherton Report was reprinted in the *San Francisco News,* March 16, 1937. For more on the investigation and its outcome, see Robert W. Cherny and William Issel, *San Francisco: Presidio, Port, and Pacific Metropolis* (San Francisco: Boyd and Fraser, 1981), 61–62.

16. Joseph J. Truxaw to Most Reverend Thomas A. Connolly, January 13, 1940; Rev. Edwin J. Kennedy to Honorable William J. Quinn, January 26, 1940; Rev. Edwin J. Kennedy to Rev. Joseph J. Truxaw, January 31, 1940; Charles W. Dullea to Rev. Edwin J. Kennedy, April 2, 1940; all in National Catholic Welfare Conference, Catholic Action Study folder, 1940, Correspondence Files, Chancery Archives; Anna E. McCaughey to Archbishop Mitty, June 5, 1941, National Council of Catholic Women/National Council of Catholic Men, 1940–1941 folder, Correspondence Files, Chancery Archives.

17. Margaret Sanger, quoted in Sue Barry, "News and Views," *People's World,* May 22, 1939; Anthony B. Diepenbrock to Board of Directors, Golden Gate International Exposition, March 4, 1939, Golden Gate Exposition folder 1 of 2, 1939–1940, Correspondence Files, Chancery Archives.

CHAPTER 8. CATHOLIC ACTION AND COMMUNISM

Epigraph: Memorandum on Communism prepared for Archbishop Mitty by Father Hugh A. Donohoe, attached to a letter from Donohoe to Archbishop Mitty, September 2, 1937, Communism 1936–1937 folder, Correspondence Files, Chancery Archives.

1. Pizzardo, "Catholic Action Aims"; generalizations about CP strategy and tactics, unless otherwise indicated, are based on Cherny, "Prelude to the Popular Front," and Robert W. Cherny, "The Communist Party in California, 1935–1940: From the Political Margins to the Mainstream and Back," forthcoming in *American Communist History,* 2010.

2. "Concise Summary on Communism by Fr. Feely, S.J.," *Monitor,* May 4, 1935; Cherny, "Communist Party in California."

3. "Mayor Rossi's letter to Gov. Merriam, requesting additional National Guardsmen for San Francisco," July 14, 1934, at http://www.sfmuseum.org/hist4/maritime13.html, accessed July 19, 2008; Rossi statement on driving Communists out of San Francisco quoted in Mike Quin [pseudonym of Paul William Ryan], *The Big Strike* (Olema, Calif.: Olema Publishing Co., 1949), 163. Robert W. Cherny describes a variety of anti-Communist offensives in California (but not those of the Catholic Church) in "Anticommunist Networks and Labor: The

Pacific Coast in the 1930s," in *Labor's Cold War: Local Politics in Global Context,* ed. Shelton Stromquist (Urbana: University of Illinois Press, 2008), 17–48.

4. Chief Quinn's testimony was given to the state Peace Officers Association, an anti-Communist organization chaired by the head of the Los Angeles Police Department's "Red Squad," William F. Hynes. Quinn served as second vice president; quoted in Charles P. Larrowe, *Harry Bridges: The Rise and Fall of Radical Labor in the U.S.,* 2nd rev. ed. (Westport, Conn.: Lawrence Hill, 1972), 34; see also *The Communist Situation in California: Report of Sub-committee on Subversive Activities of the Crime Prevention Committee* (Oakland, Calif.: Peace Officers Association, 1937), 48–49.

5. Hugh Gallagher to Your Excellency, handwritten letter, n.d., and attached report dated November 2, 1936, in Communism 1936–1937 folder, Correspondence Files, Chancery Archives; Joseph S. Connelly ("Anti-subversive Committee, American legion, Dept. Cal.") to Rev. Dr. Thomas A. Connolly, August 31, 1936; Thomas A. Connolly (chancellor-secretary) to Connelly, September 2, 1936, both in Communism 1936–1937 folder, Correspondence Files, Chancery Archives.

6. Birth certificate of Oleta O'Connor, filed May 6, 1910, San Francisco Department of Public Health; "In re: Olita [*sic*] O'Conner [*sic*]," typed report attached to handwritten letter from Hugh Gallagher to Your Excellency, n.d., in attached report dated November 2, 1936, Communism 1936–1937 folder, Correspondence Files, Chancery Archives; Oleta O'Connor Yates, June 26 testimony in transcript of 1952 trial in federal district court for violation of the Smith Act (hereafter Yates Transcript), reprinted in "What a Communist Told the Court: The Testimony of Oletta [*sic*] O'Connor Yates," *People's Daily World Extra,* August 1, 1952, 5.

7. Yates Transcript, 9; American Legion investigator quoted in *San Francisco Examiner,* August 5, 1935; memorandum from Wooster Taylor, August 6, 1935; memorandum to Mr. Chase, February 20, 1935, both in Associations, Communism File (Yates), San Francisco History Center, San Francisco Main Public Library, Civic Center (hereafter Yates File).

8. "Biographies provided by Department of Justice on Seven San Francisco Communists Arrested Today by FBI," telegram from Joshua Eppinger to Examiner, San Francisco, Calif., July 26, 1951, copy in Yates File.

9. "Address at St. Vincent De Paul Golden Jubilee Dinner Condemning Idea of Totalitarian State," January 5, 1936; *Monitor,* February 22, 1936. "Quod Apostolici Muneris" (On Socialism), is at http://www.vatican.va/holy_father/leo_xiii/encyclicals/documents/hf_l-xiii_enc_28121878_quod-apostolici-muneris_en.html.

10. "Inaugural Address at the World Catholic Press Exposition," May 12, 1936, *Monitor,* May 16, 1936.

11. *Western Worker,* November 21, November 25, and December 2, 1935; *Western Worker,* January 16, January 30, and February 10, 1936; *Western Worker,* October 26, 1936, all quoted in Cherny, "Communist Party in California," 11–13.

12. Hugh Gallagher to Archbishop Mitty, June 5 and August 3, 1936, and "Special Memorandum in Re. Harry Bridges," all in Communism 1936–1937 folder, Correspondence Files, Chancery Archives; Carmel Gannon to Monsignor Connolly, September 28, 1936, and attached two-page handwritten list of individuals under surveillance, Communism 1936–1937 folder, Correspondence Files, Chancery Archives; George Maisak to Archbishop Mitty, September 15, 1936, and Harry M. Connelly III to Fellow American, September 12, 1936, both in Communism 1936–1937 folder, Correspondence Files, Chancery Archives.

13. "Arbitration Urged by Archbishop Mitty in S.F. Waterfront Dispute," copy in Labor folder 1934–1939, Correspondence Files, Chancery Archives.

14. Larrowe, *Harry Bridges,* 98–100, 112–114; Paul C. Smith, *Personal File: An Autobiography* (New York: Appleton-Century, 1964), 156–157.

15. Attendance figures are from newspaper articles and attendance numbers included in notes on photographs: *Western Worker,* August 17, 1936; *San Francisco Chronicle,* October 25, 1936; photograph of the Feast of Christ the King Celebration (AAC-5340) and of the Eucharistic Congress, 1941 (AAC-5217), in the digital photograph collection, San Francisco History Center; the encyclical "Quas Primas" (On the Feast of Christ the King) is at http://www.vatican.va/holy_father/pius_xi/encyclicals/documents/hf_p-xi_enc_11121925_quas-primas_en.html.

16. *San Francisco News,* October 19, 1936; *San Francisco Chronicle,* October 25, 1936.

17. "An Appeal to Catholic People: A Reply to Archbishop Mitty," Communism 1936–1937 folder, Correspondence Files, Chancery Archives.

18. Ibid.

19. Ibid.

20. Election data are from http://www.joincalifornia.com/candidate/6219.

21. "Radio Address by Vernon Healy, Delivered over KGO October 24, 1936," Communism 1936–1937 folder, Correspondence Files, Chancery Archives.

22. Voter registration and election results are from Cherny, "Communist Party in California," tables 1 and 2, 45–46; J. A. Hall to Archbishop Mitty, March 19, 1937; Mitty to Rev. Bryan J. McEntegart, March 20, 1937; Bryan J. McEntegart to Mitty, March 30, 1937; Mitty to Rev. James J. McHugh, April 14, 1937; Mitty to McEntegart, April 14, 1937, all in Communism 1936–1937 folder, Correspondence Files, Chancery Archives.

CHAPTER 9. CATHOLIC ACTION, EUROPEAN CRISES, AND SAN FRANCISCO POLITICS

Epigraphs: Andriano, "Program of Catholic Action."

1. "Divini Redemptoris" (On Atheistic Communism) is at http://www.vatican.va/holy_father/pius_xi/encyclicals/documents/hf_p-xi_enc_19031937_divini-redemptoris_en.html.

2. *Monitor,* May 1, 1937; *San Francisco News,* April 29, 1937.

3. "Report on April 28, 1937 Dreamland Auditorium Meeting under Auspices of American Friends of the Soviet Union," Communism 1936–1937 folder, Correspondence Files, Chancery Archives.

4. *New York Times,* July 26, 1938; *People's World,* January 3, 1938; Clyde H. Ashen to State Officers, Deputies, Grand Knights, Officers and Members of the Knights of Columbus, California State Council Jurisdiction, July 30, 1937, Knights of Columbus folder 1937, Correspondence Files, Chancery Archives; Archbishop Mitty to Hugh Gallagher, June 13, 1938, Communism folder 1938–1939, Correspondence Files, Chancery Archives; Martin H. Carmody to Archbishop Mitty, date illegible but 1938, Knights of Columbus folder 1938, Correspondence Files, Chancery Archives.

5. Martin H. Carmody to Archbishop Mitty, date illegible but 1938, Knights of Columbus folder 1938, Correspondence Files, Chancery Archives; Louis Kenedy to Rev. Wilfred G. Hurley, C.S.F., February 25, 1939; Archbishop Mitty to Louis Kenedy, March 25, 1939; Edward J. Heffron to Archbishop Mitty, March 30, 1939, all in National Council of Catholic Men/National Council of Catholic Women 1938–1939, folder 2 of 2, Correspondence Files, Chancery Archives; José M. Sánchez, *The Spanish Civil War as a Religious Tragedy* (Notre Dame, Ind.: Notre Dame University Press, 1987), 172–198; J. David Valaik, "Catholics, Neutrality, and the Spanish Embargo," *Journal of American History* 54 (June 1967), 73–85.

6. The quotation on the breakdown of public order is from Stanley G. Payne, *The Collapse of the Spanish Republic, 1933–1936: Origins of the Civil War* (New Haven, Conn.: Yale University Press, 2006), 362; J. David Valaik, "American Catholics and the Second Spanish Republic, 1911–1936," *Journal of Church and State* 10 (Winter 1968), 13–28; Donald F. Crosby, "Boston's Catholics and the Spanish Civil War," *New England Quarterly* 44 (March 1971), 82–100; "Memorandum on Communism" (hereafter Donohoe memorandum) prepared for Archbishop Mitty by Father Hugh A. Donohoe, attached to a letter from Donohoe to Archbishop Mitty, September 2, 1937, 3, Communism 1936–1937 folder, Correspondence Files, Chancery Archives.

7. Sánchez, *Spanish Civil War,* 9; the quotation "the greatest anticlerical bloodletting Europe has ever seen" is from Mary Vincent, "'The Keys of the Kingdom': Religious Violence in the Spanish Civil War, July–August 1936," in *The Splintering of Spain: Cultural History and the Spanish Civil War, 1936–1939,* edited by Chris Ealham and Michael Richards (New York: Cambridge University Press, 2005), 68.

8. Donohoe memorandum, 3; J. David Valaik, "American Catholic Dissenters and the Spanish Civil War," *Catholic Historical Review* 53 (January 1968), 537–555.

9. Charles A. Ramm biographical information is from the University of California Web site, http://sunsite.berkeley.edu/~ucalhist/general_history/

overview/regents/biographies_r.html; for Tobin, see Lewis Francis Byington, *History of San Francisco* (Chicago: S. J. Clarke, 1931), vol. 3, 74–78.

10. "Text of Address of William F. Montavon," October 27, 1936, Communism 1936–1937 folder, Correspondence Files, Chancery Archives.

11. Aurelio M. Espinosa, *The Spanish Republic and the Causes of the Counter-Revolution* (San Francisco: Spanish Relief Committee, 1937), 19. Umberto Olivieri became an ordained Catholic priest in 1958, at the age of seventy-four, and spent the last fifteen years of his life ministering to the Otomi tribe in Mexico. See Sister Josephine Olivieri Targuini, D.C. (Olivieri's adopted daughter), "My Favorite Priest," at *Ave Maria Online,* http://avemaria.bravepages.com/articles/jan/olivieri.html.

12. Sylvester Andriano, preface to *Democracy! Which Brand, Stalin's or Jefferson's?* by Umberto Olivieri (San Francisco: Spanish Relief Committee, 1937).

13. Olivieri, *Democracy!* 15.

14. "The great scandal of silence" quotation is from Sánchez, *Spanish Civil War,* 116; F. R. Fuller to Archbishop Mitty, April 22, 1937, Communism 1936–1937 folder, Correspondence Files, Chancery Archives; F. R. Fuller to Father Raymond J. Feely, February 1, 1938, Communism 1938–1939 folder, Correspondence Files, Chancery Archives.

15. *People's World,* January 21 and October 26, 1938.

16. The encyclical "Mit Brennender Sorge" is at http://www.vatican.va/holy_father/pius_xi/encyclicals/documents/hf_p-xi_enc_14031937_mit-brennender-sorge_en.html; Maria Mazzenga, "Condemning the Nazis: Father Charles Coughlin, Father Maurice Sheehy, the National Catholic Welfare Conference, and Kristallnacht," paper presented at the American Catholic Historical Association, Washington, D.C., January 6, 2008.

17. Pius XI, "Mit Brennender Sorge"; the German ambassador quoted in Anthony Rhodes, *The Vatican in the Age of the Dictators (1922–1945)* (New York: Holt, Rinehart and Winston, 1973), 206.

18. Gribble, *Archbishop for the People,* 113–114; Rev. M. J. Ahern to Archbishop Mitty, March 13 and July 24, 1936; Archbishop Mitty to Ahern, April 14, 1936, "A" folder, 1936–1937, Correspondence Files, Chancery Archives.

19. *Monitor,* January 1, 1938; the text of Mitty's radio address is reprinted in the *Monitor,* November 19, 1938; the transcript of the entire broadcast and an audio clip is at http://libraries.cua.edu/archrcua/packets.html.

20. *Monitor,* November 19, 1938.

21. *People's World,* January 21, February 3, February 4, March 8, and March 11, 1938.

22. *People's World,* May 2, May 4, July 30, October 1, October 5, and October 24–26, 1938.

23. William Schneiderman, *Dissent on Trial: Memoirs of a Political Life* (Minneapolis: MEP Publications, 1983), 63, quoted in Cherny, "Communist Party in California," 30; Al Richmond, *A Long View from the Left* (Boston: Houghton Mifflin, 1972), 174.

24. *San Francisco Chronicle,* October 28, 1938; *San Francisco Call-Bulletin,* October 27, 1938; "Address on Catholic Action," October 29, 1938, Mitty Sermons, Chancery Archives.

25. Hugh A. Donohoe, "Communism: Anti-religious and Anti-American," *Argonaut* 117 (November 11, 1938), 7–8; the editor of the *Argonaut,* W. W. Chapin, had originally asked Archbishop Mitty to write the article on Communism, but Mitty delegated the job to Father Donohoe, warning him that "you had better be prepared, however, for some comeback to your article." Archbishop Mitty to Rev. Hugh A. Donohoe, September 2, 1938, Communism 1938–1939 folder, Correspondence Files, Chancery Archives.

26. Franck Roberts Havenner, "Reminiscences," oral history interview by Corrine L. Gilb, 1953, Regional Oral History Office, Bancroft Library, University of California, Berkeley, 91–93.

27. William Malone, oral history interview by Malca Chall, 1978, Regional Oral History Office, Bancroft Library, University of California at Berkeley, 116, 254; *San Francisco Examiner,* November 8, 1939; Stefano Luconi, "Una Quinta Colonna nell'Urna: Il Regime Fascista e le Elezioni Presidenziali del 1940 negli Stati Uniti," in *L'Italia Fascista tra Europa e Stati Uniti d'America,* ed. Michele Abbate (Civita Castellana ed Orte: Centro Falisco di Studi Storici, 2002), 47.

CHAPTER 10. ANDRIANO'S ORDEAL: THE LOYALTY HEARINGS

Epigraphs: U.S. House Committee on Un-American Activities, *Investigation of Un-American Propaganda Activities in the United States, Volume 3 of 7, Executive Hearings, San Francisco, California: July 17–August 20, 1940* (Washington, D.C.: U.S. Government Printing Office, 1940), 1443; *People's World,* May 29, 1942.

1. Rudolph J. Vecoli, "The Making and Un-making of the Italian American Working Class," in Cannistraro and Meyer, *Lost World of Italian American Radicalism,* 22–23. For the Franklin D. Roosevelt speech, a commencement address at the University of Virginia, see the Web site http://millercenter.virginia.edu/scripps/diglibrary/prezspeeches/roosevelt/fdr_1940_0610.html.

2. *Monitor,* November 2, 1935; Michael P. Carroll, *American Catholics in the Protestant Imagination: Rethinking the Academic Study of Religion* (Baltimore: Johns Hopkins University Press, 2007), 71–77. Communist Party anti-Catholicism during this period deserves more attention from historians than it has received thus far; George Sirgiovanni discusses Catholic anti-Communism in *An Undercurrent of Suspicion: Anti-Communism in America during World War II* (New Brunswick, N.J.: Transaction, 1990), 147–163.

3. *Il Corriere del Popolo,* May 29, 1930, quoted in De Medici, "Italian Language Press," 54–55.

4. Martin Dies, *The Trojan Horse in America* (New York: Dodd, Mead, 1940), 333. See also Francis MacDonnell, *Insidious Foes: The Axis Fifth Column and the American Home Front* (Guilford, Conn.: Lyons Press, 2004), 75–76. The HUAC

hearings transcripts are published in U.S. House Committee on Un-American Activities, *Investigation of Un-American Propaganda Activities in the United States,* 1437–1463. *Un-American Activities in California,* 282–321.

5. Claire Phillips and Myron B. Goldsmith, *Manila Espionage* (Portland, Ore.: Binfords and Mort, 1947); *New York Times,* "Spy Story Opens at the Holiday," July 4, 1951; U.S. House Committee on Un-American Activities, *Investigation of Un-American Propaganda Activities,* 1439, 1442–1443.

6. U.S. House Committee on Un-American Activities, *Investigation of Un-American Propaganda Activities,* 1439, 1442–1443.

7. Ibid., 1444–1445.

8. Ibid., 1446, 1457; *Un-American Activities in California,* 301; Baccari et al., eds., *Saints Peter and Paul Church,* 158–159; Canepa, "Profilo della Massoneria," 97–100. Antonio Cogliandro and Andriano each merited a full-page biography and portrait in an expensively produced coffee table book. See G. M. Tuoni, *Attività italiane in California* (San Francisco: Mercury Press, 1929), 48, 54. Catholic success in persuading Italian Masons to raise their children in the church can be seen in the case of Joseph L. Alioto, the son of a Sicilian fisherman member of the Speranza Italiana Masonic lodge. Alioto attended Sacred Heart High School, became a protégé of Andriano's colleague James L. Hagerty at St. Mary's College, received a law degree at Catholic University, worked with Archbishop Mitty on Catholic Action projects, and later became mayor of San Francisco. See William Issel, "'The Catholic Internationale': Mayor Joseph Alioto's Urban Liberalism and San Francisco Catholicism," *U.S. Catholic Historian* 22 (Spring 2004), 99–120.

9. U.S. House Committee on Un-American Activities, *Investigation of Un-American Propaganda Activities,* 1448–1451; Jim Newton, *Justice for All: Earl Warren and the Nation He Made* (New York: Riverhead Books, 2006), 112–120.

10. Edward L. Barrett Jr., *The Tenney Committee: Legislative Investigation of Subversive Activities in California* (Ithaca, N.Y.: Cornell University Press, 1951), 13. See also M. J. Heale, *McCarthy's Americans: Red Scare Politics in State and Nation, 1935–1965* (Athens: University of Georgia Press, 1998); Heale, "Red Scare Politics: California's Campaign against Un-American Activities, 1940–1970," *Journal of American Studies* 20 (1986), 5–32; Ingrid Winther Scobie, "Jack B. Tenney and the 'Parasitic Menace': Anti-Communist Legislation in California 1940–1949," *Pacific Historical Review* 43 (1974), 188–211.

11. *Report on Un-American Activities in California,* 292, 298–299; the May 1942 hearings received front-page coverage in San Francisco newspapers, and detailed articles appeared in the two morning newspapers, the *San Francisco Examiner* and *San Francisco Chronicle,* on May 26, 27, 28, 29, 1942; in the paragraphs to follow, reference to testimony is based on the *Hearing Transcripts,* California State Assembly Fact Finding Committee on Un-American Activities in California, Investigation into Matters Pertaining to Un-American Subversive Activities, St. Francis Hotel, San Francisco, May 25, 26, and 27, 1942, 3335–3717.

12. *Pittsburg Post Dispatch,* February 2, 1942.

13. John S. Owens, O.P., to Archbishop Mitty, February 3, 1942, "A–C" folder, 1941–1942 (Alien Enemy Registration, Evacuation), Correspondence Files, Chancery Archives.

14. Andriano sent the archbishop "a brief summary of my statements to you the other day," in Sylvester Andriano to Archbishop Mitty, February 9, 1942, "A–C" folder, 1941–1942 (Alien Enemy Registration, Evacuation), Correspondence Files, Chancery Archives.

15. Archbishop Mitty to Right Rev. Michael Ready, February 7, 1942; Monsignor Ready to Archbishop Mitty, February 16, 1942; Francis Biddle to Monsignor Ready, February 16, 1942, all in "A–C" folder, 1941–1942 (Alien Enemy Registration, Evacuation), Correspondence Files, Chancery Archives.

16. Tetsuden Kashima, *Judgment without Trial: Japanese American Imprisonment during World War II* (Seattle: University of Washington Press, 2004), 49–56, 137–139; Arnold Krammer, *Undue Process: The Untold Story of America's German Alien Internees* (Lanham, Md.: Rowman and Littlefield, 1997), 56–57; Greg Robinson, *By Order of the President: FDR and the Internment of Japanese Americans* (Cambridge, Mass.: Harvard University Press, 2001), 112–124, 257–258.

17. *Hearing Transcripts,* 3335–3336; *San Francisco Examiner,* May 26, 1942; *San Francisco Chronicle,* May 26, 1942.

18. "Curriculum of Carmelo Zito," n.d., Carmelo Zito Papers, Italian American Collection, Immigration History Research Center, University of Minnesota, Minneapolis; Armida Zito to Honorable Mayor Rossi, n.d., but June 1942, "A" folder, 1943, Correspondence Files, Chancery Archives; "Chronology of Arturo Giovannitti's Life," at http://www.quale.com/Giovannitti.html.

19. "Curriculum of Carmelo Zito"; Armida Zito to Mayor Rossi; *Il Corriere del Popolo,* January 14, 1937; De Medici, "Italian Language Press," 57–60; for a sympathetic account of Zito's political philosophy and defense of his tactics that uncritically accepts the truth of his charges against Rossi and Andriano, see Bénédicte Deschamps, "Opposing Fascism in the West: The Experience of *Il Corriere del Popolo* in San Francisco in the Late 1930s," in *Italian Immigrants Go West: The Impact of Locale on Ethnicity,* ed. Janet E. Worrall, Carol Bonomo Albright, and Elvira G. Di Fabio (Cambridge, Mass.: American Italian Historical Association, 2003), 109–123.

20. *People's World,* October 13, 24, 25, 26, 1938; according to Stephen Schwartz, who interviewed Zito and used his files for a book on West Coast radicalism, Zito "was as anticlerical as he was antifascist, and he doubtless considered support for the Vatican tantamount to support for the fascists." Stephen Schwartz, "Catholic Action in 30s S.F. North Beach," e-mail letter to Bill Issel, January 22, 2004; see also Schwartz, *From West to East: California and the Making of the American Mind* (New York: Free Press, 1998), 274–275. John P. Diggins drew on interviews with Zito to conclude that his testimony represented the culmination of one of several "noisy ideological feuds that had been going on for almost a decade" across the country: John P. Diggins, *Mussolini and Fascism: The*

View from America (Princeton, N.J.: Princeton University Press, 1972), 347. Diggins mistakenly asserts that the Tenney Committee investigated San Francisco's "Italian American police chief." The city's chief of police was not Italian American; the reference is probably to Andriano, a former police commissioner. Ironically, the Military Intelligence Division of the War Department and the Office of Naval Intelligence included Carmelo Zito on its so-called "ABC List" of suspected individuals tagged for investigation by the FBI in the event of war: Stephen Fox, *The Unknown Internment: An Oral History of the Relocation of Italian Americans during World War II* (Boston: Twayne, 1990), 174.

21. *San Francisco Examiner,* June 12, 1940; Diggins, *Mussolini and Fascism,* 107; U.S. House Committee on Un-American Activities, *Investigation of Un-American Propaganda Activities,* 1439.

22. *Hearing Transcripts,* 3345–3347.

23. Ibid., 3352–3353.

24. Ibid., 3362–3363.

25. Ibid., 3364, 3375.

26. *People's World,* May 26, 1942; *Hearing Transcripts,* 3395–3396.

27. *Hearing Transcripts,* 3397–3398, 3402.

28. Ibid., 3403.

29. Ibid., 3404–3406.

30. Ibid., 3413–3421.

31. Ibid., 3446–3450.

32. Ibid., 3454–3456. Historian Stefano Luconi researched the papers of the Segreteria Particolare del Duce, located in the Archivio Centrale dello Stato in Rome, and found "just a thin file" pertaining to Mayor Rossi, with documents proving, contrary to charges made at the Tenney Committee hearings, that the mayor "did not ask for the picture" [an autographed photograph of Mussolini that Rossi had in his office before Italy declared war]; e-mail letter from Stefano Luconi to Bill Issel, September 17, 2002. Communist Party members and publications denounced socialists as well as Catholic Action activists during World War II. African American socialist A. Philip Randolph, head of the Brotherhood of Sleeping Car Porters, was accused of having "guaranteed the triumph of fascism." See *Daily Worker,* December 18, 25, 1942. On the Bridges deportation order, see *People's World,* May 29, 1942, and *People's World Extra,* May 30, 1942.

33. *Hearing Transcripts*; U.S. House Committee on Un-American Activities, *Investigation of Un-American Propaganda Activities,* 1446–1462; *Report on Un-American Activities in California,* 284–319.

34. Italian historians Stefano Luconi and Matteo Pretelli searched in vain in the collections of the Archivio Storico Diplomatico del Ministero degli Affari Esteri in Rome for documentary evidence that Sylvester Andriano cooperated in Fascist government attempts to influence the Italian American community; e-mail letter from Stefano Luconi to Bill Issel, September 17, 2002; letter from Stefano Luconi to Bill Issel, January 13, 2003; e-mail letter from Matteo Pretelli to Bill

Issel, April 22, 2004; see also Luconi, "Una Quinta Colonna nell' Urna"; Matteo Pretelli, "Italian Language and Culture as Tools of Fascist Propaganda and Affirmation of the Italian Character among Italian Immigrants and Their Sons in the USA," unpublished paper in author's possession.

35. Alfonso Zirpoli Oral History, in Fox, *Unknown Internment,* 167.

36. *Hearing Transcripts*; *Report on Un-American Activities in California,* 298; *San Francisco Examiner,* May 27, 1942. For an account of Mayor Rossi's politics that accepts at face value the truth of the pro-Fascist charges against him and Andriano, see Stefano Luconi, "Mussolini's Italian-American Sympathizers in the West: Mayor Angelo J. Rossi and Fascism," in Worrall et al., *Italian Immigrants Go West,* 124–133. The judgment about Andriano's personal style is based on reading his extensive correspondence with James L. Hagerty, his correspondence (over a period of nearly three decades) with Archbishops Hanna and Mitty, and the Cicoletti interview.

37. Andriano to Hagerty, March 10, 1943; James L. Hagerty to Dear Syl [Andriano], Feast of Christ the King, 1942 (October 25), both in Hagerty Papers.

38. Andriano to Hagerty, March 10, 1943, Hagerty Papers. As Peter Ackroyd puts it in his 1998 biography, Thomas More "simply did not believe that the English parliament could repeal the ordinances of a thousand years." Peter Ackroyd, *The Life of Thomas More* (New York: Anchor Books, 1998), 400.

39. *Hearing Transcripts,* 3715–3716; Fox, *Unknown Internment,* 123. The unscrupulous tactics used by the Tenney Committee were exposed in 1951 by a University of California law professor in a report underwritten by the Rockefeller Foundation. See Barrett, *Tenney Committee,* 330–354.

CHAPTER 11. ANDRIANO'S ORDEAL: EXCLUSION AND EXILE

Epigraphs: John Edgar Hoover to SAC, San Francisco, November 21, 1942, 100-32005-72, letter marked "*Personal Attention,*" Andriano FBI file; Attorney General Francis Biddle, "Memorandum for the President," April 17, 1943, Appendix 12, Michi Weglyn, *Years of Infamy: The Untold Story of America's Concentration Camps* (New York: Morrow Quill Paperbacks, 1976), 200–201.

1. "Rossi Denies Giving a Fascist Salute," *New York Times,* May 27, 1942.

2. Archbishop Mitty to Monsignor Ready, May 27, 1942, "A" folder, 1942–1943, Correspondence Files, Chancery Archives; Mitty did not name the person he characterized as "the principal witness," but his description would have applied to either Cogliandro or Zito.

3. Ibid.

4. Ibid.

5. *People's World,* May 27, 1942.

6. *Il Corriere del Popolo,* May 28, 1942; *People's World,* May 28, 29, 30, 1942.

7. Mitty to Ready, May 27, 1942; *Monitor,* May 30, 1942.

8. *Monitor,* May 30, 1942.

9. Copy of telegram to Honorable Franklin D. Roosevelt, in box 237, Hagerty Papers.

10. San Francisco City and County Board of Supervisors, *Journal of Proceedings,* June 8, 1942, 1376; Monsignor Ready to Archbishop Mitty (confidential), June 17, 1942, Archbishop Mitty to Monsignor Ready, June 24, 1942, both in "A" folder, 1942–1943, Correspondence Files, Chancery Archives; Sylvester Andriano to James Hagerty, June 22, 1942, box 237, Hagerty Papers.

11. *Il Corriere del Popolo,* July 9, 1942.

12. *Il Corriere del Popolo,* July 23, 1942.

13. Sylvester Andriano to Dear Member in Catholic Action, July 25, 1942, Catholic Lay Organizations/Catholic Men of San Francisco folder, Correspondence Files, Chancery Archives.

14. Kashima, *Judgment without Trial,* 136–137; "Andriano, Sylvester—Fascist," 100-32005-X, Sylvester Andriano FBI file (hereafter only the document numbers are listed); names of many of the confidential informants have been redacted, so it is not possible to determine their identity, but it is highly probable that Carmelo Zito was the single most frequent informant, both because of the match between the material in the reports and Zito's public accusations and because the 7/16" space of the blacked-out area could accommodate little more than a name of four letters or less given the font size of the typewritten reports. All FBI and Military Intelligence documents are in the author's possession and were obtained through the Freedom of Information Act.

15. Athan G. Theoharis and John Stuart Cox, *The Boss: J. Edgar Hoover and the Great American Inquisition* (Philadelphia: Temple University Press, 1988), 151; Kashima, *Judgment without Trial,* 21–22. Hoover's zeal in seeking to increase his bureau's power and public prominence by expanding its intelligence-gathering role has been documented by several other historians in addition to Theoharis and Cox: see Richard Gid Powers, *Secrecy and Power: The Life of J. Edgar Hoover* (New York: Free Press, 1987); Katherine A. S. Sibley, *Red Spies in America: Stolen Secrets and the Dawn of the Cold War* (Lawrence: University Press of Kansas, 2004); Raymond J. Batvinis, *The Origins of FBI Counterintelligence* (Lawrence: University Press of Kansas, 2007).

16. Kashima, *Judgment without Trial,* 22, 27–29; J. Edgar Hoover to Lawrence M. C. Smith, March 31, 1941, 100-32005-X, 100-32005-1; Memorandum Re. Sylvester Andriano, June 7, 1942, Memorandum for the Commanding General, June 22, 1942, both in Record Group 181, Twelfth Naval District, District Intelligence Office, FBI Reports on Euro-Ethnic Organizations, box 1, folder 1438 A8-5/EF/16 (13A) FBI List of Pro-Axis Sympathizers Recommended for Internment.

17. N. J. L. Pieper to Director, June 29, 1941, 100-32005-2; "Report on Sylvester Nathaniel Andriano," August 14, 1941, 100-32005-3.

18. Wendell Berge to J. Edgar Hoover, December 24, 1941, 100-32005-8X; J. Edgar Hoover to Edward J. Ennis, January 13, 1942, 100-32005-8; N. J. L. Pieper to Director, February 12, 1942; J. Edgar Hoover to SAC Pieper, March 7, 1942, 100-32005-10; J. Edgar Hoover to SAC Pieper, March 25, 1942, 100-32005-17.

19. Memorandum for Assistant Attorney General Wendell Berge from J. Edgar Hoover, May 25, 1942, 100-32005-16; John Edgar Hoover to Major General Lewis B. Hershey, June 6, 1942, 100-32005-24; memorandum for the Director from Wendell Berge, June 11, 1942, 100-32005-[last digits illegible]; N. J. L. Pieper to Director, July 28, 1942, 100-32005-[last digits illegible].

20. Report of Special Agent [redacted], August 14, 1942, file number illegible, 1.

21. Ibid., 43–47.

22. C. G. Parker Jr. to John Edgar Hoover, August 6, 1942, 100-32005-37; John Edgar Hoover to Colonel C. G. Parker Jr., September 5, 1942, 100-32005-37; E. P. Coffey, memorandum for Mr. Tracy, September 22, 1942, 100-32005-47; E. P. Coffey, memorandum for Mr. Tracy, September 23, 1942, 100-32005-48; John (Hoover) to Walter Winchell, September 10, 1942, 100-32005-45; Jack B. Tenney to Walter Winchell, September 23, 1942; letter marked "*Confidential and Personal,*" no file number; J. L. De Witt, Individual Exclusion Order, No. B-7, September 28, 1942, copy in "A" folder, 1942–1943, Correspondence Files, Chancery Archives.

23. According to Zirpoli, when Andriano's supporters urged him to challenge the army's relocation order in court, he replied, "No. I don't want to do anything that detracts in the slightest degree from the war effort." Zirpoli Oral History in Fox, *Unknown Internment,* 167; James L. Hagerty to Dear Syl [Andriano], November 20, 1942, box 237, Hagerty Papers.

24. *Il Corriere del Popolo,* October 15, 1942.

25. *San Francisco Chronicle,* October 27, 1942; *Il Corriere del Popolo,* October 29, 1942. Andriano to Very Reverend Bishop Thomas A. Connolly, May 29, July 9, 1942, in "A" folder, 1942–1943, Correspondence Files, Chancery Archives; Andriano to Most Reverend and dear Archbishop [Mitty], July 29, 1943, "A" folder, 1942–1943, Correspondence Files, Chancery Archives; Andriano to Dear Jim [Hagerty], Feast of Corpus Christi (June 24, 1943), box 237, Hagerty Papers.

26. The details in this paragraph are based on various memoranda and reports in the Andriano FBI file. The quotation is from John Edgar Hoover to SAC, San Francisco, November 21, 1942, 100-32005-72, letter marked "*Personal Attention.*"

27. "John" to Walter Winchell, September 10, 1942, 100-32005-45; the *March of Time* broadcast is discussed in a teletype from Pieper to Director, October 9, 1942, 100-32005-69; "RoBerTo Checked," *Time,* October 19, 1942.

28. Interview, name redacted, quoted in Report from the San Francisco Office, September 16, 1941, 100-32005-29.

29. N. J. L. Pieper to Director, F.B.I., February 11, 1943, 100-32005-[last two digits illegible]; teletype from Pieper to Director, February 10, 1943, 100-32005-84.

30. S. J. Drayton interview with Sylvester Andriano, quoted in Report from the Chicago Office, March 9, 1943, 100-32005-[last two digits illegible].

31. D. M. Ladd, "Memorandum for Director," March 30, 1943, 100-32005-97; D. M. Ladd to the Director, March 31, 1943, 100-32005-100; John Edgar Hoover, "Memorandum for the Attorney General," April 12, 1943, 100-32005-95. The constitutionality of the executive order was eventually decided by the Supreme Court in the Hirabayashi and Yasui cases, June 21, 1943, and the Korematsu case, December 18, 1944.

32. Secretary of War Henry L. Stimson to President Roosevelt, March 31, 1943, OF 5262, FDR Library, Hyde Park, New York, quoted in Appendix 12, Weglyn, *Years of Infamy,* 201; Attorney General Francis Biddle, "Memorandum for the President," April 17, 1943, copy in Appendix 12, Weglyn, *Years of Infamy,* 200–201; Francis Biddle, *In Brief Authority* (Garden City, N.Y.: Doubleday, 1962), 220.

33. *San Francisco Chronicle,* December 31, 1943; *Il Corriere del Popolo,* January 6, 1944; Sylvester Andriano to Dear Jim [Hagerty], November 12, 1943, box 327, Hagerty Papers. During his months of exile Andriano and his supporters in San Francisco discussed the possibility that a partisan political dynamic played a role in the *San Francisco Chronicle*'s sensationalistic condemnation of him in its reporting and editorials. They suspected that the Republican Party–oriented publisher and his editor wanted Andriano out of the way until after the gubernatorial election in November 1942 because he and his Democratic Party supporters favored incumbent Culbert Olson while the paper backed the challenger, state attorney general Earl Warren.

The suspicions of Andriano and his supporters cannot be proved one way or the other, but it is true that the *Chronicle* sided with the finger-pointers and equated charges of subversion with evidence of guilt. The *Examiner* and the afternoon papers covered the same events differently; they reported the political character, lack of evidence, and inconclusive nature of the witnesses' testimony. The *Monitor* went even further, forthrightly criticizing the hearings in a front-page editorial and condemning the motivations of Andriano's accusers. The *Chronicle* consistently parroted the attackers' charges and called for Andriano's exclusion, his removal from the draft board, and even the revocation of his U.S. citizenship. See John P. Doran to Hon. Frank J. Hennessy, October 22, 1942; Andriano to Dear Jim [Hagerty], October 28, 1942; Hagerty to Dear Syl [Andriano], November 15, 1942, all in box 237, Hagerty Papers; *Monitor,* editorial, May 30, 1942.

34. "Exclusion Case: Sylvester Andriano," August 9, 1943, Records of the Office of the Secretary of War, Record Group 107, box 7, National Archives and Records Service, Washington, D.C.; "Exclusion of Non-Japanese," Supplemental Report, Part III, 854–855, Records of U.S. Army Operational, Tactical, and Support Organizations (World War II and Thereafter), Record Group 338, box

9, National Archives and Records Service, Washington, D.C.; J. Edgar Hoover to Assistant Attorney General Tom C. Clark, February 12, 1944, 100-32005-121; Tom C. Clark to the Director, April 13, 1944, 100-32005-134.

EPILOGUE

Epigraphs: Sylvester Andriano to Dear Jim [Hagerty], November 12, 1943, box 327, Hagerty Papers; "Catholicism in San Francisco," mimeographed typewritten report given at the County Convention, July 10–11, 1948, 2, 3, copy in Subject File, CP 1948, Southern California Library for Social Studies and Research, Los Angeles, California.

1. Andriano to Dear Jim [Hagerty], November 12, 1943; Andriano to Dear Jim, August 1, 1945; John J. Mitty to Sylvester Andriano, March 2, 1946, Catholic Action File, 1945–1946, AASF.

2. "Catholicism in San Francisco"; details about the Civic Unity Committee are from the papers of Robert Browning Flippin, an African American member of the committee: Mayor's Committee Miscellaneous Papers, 1944–1945 folder; Mayor's Committee Minutes, 1944–1945 folder, Stewart-Flippin Papers, Moorland-Spingarn Research Center, Howard University, Washington, D.C. On the postwar competition between Catholics and the Communist Party in San Francisco, see Issel, "Catholic Internationale"; see also Richard Gid Powers, "American Catholics and Catholic Americans: The Rise and Fall of Catholic Anticommunism," *U.S. Catholic Historian* 22 (Fall 2004), 17–35.

3. *Il Bollettino,* October 1, 1946; *San Francisco Chronicle,* August 13, 1955.

4. *San Francisco Call-Bulletin,* photo of Archbishop John J. Mitty, Sylvester Andriano, and John F. Henning at the dinner celebrating Mitty's fifty years as a priest, October 26, 1956; *San Francisco Examiner,* March 3, 1964.

5. Arturo Giovannitti, *Quanda canta il gallo* (Chicago: E. Clemente, 1957); "Curriculum of Carmelo Zito"; Msgr. Luigi Civardi, *Christianity and Social Justice,* translated by Sylvester Andriano (Fresno, Calif.: Academy Guild Press, 1961); Civardi, *How Christ Changed the World: The Social Principles of the Catholic Church* (Rockford, Ill.: Tan Books, 1991). I am indebted to David Cicoletti for the information about the circumstances of the death of his great-uncle. Sylvester Andriano's wife, Leonora, died in 1989. Carmelo Zito died in 1981; Schwartz, *From West to East,* 376, describes the editor's bafflement at the behavior of the new cultural radicals.

6. Roger W. Lotchin, "California Cities and the Hurricane of Change: World War II in the San Francisco, Los Angeles, and San Diego Metropolitan Areas," *Pacific Historical Review* 63 (1994), 393–420; Mark S. Massa, S.J., *Anti-Catholicism in America: The Last Acceptable Prejudice* (New York: Crossroad Publishing Co., 2003); Philip Jenkins, *The New Anti-Catholicism: The Last Acceptable Prejudice* (New York: Oxford University Press, 2003).

7. Andriano's seems to have been an exceptional case; a search through the literature on American cities during World War II and in studies of the FBI's and

the army's implementation of the wartime restrictions has not yielded similar cases in which a leading citizen became the victim of an anti-Catholic political attack, aided and abetted by witch-hunting legislative committees with the cooperation of the FBI and the army. See Rose D. Scherini, "Executive Order 9066 and Italian Americans: The San Francisco Story," *California History* 70 (1991/92), 367–377, 422–424; Scherini, "The Fascist/Anti-Fascist Struggle in San Francisco," in *New Explorations in Italian American Studies,* ed. Richard N. Juliani and Sandra P. Juliani (Staten Island, N.Y., 1994), 63–71; Gloria Ricci Lothrop, "A Shadow on the Land: The Impact of Fascism on Los Angeles Italians," *California History* 75 (1996/97), 338–353, 385–387.

8. San Franciscans of Irish birth or ancestry still dominated much of the city's public life during World War II; see Stephen C. Fox, "General John DeWitt and the Proposed Internment of German and Italian Aliens during World War II," *Pacific Historical Review* 57 (1988), 407–438; Stephen Fox, *Fear Itself: Inside the FBI Roundup of German Americans during World War II; The Past as Prologue* (New York: iUniverse, 2007), xxii–xxxix; Arnold Kramer, *Undue Process: The Untold Story of America's German Alien Internees* (London: Rowman & Littlefield, 1997); Kashima, *Judgment without Trial.*

9. Stephen Fox, "General John De Witt," 419.

10. Richard Hofstadter, *The Paranoid Style in American Politics and Other Essays* (New York: Alfred Knopf, 1965); Michael Rogin, *Ronald Reagan: The Movie; and Other Episodes in Political Demonology* (Berkeley and Los Angeles: University of California Press, 1987); M. J. Heale, "Red Scare Politics"; John Sbardellati and Tony Shaw, "Booting a Tramp: Charlie Chaplin, the FBI, and the Construction of the Subversive Image in Red Scare America," *Pacific Historical Review* 72 (2003), 495–530.

11. Schwartz, *From West to East,* 376; Sylvester Andriano to Right Rev. Leo Maher, August 1, 1960, *The Monitor* folder, Correspondence Files, Chancery Archives.

Index

Italic letter *f* following a page number refers to a figure on the page.

William Issel is Professor of History Emeritus at San Francisco State University and Visiting Professor of History at Mills College. He is the author of *Social Change in the United States, 1945–1983,* co-author of *San Francisco, 1865–1932: Politics, Power, and Urban Development,* and co-editor and contributor to *American Labor and the Cold War: Grassroots Politics and Postwar Political Culture.*